Contemporary China

Contemporary States and Societies

This series provides lively and accessible introductions to key countries and regions of the world, conceived and designed to meet the needs of today's students. The authors are all experts with specialist knowledge of the country or region concerned and have been chosen also for their ability to communicate clearly to a non-specialist readership. Each text has been specially commissioned for the series and is structured according to a common format.

Published

Contemporary Russia
Edwin Bacon with
Matthew Wyman

Contemporary South Africa (2ed)
Anthony Butler

Contemporary America (3ed)
Russell Duncan
and Joseph Goddard

Contemporary China
Alan Hunter and John Sexton

Contemporary Japan (2ed)
Duncan McCargo

Contemporary Britain (2ed)
John McCormick

Contemporary Latin America (2ed)
Ronaldo Munck

Forthcoming

Contemporary India
Katharine Adeney
and Andrew Wyatt

Contemporary France
Helen Drake

Contemporary Spain
Paul Kennedy

Contemporary Asia
John McKay

Contemporary Ireland
Eoin O'Malley

Also planned

Contemporary Germany
Contemporary Italy

Contemporary States and Societies
Series Standing Order
ISBN 978–0–333–75402–3 hardcover
ISBN 978–0–333–80319–6 paperback
(outside North America only)

You can receive future titles in this series as they are published by placing a standing order. Please contact your bookseller or, in the case of difficulty, write to us at the address below with your name and address, the title of the series and the ISBN quoted above.

Customer Services Department, Palgrave Ltd
Houndmills, Basingstoke, Hampshire RG21 6XS, England

Contemporary China

Alan Hunter
and
John Sexton

First published 1999 by
MACMILLAN PRESS LTD
Houndmills, Basingstoke, Hampshire RG21 6XS
and London
Companies and representatives
throughout the world

ISBN-13: 978-0-333-71002-9   paperback
ISBN-10: 0-333-71002-9   paperback

ISBN-13: 978-0-333-71003-6   paperback
ISBN-10: 0-333-71003-7   paperback

This book is printed on paper suitable for recycling and made
from fully managed and sustained forest sources. Logging,
pulping and manufacturing processes are expected to conform
to the environmental regulations of the country of origin.

A catalogue record for this book is available
from the British Library.

Copy-edited and typeset by Povey–Edmondson
Tavistock and Rochdale, England

Printed and bound in Great Britain by
CPI Antony Rowe, Chippenham and Eastbourne

 Published in the United States of America 1999 by
ST. MARTIN'S PRESS, INC.,
Scholarly and Reference Division,
175 Fifth Avenue, New York, N.Y. 10010

ISBN 0–312–22146–0 hardcover
ISBN 0–312–22147–9 paperback

Contents

List of Figures, Maps, Tables, and Boxes

Figures

Maps

Tables

Boxes

Preface and Acknowledgements

In line with the series style, references in the text have been kept to a minimum. Some of the issues raised are controversial, and there are many areas of disagreement among specialists about finer points of analysis. Moreover, statistical information about China should be treated with caution, although its accuracy is certainly improving. Given space constraints we are unable to report all divergent points of view, but in the 'Recommended Reading' section (p. 211) readers will find a range of works which provide a basis for further study.

Much of *Contemporary China* focuses on China in the late 1990s, although background information on modern history and politics is included. The economy in particular is changing so rapidly that we have used current data sources including the Internet, which now provides much information about China. We cover many trends up to spring 1998. Beyond that, China may be relatively stable for a few years, in which case most of the patterns and policies described here could remain in force. Or, it may enter a period of significant political and economic upheaval. If so, readers will have to provide their own updates, and may find the Internet a good first stop for news and views.

Chinese terms have been kept to a minimum. Where Chinese words and names are used, they are given in the transliteration system known as 'hanyu pinyin', with the exception of a very few proper names, like Hong Kong, for which a different international usage has been established. Many syllables in hanyu pinyin can be pronounced more or less as in English. Important exceptions are:

'c' followed by a vowel is pronounced like 'ts' as in 'rats' (so 'cai' is something like 'tsai');
'q' like 'ch' in 'cheese' ('qiu': 'chew');
'x' like 'sh' in 'ship' ('xu': 'shoe');
'z' like 'dz' in 'buds' ('ze': 'dze');
'zh' like 'j' in 'jam' ('zhou': 'Joe').

The Chinese currency is known by two terms, 'renminbi' and 'yuan': we have opted to use the former. As explained in Chapter 3, it is often difficult to make meaningful comparisons between Chinese and international prices.

The authors would like to thank Greg Benton for his encouragement and advice; Jane Bell, Joy Hunter, and Julian Szego for their helpful comments and criticism; and Johanne Goring for her assistance with the Bibliography.

ALAN HUNTER
JOHN SEXTON

List of Abbreviations and Acronyms

ADB	Asian Development Bank
APEC	Asia Pacific Economic Cooperation
ASEAN	Association of South East Asian Nations
BBC	British Broadcasting Corporation
BCE	Before the Common Era (BC)
BJP	Bharatiya Janata Party
CCP	Chinese Communist Party
CE	Common Era (AD)
CIA	Central Intelligence Agency
CMC	Central Military Commission
CNN	Cable News Network
Comintern	Communist International
CPPCC	Chinese People's Political Consultative Conference
CPSU	Communist Party of the Soviet Union
FDI	foreign direct investment
FSU	Former Soviet Union
GATT	General Agreement on Tariffs and Trade
GDP	gross domestic product
GMD	Guomindang (Nationalist Party)
GNP	gross national product
IBRD	International Bank for Reconstruction and Development (World Bank)
ICBM	Inter Continental Ballistic Missile
IDA	International Development Association
IMF	International Monetary Fund
MAC	Military Affairs Commission
MFN	Most Favoured Nation
MTV	MTV (Music Television) Network
NATO	North Atlantic Treaty Organization
NEPA	National Environmental Protection Agency
NPC	National People's Congress

NRA	National Revolutionary Army
PBC	People's Bank of China
PLA	People's Liberation Army
PPP	Purchasing Power Parity
PRC	People's Republic of China
ROC	Republic of China
SAR	Special Administrative Region (Hong Kong)
SEZ	Special Economic Zone
TVE	Township and Village Enterprise
UK	United Kingdom
UN	United Nations
USA	United States of America
US	United States
USSR	Soviet Union
WTO	World Trade Organization

Note: The term 'the Party' is also used to refer to the Chinese Communist Party.

Note to map: Although numerous adjustments have been made to internal administrative boundaries over the centuries, many of modern China's provinces and provincial capitals are of ancient origin. There are currently twenty-three provinces (including the island of Taiwan over which China claims sovereignty), many of them the size of major European countries. The largest, Sichuan, has a population of 120 million. Equivalent in status to provinces are five 'autonomous regions' (Guangxi, Inner Mongolia, Ningxia, Tibet, and Xinjiang) and four municipalities (Beijing, Chongqing, Shanghai, and Tianjin). In July 1997, Hong Kong reverted to China and in 1999 the former Portuguese colony of Macao will follow. These territories will have the status of 'Special Administrative Regions' (SARs).

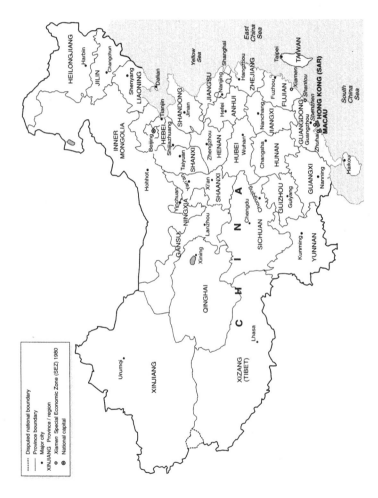

China's provinces and major cities

Disputed national boundary
Province boundary
Major city
XINJIANG Province / region
Xiamen Special Economic Zone (SEZ) 1980
National capital

HEILONGJIANG
Harbin
JILIN
Changchun
Shenyang
LIAONING
Dalian
INNER MONGOLIA
Beijing
HEBEI Tianjin
Shijiazhuang
SHANDONG
Jinan
Zhengzhou
HENAN
Taiyuan
SHANXI
Xian
SHAANXI
Hohhot
Yinchuan
NINGXIA
Lanzhou
GANSU
Xining
QINGHAI
Urumqi
XINJIANG
Lhasa
XIZANG (TIBET)
Chengdu
SICHUAN
CHINA
HUBEI
Wuhan
Changsha
HUNAN
Chongqing
GUIZHOU
Guiyang
Kunming
YUNNAN
GUANGXI
Nanning
Nanchang
JIANGXI
ANHUI
Hefei
JIANGSU
Nanjing
Shanghai
Hangzhou
ZHEJIANG
Fuzhou
FUJIAN
Xiamen
Shantou
GUANGDONG
Guangzhou
Shenzhen
Zhuhai
HONG KONG (SAR)
MACAU
Haikou
Taipei
TAIWAN
Yellow Sea
East China Sea
South China Sea

xiii

Introduction

China is home to about one fifth of the world's population. It has had a turbulent, bloody history in the twentieth century, and until the late 1970s was regarded as an intractable and radical communist state. Yet in the past two decades, a wide-ranging series of reforms has transformed the economy into a unique hybrid of state control and free-wheeling capitalism, and the political system into a mix of authoritarian one-party rule and local factionalism.

Economic growth has been spectacular, but has brought with it equally spectacular problems. Since the late 1970s, the Chinese economy has been growing at an average annual rate of more than 9 per cent; put another way, output has more than quadrupled over the last twenty years. Projecting relative growth rates of 8.7 per cent and 2.3 per cent respectively, China will overtake the USA early in the next century, to become the world's largest economy (*The Economist*, 28 November 1992). Analysts now take the prospect of China as an industrial superpower extremely seriously. It has become commonplace to talk of a Chinese miracle. According to one expert, if China's growth continues, 'the world is in for the biggest change since the industrial revolution' (Krugman, 1994: 76).

Yet, however impressive in terms of raw output, the Chinese system has been characterized by an economist as 'a young, rough-hewn, uncouth, neomercantilist, rule-bebarnacled, rule-breaking, corporatist, insider, quasi-capitalism; wheeling, dealing, networking, and bribing its way within a market-friendly Leninist political power structure' (Prybla, 1997: 4). The economic structure is immature and vulnerable to extra-economic factors, in particular to flaws in the legal and political system and to volatility in global markets. China may succeed in deepening and consolidating its gains, but an alternative scenario is quite feasible, namely that 'corruption and regionalism will turn it into another Nigeria' (Kristof and WuDunn, 1994: 187). The assumption that China can maintain its recent growth rate should not by any means be taken for granted, although its undoubted successes should not be minimized either.

1

The political outlook is uncertain. In 1989, the Chinese government was badly shaken by protest movements in most major cities, which it eventually crushed in a brutal manner by deploying military forces against unarmed citizens. The immediate aftermath was a crackdown on political activism, and many expected a return to hard-line communism. Instead, the response of the Chinese government was far more sophisticated. The top leadership stabilized around the figure of Jiang Zemin, and the death of Deng Xiaoping in 1997 caused hardly a ripple of instability. The government proved capable of managing the economy, and political opposition remained fragmented and marginalized. The recovery of Hong Kong from British rule was presented in the media as a culmination of national prestige, a marker of success and power. There is no way to ascertain the true state of public opinion about politics in China, since there is no real freedom of debate, publication, or association. It should be safe to say that the central government now has far more support from the populace than it did in 1989; yet many anticipate further explosions of public dissent when the opportunity arises.

Apart from the domestic economy and politics, two issues are likely to dominate international reporting on China in the next few years. First, China is now a great power in Asia. Until perhaps the late 1980s, the international community was uncertain whether China's reforms would deliver the economic growth necessary to support military and political influence outside its borders. By the late 1990s, there was no question. China must be counted among the leading players in any analysis of Asian politics. It appears to be far stronger than the emasculated Russia, and rivals Japan and the USA. Its influence is now felt throughout east and southeast Asia, and it looks set to become regional hegemon soon, or at least to challenge Japan for this role. Second, China is an environmental disaster. Its rapid industrialization was achieved with very little concern for environmental protection and, as we shall see, it has appalling indicators for water and air pollution, soil degradation, and other factors. The grave domestic problems are being inadequately addressed. Further, many of the factors (for example, sulphur emissions or use of CFCs) cause global as well as local problems. Yet like other developing countries, the Chinese government, possibly supported by much of its population, argues strongly against Western hypocrisy in demanding standards that the West did not implement during its own industrialization.

This book is intended as an introduction to China, and is inevitably short on details of particular issues, while many interesting facets of Chinese life had to be omitted altogether. China is a complex society, with a unique history and culture; indeed, many non-Chinese may have been brought up to regard China as exotic, remote, and impenetrable. Yet we believe it is possible to gain a reasonable overview of its central political and economic structures, complemented by a preliminary understanding of social and cultural issues, such as the role of the family, art, and religion. When reading, you may find in Chinese life a continual overlap of different strands, interacting so multifariously that it is often difficult to say which is dominant. In a stimulating study (Ogden, 1989), Ogden examines China's unresolved dilemmas through three main lenses:

First, China has a powerful historical and cultural legacy. It has a recorded imperial history of some 3000 years, and a social structure which, according to most Western observers at least, tends towards hierarchy if not despotism and to which democracy and freedom are alien. In many respects, society and culture differ from those of other countries: eating habits, the writing system, the literary and artistic tradition, the role of religion, family relations, and many other facets of daily life are unintelligible to the uninformed foreigner. Incidentally, one should remember that outsiders' habits and customs may appear equally strange to many Chinese, although Chinese, especially educated urbanites, are often better informed about foreign countries than foreigners are about China.

Second, China is a developing country. In 1949, China was among the weakest and most war-devastated countries in the world. Its standard of living and economic output was below that of India, ranking with the poorest African and South American states. It is a notable achievement of the Chinese Communist Party (CCP) that, in fifty years, life expectancy and standards of living have risen tremendously, despite continuing poverty in rural areas. However, in many respects its social indicators are still those of a developing country – for example, in terms of transport, healthcare, education, and rural incomes. China's present and, still more, its recent past should be understood in terms of a developing economy, and a very large one at that: India is an obvious point of comparison.

Third, China was, and to some extent still is, a 'socialist' or 'communist' country. We put the terms in inverted commas, because there is no definition that could encompass the extraordinary variety of policies and disasters created in their names. Yet, undeniably,

China's development has been driven by the CCP, whose ideology was derived largely from that of the Communist Party of the Soviet Union (CPSU), notably from its Stalinist era. From 1949, when the CCP took power, up to the present day, Chinese government, politics, and social life have been dominated by the Party. The Party's influence extends into almost all aspects of life, including education, industry, commerce, and the military. There are Party branches in most institutions, including factories, offices, shops, schools, colleges, and army units. Although there were serious challenges to its ideology by the late 1980s, the CCP is still an overwhelming force; and one cannot begin to understand contemporary China without an appreciation of its role.

In the 1990s, powerful new factors came into play following the reforms promoted by Deng Xiaoping, and the creation of a radically new kind of economic structure that is part state-socialist, and part free-market capitalism. The reforms led to the de-collectivization of agriculture and the promotion of small-scale private enterprises; the one-child family; massive investment by overseas Chinese and foreign businesses; saturation by mass media from Hong Kong, Taiwan, and beyond; internal and international migration; and the virtual collapse of communist ideals.

Another important consideration for the student of China is that outside analysis and Chinese self-perceptions often differ widely. On the one hand, there is a highly knowledgeable international body of expertise about China, particularly in the USA, and dozens of English-language specialist studies are published every year. At least until very recently, such studies were generally more carefully researched and more incisive than those produced in China, partly because Chinese social scientists and intellectuals, as we shall see later, have been censored or obliged to self-censor. But in some Western writing one may observe an assumption that Westerners know best how to deal with Chinese problems, and regret that Chinese display a perversely frustrating reluctance to heed Western lectures. To an earlier generation of Christians, China was the greatest mission-field in the world, but the number of converts was disappointingly low. In the 1980s, it appeared self-evident to most Western commentators and politicians that China should speed up its economic reforms, implement far-reaching democratization, and create an optimum environment for foreign business interests. But the experience of the Soviet bloc suggests that the Chinese government's policies were on the whole far more successful in preserving national integrity, social stability, and economic growth than the East European and Russian attempts at immediate transition to democracy and a free market. It is true that the government was brutal, clumsy, and self-seeking when it crushed the 1989 student movement, but many Chinese dislike being preached at by outsiders who may be profoundly ignorant of Chinese realities.

Perhaps because of the differences of language and culture, the legacy of anti-communism, China's huge population, its growing economic and military power, and the uncertainty of future security regimes in Asia, China is more frequently portrayed as a potential threat than a potential partner. Foreign commentators justifiably raise the problems of business piracy, the gulag, human rights abuses, and corruption. Yet one seldom sees references to China's profound historical contributions to science, medicine, and technology; to its resourceful, determined, and inventive population; or to the tremendous advances in overall social welfare achieved since 1949. Should the national interests of China and foreign powers be represented as ultimately irreconcilable and likely to lead to conflict? Or are we still in danger of harbouring dated attitudes and stereotyping a great civilization? Least of all are we kept informed of the rapidly changing relations between China and its neighbours: India, Russia, Japan, and other Asian states. Yet these relations may well determine the future of geo-politics into the next century.

After studying China, you may conclude that its unique characteristics – in size, culture, history, and economic system – mean that any comparisons with other countries are problematic. Yet apart from the intrinsic importance of learning about contemporary Chinese society, there are significant broader issues that may be addressed in the light of the Chinese experience. As already mentioned, so far at least, the Chinese reform process seems to have been far more successful than the Russian, arguably than most East European ones. Was this due to appropriate policies or to other factors? Are there lessons for other economies in transition? Another question is the overall development strategy, including population control and the crushing of political dissent. Why have there been such abuses of human rights in China? Are they justified by economic success, or should dissident groups and foreign governments step up their criticism?

China is also by far the most important communist state remaining in the late 1990s. What does its recent experience tell us about

Marxism as a political philosophy? Is it completely redundant, or does a Chinese-style neo-Marxism have a future as programme of revolution, or system of government? Ironically, an influential development of neo-Marxist thought since the 1960s was the world-capitalism theory, which argues that poor countries on the periphery of the world economy will never be able to break out of their dependency and exploitation by imperialist economic forces. Yet China appears to have done precisely that, and may soon become a strange hybrid: a fully fledged, internationally successful capitalist economy – although doubtless riddled with internal weaknesses and problems – managed by a communist party.

The purpose of this book is to serve as an introduction to China for the non-specialist reader. We have tried to strike a balance between various topics: it is important even for a basic grasp of the country to realize the connections between history, the social system, and the economy; and between the intellectuals' concerns and those of politicians. Chapters 1–4 focus on history, geography, the economy, and politics. Chapters 5 and 6 introduce the reader to the Chinese social system and ways of thought, ranging from traditional approaches to the intellectual currents of the 1980s and 1990s. Chapter 7 discusses China's international relations, which are an integral part of its development strategy and, of course, of the utmost importance to the rest of the world. Chapter 8 concludes with some observations on China as it moves into the twenty-first century.

1
The History of Modern China

Imperial and Republican China continue to mould – and to haunt – the People's Republic (PRC). The political leadership frequently invokes the 'century of humiliation', when China was attacked by Japan and the Western powers, as a reason for anti-foreign policies (Box 1.1). The decay of the Qing empire, the movement for cultural regeneration in the 1910s, the disintegration of 1920s' China into warlord fiefdoms, the brutality of the Japanese occupation, the corruption of the Nationalist regime in the late 1940s, and many other issues and events, some dating back many centuries, are frequently cited in current debates. The Chinese have a tradition of historiography dating back to at least the fifth century BCE; our narrative here starts with a brief overview of events leading to the formation of the Republic of China in 1911, and traces the story down to the immediate aftermath of the 1989 democracy movement.

The Collapse of the Old Regime

China's last imperial dynasty, the Qing, was established by foreign conquest in 1644 when a coalition of tribes from the northeast region of Manchuria swept away the failing Ming dynasty. The Qing rulers made sure the armed forces remained under Manchu control and imposed certain of their customs such as the wearing of hair-braids (which foreigners often mistook to be a quintessentially Chinese fashion), but made no fundamental changes to the structure of Chinese society. On the contrary, in the eighteenth century traditional China reached its full flowering. China was at this time one of the richest and most powerful countries in the world, and its manner of civilian governance by a gentry caste of Confucian scholar-officials was much admired by European philosophers of the enlightenment, for whom it embodied an ideal of rational and stable government.

Box 1.1 Key dates in imperial and republican Chinese history, 1842–1949

1842 29 August – China cedes Hong Kong to Great Britain in the Treaty of Nanjing that concludes the Opium War.

1853 29 March – Taiping rebels led by the Christian mystic Hong Xiuquan seize Nanjing.

1900 14 August – foreign troops occupy Beijing to suppress the Boxer Rebellion.

1911 After uprisings against the Qing dynasty, Sun Yatsen is proclaimed President of the Republic of China on 29 December.

1912 14 February – Sun resigns as President in favour of the former Qing official Yuan Shikai.

1919 4 May – students march to Tian'anmen in protest at concessions to Japan in the Versailles treaty.

1921 23 July – first congress of the Chinese Communist Party begins in Shanghai.

1925 The May 30th movement sweeps China after British police shoot down strikers in Shanghai.

1926 1 July – With Soviet aid and in alliance with the CCP, Chiang Kaishek launches the Northern Expedition to suppress warlordism.

1927 12 April – Chiang Kaishek's troops and underworld gangs massacre CCP members and trades unionists in Shanghai.

1932 February – Japan sets up the puppet state of Manzhouguo (Manchukuo), nominally ruled by the former Qing emperor Puyi.

1935 6–8 January – CCP conference held at Zunyi during the Long March elects Mao Zedong Secretary of the Politburo Standing Committee.

1936 12 December – Chiang Kaishek is kidnapped by dissident officers. Following his release he agrees to a united front with the CCP against the Japanese.

1937 7 July – the Marco Polo Bridge incident sparks Japan's invasion of China.

1945 14 August – unconditional surrender of Japan.

1946 July – Guomindang (GMD) forces initiate civil war against communist People's Liberation Army (PLA).

1949 1 October – Mao Zedong proclaims the People's Republic of China.

While foreigners admired China's apparent stability and continuity, Chinese court historians saw history as a circular process of the rise and fall of dynasties. They believed that after an initial period of vigorous and beneficent rule, indolent or wicked successors to the energetic dynastic founders would eventually lose the mandate of heaven, provoking a popular rebellion from which a new lineage would emerge to recommence the cycle. According to this view, by the early nineteenth century the Qing appeared to have started their predestined descent. It took the regime nearly a decade to suppress a rebellion by millenarian Buddhists of the White Lotus sect as the century dawned; that uprising was itself dwarfed by the great Taiping Rebellion which engulfed China in the 1850s. Led by the religious mystic Hong Xiuquan, who claimed to be the younger brother of Jesus Christ, the Taiping rebellion was by far the bloodiest military conflict of the nineteenth-century world. More than a decade of civil war and famine left 20 million dead. The Qing regime, within an ace of being overthrown, was forced to sanction the creation of native Chinese armed forces to suppress the rebellion and accept foreign military aid. It emerged from the crisis gravely weakened.

If internal rebellions threatened the dynasty, the imperial system itself was threatened by growing foreign pressure. Britain, in particular, was keen to open up China and impatient with the conservative Beijing regime which, until the 1830s, restricted foreign trade to the single port of Guangzhou (Canton). The imperial government responded poorly to Britain's challenge. Its problem was that China had for so long dominated East Asia that it had neither the military capability nor political mechanisms for dealing with powerful opponents from outside its traditional sphere. Foreigners were traditionally regarded as barbarians whose place was to pay tribute to the Emperor and accept his sage advice. These illusions were destroyed by Britain's infamous Opium War of 1839–42, started after Chinese officials, seeking to suppress addiction, seized and destroyed opium owned by British merchants. The war exposed the military impotence of the Qing government, which was forced to cede Hong Kong in the first of many unequal treaties. Foreign powers eventually gained jurisdiction in dozens of treaty ports and concession areas, won the right to station troops in Beijing and other cities, the exemption of their citizens from Chinese law, and control of the Chinese customs service. As the colonialist scramble accelerated, British, French, Russian, German, and Japanese forces piled defeat upon humiliation until in 1900, following an outburst of anti-foreign feeling in the Boxer Uprising, the imperial government was expelled from Beijing by a joint expeditionary force headed by a German general. At this stage the colonialist powers actively considered partition, but preferred rough commercial equality to the risk of exclusion from each others' spheres of influence, and therefore revived the moribund Qing regime. The most enthusiastic supporter of this 'open-door' policy was the USA, whose military position in China was weakest.

Even in the face of mounting crisis the Qing regime made no sustained effort to reform itself. A 'self-strengthening' movement associated with the reformer Li Hongzhang, who had helped suppress the Taipings, imported modern military technology, and in 1861 the regime established a ministry of foreign affairs. But the court was dominated by the reactionary dowager empress Cixi from the 1860s until the early 1900s. Cixi's most significant political act was to order the execution of ministers who gained control of the government during a period known as the Hundred Days of Reform in 1898. As Cixi's grip on power weakened, limited institutional reform was finally undertaken. The traditional civil service examination based on knowledge of the Confucian classics was abolished, modern army units known as the New Army were formed, and in 1909, in response to pressure for constitutional reform, elections were held to regional assemblies. These belated concessions did not strengthen the regime, however, but merely put in place the mechanisms for its removal.

Republican China, 1911–49

Sun Yatsen and the 1911 Revolution

A new bourgeois class was slowly evolving from the traditional scholar-bureaucrats and landowners who, despite the low social status accorded to merchants in Confucian tradition, had begun to involve themselves in commerce and industry. Usually referred to as the gentry, this class dominated the provincial assemblies. Its majority was in favour of a peaceful evolution towards a constitutional monarchy. More radical voices calling for the overthrow of the Manchu regime also gathered considerable support, especially in the south and among overseas Chinese. The acknowledged leader of

---

Box 1.2   Sun Yatsen, 1866–1925
         (Sun Zhongshan or Sun Yixian in hanyu pinyin spelling)

Sun received medical training in Hong Kong and Hawaii and was influenced by Christianity and Western political thought. He organized several revolutionary groups, with support from overseas Chinese; the 1911 revolution, however, took him by surprise. He promulgated 'Three People's Principles': nationalism, people's rights, and people's livelihood. In December 1911, Sun became president of the Republic of China, and the following year formed the Guomindang, or Nationalist Party (GMD), which won elections to a national assembly in 1912. Sun was forced to flee to Guangdong in 1913 after a military coup. He remained there, while north China was dominated by warlords, until his death in 1925. He succeeded in building up forces, partly with Soviet support, which eventually ousted the warlords after the Northern Expedition of 1926. Sun is revered in both the PRC and Taiwan as the founding father of Republican China.

China's revolutionaries and the outstanding figure in early twentieth-century politics was Sun Yatsen (Box 1.2). Sun, born in Guangdong province in 1866, was educated in Hawaii and Hong Kong, where he absorbed many Western influences and became a Christian. He had a somewhat poorly defined vision of a modernized China, formulating his ideas as the 'Three People's Principles': nationalism, people's rights, and people's livelihood, the latter usually understood to mean a mild form of socialism. His conspiratorial political methods, however, were rooted in the Chinese tradition of secret societies, and he organized a number of underground groups and failed putsches. The 1911 uprising in fact took him by surprise, although some members of his Tongmenghui organization played leading roles in it.

The final collapse of the regime was triggered when it attempted to nationalize China's railways to speed up stalled private construction projects. Enraged by poor compensation terms, gentry in Sichuan fomented a patriotic hue and cry on the grounds that nationalization by the Manchu, with the aid of foreign loans, amounted to the seizure of China's railways by foreigners. During the ensuing disorders and troop movements, pro-Tongmenghui officers seized the city of Wuhan in October 1911, and declared its independence of Beijing. The Qing officials fled, and provinces around China soon made similar declarations, usually announced by coalitions of local assembly leaders and New Army officers. In December a provisional government in Nanjing named Sun Yatsen first President of the Republic of China.

Yuan Shikai Attempts to Found a New Dynasty

The Qing regime in Beijing thought that it could rely on the Beiyang Army – the northern divisions of the New Army – and recalled its former general, Yuan Shikai, into service. But Yuan immediately betrayed the government and seized power for himself. In secret negotiations, Sun Yatsen agreed to hand over the presidency to Yuan in return for the abdication of the infant emperor Puyi and the abolition of the monarchy. For a brief period China had the institutions and appearance of a parliamentary republic. The Tong-menghui, expanded and renamed as the Guomindang (National People's Party, GMD), won elections held at the end of 1912. However, as the GMD's new leader, Song Jiaoren, prepared to take over the premiership, Yuan ordered his assassination and, after a brief civil war, banned the GMD and dissolved parliament. The vast majority of Chinese, for the most part illiterate peasants, had not been permitted to vote and were indifferent to the parliament's fate. In 1916, having no other political reference points, Yuan attempted to establish a new dynasty. However neither the provincial authorities nor his own subordinates in the army were prepared to tolerate his coronation. Faced with mounting chaos, a humiliated Yuan reinstated the Republic and died shortly afterwards.

Warlords

After Yuan's death, the Beijing government was reduced to impotence, a creature of whatever military force currently occupied the city. Real power was in the hands of provincial military leaders. These warlords waged intermittent, inconclusive, and destructive war against each other over the next decade or so, in a bewildering story of alliance and betrayal. The period, for many Chinese, still exemplifies national disintegration and meaningless slaughter; a perception that favours centralized government, and one that was reinforced in the early 1990s by media coverage of events in Russia and Yugoslavia.

For the most part the warlord armies emerged out of the New Armies of the old regime. Some warlords such as Duan Qirui and Feng Guozhang had been military subordinates of Yuan in the Beiyang Army. Yan Xishan, who ruled Shanxi province, was a former Tongmenghui revolutionary and New Army officer who had seized control of the province in the revolution of 1911. Others were former bandits such as Zhang Zuolin, who controlled Manchuria with Japanese backing. A few were idealist and even reformist, such as Feng Yuxiang, the 'Christian General', who was reported to baptize whole regiments using a hosepipe. Most were corrupt and reactionary, like Zang Zongchang, warlord of Shandong in the late 1920s, who reduced the province to anarchy and earned the sobriquet of 'Dog Meat General' for his brutality.

Whatever their origins, all warlords required money to pay their troops and buy modern weapons, which foreign arms dealers were eager to supply. The larger the population under a warlord's control, the greater the tax revenue he could extract, and this gave him a strong incentive to expand his territory. Taxation was supplemented by plunder and forced labour. All were destructive of the economy, as were other common money-raising schemes such as opium cultivation, or the 'purchase' of goods with the warlords' own worthless paper currencies. From the half-million or so troops inherited from the New Armies in 1916, the number of men under arms gradually rose to a peak of around 2 million by 1929. Some large-scale battles were fought, particularly as Duan Qirui, Feng Guozhang and Zhang Zuolin fought for control of the Beijing government, an institution reduced to irrelevance in the process. At the other extreme, a myriad of minor warlords, some controlling little more than guerrilla bands, wreaked havoc in many places.

The May 4th Movement

In contrast to this pointless destruction, a slower process had been ripening in the treaty ports and concession areas controlled by the foreign powers. Peaceful conditions allowed both foreign and Chinese-owned business to prosper in these mainly coastal regions. A class with some characteristics of a modern bourgeoisie was beginning to take shape, and alongside it, an urban working class. In the long run, these developments were of more significance for China than the military competition between the warlords, although

---

Box 1.3   Chen Duxiu, 1879–1942

An outstanding intellectual and writer, Chen was editor of the journal *New Youth*, and a leading figure in the May 4th movement. He became the founder and first general secretary of the CCP in 1921, but was removed from its leadership in 1927; his achievements were then systematically denigrated by CCP historians until the 1980s. In 1931, after corresponding with the exiled Russian revolutionary, Leon Trotsky, Chen became leader of the Left Opposition to the official CCP leadership. He was imprisoned by the Guomindang from 1932 to 1937. He died a few years later in relative obscurity. In 1941 Chen left the Trotskyist movement; in his final writings, he rejected Leninism and Bolshevism in favour of a synthesis of radical democracy and socialism.

---

this is not how it appeared at the time, either to the outside world or to the long-suffering Chinese.

The New Culture Movement of the 1910s saw the rapid spread of radical ideas, many taken from progressive Western thinkers such as John Dewey. The journal *New Youth* epitomized this ferment, promoting radical arguments against the entire Confucian tradition. Its editor, Chen Duxiu (Box 1.3), believed that China could be transformed by science and democracy, perfectly expressing the optimistic mood of the time and the intellectual fashion for embracing all that was new and rejecting all that was old. Confucianism which, in various guises, had remained the world view of the educated elite, now had to compete with a new and heady brew of liberalism, anarchism, feminism and socialism. Chen himself became the founder and first General Secretary of the Chinese Communist Party (CCP) in 1921.

In 1917, the Beijing government of Duan Qirui declared war on Germany in the hope of regaining the German-controlled province of Shandong at the end of the first World War. The allies, however, had already promised Shandong to Japan in a secret treaty, a policy confirmed at Versailles in 1919. Public opinion was outraged at this national humiliation, and on 4 May 1919 thousands of Beijing students marched to Tian'anmen and staged the first protest of its kind in China's political history. Their action had profound resonance seventy years later, when students again marched to Tian'anmen to confront their government.

Table 1.1   CCP membership, 1921–97

Year	Membership	Year	Membership
1921	53	1945	1 210 000
1922	195	1956	10 730 000
1923	432	1973	28 000 000
1925	950	1977	35 000 000
1927	57 900	1982	39 650 000
1928	40 000	1997	58 000 000

The CCP grew strongly during an upsurge of working-class militancy in the mid-1920s but suffered a severe setback when Guomindang forces attacked the labour movement in 1927. The Party went on to build a mass membership in rural areas. Today, one in twenty Chinese are members.

Source: Christiansen and Rai, 1996: 94.

Much of China's urban population supported the students' demands, and, under pressure from the mass movement, the government refused to ratify the Versailles treaty. The victory was a defining moment of Chinese politics, inspiring the radicalization of a whole generation of youth, who became both leaders and foot-soldiers in the parties which went on to shape the future of the country. Sun Yatsen re-launched the GMD to admit thousands of young militants, many of whom later transferred their allegiance to the Communist Party.

The First United Front

The Communist International (Comintern) encouraged Chen Duxiu and his Beijing university colleague Li Dazhao to set up the CCP in 1921. But Comintern policy was not exclusively directed towards building up the CCP (Table 1.1). For one thing, many Marxists believed that socialist revolution was not on the agenda in such a backward country as China, and did not expect the CCP to grow rapidly. In the meantime the Soviet state was keen to establish military and political alliances in China, partly to build up a counterweight to Japan which threatened its far eastern provinces. Comintern theory spoke of a forthcoming 'national-democratic' revolution in China and nominated the GMD as the political force most likely to carry it through. Lengthy negotiations between Soviet

Ambassador Joffe and Sun Yatsen accompanied parallel efforts by the Dutch Comintern agent Sneevliet (alias Maring) to persuade reluctant CCP leaders to submerge their new party in the GMD. In 1923 an agreement was reached whereby CCP members were to establish a 'united front' with the GMD: they would join the GMD while retaining their own distinct organization. The Soviet Union began to ship large quantities of military aid to the GMD stronghold of Guangzhou, and Comintern advisors led by Mikhail Borodin established a military academy at nearby Huangpu to build up the GMD's new model army, the National Revolutionary Army (NRA). Soviet aid to the GMD was decisive in transforming it from a regional to a national force; by comparison, aid provided directly to the CCP was miserly.

The Northern Expedition and Chiang's Coup against the CCP

In 1925 an upsurge of working class militancy hit the foreign concession areas. The 'May 30th movement', named after a massacre of striking cotton workers by British police in Shanghai, spread rapidly. CCP membership soared. A prolonged general strike in Hong Kong spread to Guangzhou, where the Party-led strike committee began to challenge GMD authority. Such worker or peasant militancy placed the CCP–GMD alliance under strain, since it threatened the material interests of landowners and businessmen amongst the GMD leaders.

As long as Sun Yatsen was alive, the tensions remained manageable, but his premature death in 1925 removed the united front's chief advocate within the GMD. Sun's political heir-apparent was Wang Jingwei, who favoured the Soviet alliance; but real power lay in the hands of Chiang Kaishek (Jiang Jieshi in hanyu pinyin spelling), head of the Huangpu military school and commander of the NRA. While Chiang valued Soviet military aid he had no sympathy with communism or worker–peasant militancy. In early 1926 he disarmed the Hong Kong–Guangzhou strike committee, and effectively ousted Wang Jingwei as GMD leader. Despite the attack on the strike committee, relations with the Comintern were patched up, and Soviet aid continued.

Sun Yatsen's purpose in building up the NRA had been to confront the warlord armies to the north and re-unify China. Chiang now felt powerful enough to implement this project, and in July 1926 announced a Northern Expedition. The NRA, accompanied by Russian advisors, advanced into Hunan province where, combining mobile warfare with propaganda, it rapidly defeated or absorbed numerically superior warlord forces, taking Wuhan in September and Nanchang in November. As the Northern Expedition built up momentum, it energized the local populace. Its arrival was often accompanied by strikes and land seizures which the CCP sometimes encouraged, but more often attempted to restrain for the sake of its alliance with the GMD.

As Chiang's forces approached Shanghai in spring 1927, armed detachments of the CCP-led trades unions, under the direction of Chen Duxiu and Zhou Enlai, staged an uprising and prepared to welcome the advancing NRA, while reminding the GMD leaders of the power of the labour movement. By this time, however, Chiang had decided that the advantages of the Soviet alliance were exhausted, and he turned decisively against the CCP. After entering the city he conspired with powerful underworld organizations to destroy the Shanghai labour movement. Thousands of trades unionists were slaughtered by Chiang's henchmen while NRA troops held the ring. The CCP organization in the city was destroyed.

Similar attacks took place across China, marking the start of a 'white terror' that effectively smashed urban radical and even liberal political life. In Beijing, warlord troops stormed the Soviet embassy and killed dozens of Communists who had been sheltering there, including the party's co-founder Li Dazhao. While Wang Jingwei remained at the head of a GMD government in Wuhan, the Comintern had some hopes of retaining a foothold. But as commander of the NRA, Chiang held all the cards and Wang soon fell into line. In July 1927 Wang expelled all Soviet advisors and began to arrest CCP members. The first united front ended in a disaster for the Communists that they contrived to compound by ill-fated attempts to retrieve the situation through a series of poorly planned uprisings.

The Nanjing Regime

For a decade from 1927, Chiang Kaishek's Nationalist government ruled China from its new capital at Nanjing (Box 1.4). The government was rooted in the eastern seaboard and along the Yangzi, the richest and most populous regions of the country. In the coastal

---

Box 1.4   Chiang Kaishek, 1887–1975
(Jiang Jieshi in hanyu pinyin spelling)

A protege and son-in-law of Sun Yatsen, Chiang became leader of the Guomindang in 1926 and commander of its armed forces. A key leader of the Northern Expedition, he implemented a campaign of terror against his communist allies, and became President of the Republic of China in 1927. Chiang's government ruled from its capital in Nanjing until 1937, when it was forced to retreat to Chongqing to escape the Japanese invasion. Chiang received substantial US aid, and survived the Second World War as an ally of the USA and Britain. However, he was thoroughly defeated in the Civil War against the Chinese Communists between 1945 and 1949, and fled to the island of Taiwan. He ruled the island under martial law until his death in 1978, when he was succeeded by his son, Chiang Ching-kuo, who turned out to be a successful reformer.

---

cities under its control, economic growth was lively (although no more than it had been during the warlord era), especially in Shanghai where all the trappings of twentieth-century life were soon in evidence. The new government, with support from the Western powers, reversed the worst excesses of the unequal treaties, regaining control over the customs service and many of the concession areas. It also started to revoke the privileges of extra-territoriality which foreigners had enjoyed since the nineteenth century.

Overall, however, the Nationalist period in government was a failure, that ended in chaos and ignominious defeat. The government failed in its principal objective, to re-unify China. Chiang never directly controlled more than 10 per cent of the territory and 25 per cent of the population of the country, despite fighting numerous campaigns to incorporate the rest. In part, this was because of the way the Northern Expedition had been conducted. Although the NRA had defeated some warlord armies, it had won over and absorbed many more, entering into alliances with Yan Xishan, Feng Yuxiang and others. The new government consequently stood at the head of an unstable coalition of forces which began to splinter almost as soon as victory had been achieved.

The government's finances were in a state of perpetual crisis. The huge number of men under arms, who had to be paid or reintegrated into civilian life, was a major problem. In addition, many of the government's newly acquired warlord supporters expected to profit from their support of the Northern Expedition: the influx of former warlord officials, who travelled from north to south in search of new jobs, was satirized as a new Southern Expedition. Former allies had to be rewarded and potential enemies bought off. Nanjing conceded to provincial leaders the right to collect and retain land taxes, which had been the traditional source of revenue for Chinese governments. The resulting fiscal shortfall was covered by bond issues which stimulated the growth of a thriving commercial banking sector; its success, however, merely reflected the essentially parasitic nature of the GMD bureaucracy and military establishment.

Perhaps the most crucial factor in the decline of the regime was the political exhaustion of the GMD itself. The anti-communist purge, by removing its most active and idealistic members, finished it off as a campaigning organization. Henceforth, it became little more than a vehicle for advancement to lucrative posts in the bureaucracy. Politics was occasionally enlivened by factional struggles, fuelled by the continuing resentment of Wang Jingwei, but largely remained moribund. Chiang preferred to rule through officer corps' connections nurtured since the days of the Huangpu academy rather than risk open political competition. Impressed by the growth of European fascism, he briefly toyed with the creation of a similar movement in China, but his 'blueshirts' attracted little support. The regime failed to put down deep roots amongst the people in the cities. In the villages, its policy of leaving local power in the hands of village chiefs and 'evil gentry' closed off the possibility of building support among the peasantry and opened the door to the CCP. As time passed, the growing corruption of GMD officials made the government deeply unpopular.

The Long March and Mao's Rise to Leadership of the CCP

The Long March is the defining, inspirational myth of the CCP. It also marks Mao Zedong's rise to leadership of the party and the defeat of the slavishly pro-Soviet '28 Bolsheviks' appointed by Stalin. Under Mao's leadership, China's Communists pursued their path to power and their conduct of government independently of Moscow's directives, which bitter experience had taught them to mistrust. While employed by the GMD as a rural organizer during the united front, Mao had begun to recognize the revolutionary potential of the poor peasants, modifying previous Party emphasis on the leading role of urban workers. After the Shanghai massacre and the collapse of the government in Wuhan, he played a leading role in a peasant rebellion in Hunan, the so-called 'Autumn Harvest' uprising. The rebellion was defeated, but Mao regrouped his forces and gradually won control first of the Jinggang mountains and later of large parts part of Jiangxi province, winning the support of the poorer peasants by carrying out moderate land reforms. The Communists controlled much of Jiangxi until 1934 when Chiang Kaishek's forces, at the fifth attempt, drove them out. About 100 000 Red Army troops then set off on a retreat of several thousand miles through remote parts of China; fewer than 10 per cent finally arrived in the northwest, where they eventually established their new capital in Yan'an. The heroic endurance of the survivors transformed this apparent defeat into a propaganda triumph, and during the march a new leadership group crystallized around Mao. The 'Yan'an spirit', mythologized in later propaganda, was often used in later decades to legitimize CCP power by invoking its days of glory, symbolizing revolutionary idealism and self-sacrifice; however, recent research has discerned in Yan'an signs of the cynical manipulation and self-seeking that were to characterize CCP politics in later years.

Japanese Invasion and the Second United Front

Japan had been encroaching on Chinese territory for decades, having won Taiwan in the war of 1894–5, and established a bridgehead in Manchuria in the Russo–Japanese war of 1904–5. On the outbreak of the First World War, Japan seized the German concession area of Shandong, and in 1915, presented twenty-one demands to Yuan Shikai that, if acceded to, would have handed control over China's government to Tokyo. After 1918, the Japanese dominated Manchuria via warlord proxies, and in 1931 they conquered the whole of the province, installing the deposed Qing emperor Puyi as head of the puppet state of Manchukuo (Manzhouguo). Japanese troops roamed freely through northern China on 'manouvre' eliciting only feeble protests from the Nationalist government despite mounting public outrage. Chiang Kaishek famously remarked that whereas the Japanese were a disease of the skin, communism was a disease of the bone, and tied up his forces in 'bandit extermination campaigns' directed against the CCP.

In the mid-1930s, the CCP exploited the Nationalists' refusal to confront the Japanese, presenting themselves as true patriots and calling for a new anti-Japanese united front. They succeeded in winning over some senior commanders of the NRA, and on 12 December 1936 a group of senior officers kidnapped Chiang and placed him at the mercy of his Communist enemies. Some observers claim that Mao initially wanted to execute Chiang and that Moscow dissuaded him. Whatever the truth of these claims, Chiang was eventually released after agreeing to join an anti-Japanese united front with the Communists. The new deal was formalized in September 1937. In theory, it called for the incorporation of the Communist armed forces into the NRA but, mindful of the debacle of the first united front, Mao ensured that his armies retained their independence.

The Conduct of the War

In July 1937 a minor skirmish between Chinese and Japanese troops at the Marco Polo Bridge near Beijing led to a full-scale invasion by Japanese forces. The incident marked the opening of war in the Pacific that lasted until 1945. In 1941 the USA became a combatant after Japan attacked its fleet at Pearl Harbor. Between 1941 and 1945, China was a theatre of war in the greater context of the Second World War. The Allies provided material assistance to the Chinese government, and effectively ended the war by nuclear attacks on Hiroshima and Nagasaki. The fact that many Japanese army units were tied down in China was an important element in the Allied war effort in Asia.

The Japanese swiftly captured the heartland of Nationalist China, but since they lacked sufficient troops to control the whole of China, the occupation was mainly restricted to the east of the country. Chiang's government retreated to Chongqing in Sichuan province where it remained until the end of the war in 1945, out of reach of enemy land forces although subject to heavy bombing. As the Japanese advanced south in pursuit of retreating Nationalist forces, large areas in northern China fell into the hands of the Communists. Eventually the CCP controlled an area populated by 90 million people and a regular army of 1 million backed up by twice as many irregulars. Communist-led guerrillas caused severe problems to the Japanese military, who were restricted to defending towns and lines of communications. Japanese forces responded to guerrilla attacks with raids on defenceless villages, conducted with maximum brutality. Military and civilian casualties are incalculable, and run into many millions: the Japanese occupation has left scars which are far from healed.

The experience of governing the 'liberated areas' and 'base areas' behind enemy lines allowed the Party to test and refine such elements of emerging 'Mao Zedong thought' as the 'mass line', according to which the Party was supposed to formulate policy after wide consultation, and implement it by mass mobilization rather than by bureaucratic fiat. The CCP had time and space for such experimentation. After the USA entered the war, both Chiang and Mao realized that eventually Japan would be defeated with or without their help and concentrated on conserving their forces for the competition over the post-war settlement. The Party position was considerably strengthened after the Soviet Union entered the war against Japan in 1945. The Soviets seized Manchuria and allowed Communist troops led by Lin Biao to position themselves across the northeast: this became a factor of some significance in the ensuing civil war.

Civil War and Communist Victory

The second united front broke down as early as 1941, and large-scale armed conflict between the CCP and the GMD erupted in 1946. Chiang Kaishek took the initiative in the civil war, hoping to capitalize quickly on a three-to-one advantage in manpower. He seized the Party's capital in Yan'an in February 1947 and sent hundreds of thousands of troops north to clear the Communist forces out of Manchuria. But, like the Japanese before them, the Nationalist troops were unable to eliminate the Communists' rural bases. Instead, they remained holed up in their city strongholds where mounting inflation and corruption demoralized the civilian population while the Communists cut their supply lines at will. Towards the end of 1948 in Manchuria and the North China plain, a million-strong Nationalist army crumbled in the face of Communist offensives. The Communist forces, now renamed as the People's Liberation Army (PLA), absorbed many surrendering Nationalist units and swept south, meeting little resistance. As Chiang Kaishek retreated to the island of Taiwan with his remaining troops, Mao Zedong proclaimed the formation of the People's Republic of China in Beijing on 1 October 1949.

The People's Republic, 1949–89

Consolidation of the New Regime

During 1950–1, CCP forces mopped up all remaining pockets of Nationalist resistance on the mainland. China was now re-united under an effective government, and this achievement in itself, reinforced by the contrast between its relatively honest officials and the widespread corruption of the GMD's final years, helps to explain the initial popularity of the regime. The government demonstrated financial and administrative competence by dealing quickly with hyper-inflation inherited from the Nationalists. The transport network was restored and economic life started to recover.

The political institutions of the new state were designed to conform with the CCP theory of 'New Democracy', according to which a coalition of all the patriotic classes would rule the country under the leadership of the CCP during the first stage of the revolution. 'Patriotic forces' were defined as workers, peasants, petty bourgeoisie and the national bourgeoisie, but excluded landlords, 'bureaucratic capitalists' associated with the Nationalist regime, and the *comprador* bourgeoisie closely associated with foreign interests. The political forms of 'New Democracy' resembled those adopted in the 'People's Democracies' of Eastern Europe. In coalition with the CCP were a small number of officially tolerated and controlled 'democratic parties' including a splinter group from the GMD. A constituent assembly, the Chinese People's Political Consultative Conference (CPPCC) drew up basic political guidelines in a Common Programme, a kind of proto-constitution, adopted in 1949. Details of political institutions may be found in Chapter 4; for now it is important to note that the PRC government achieved power by force of arms, and claimed legitimacy on the basis of massive popular support. Its constitutional arrangements started from scratch, and made no pretence at institutional continuity with the previous regime.

The regime consolidated its position in the countryside by extending the land reform already carried out in the previously liberated areas. The reform was implemented by work-teams sent to each village to mobilize the population using the Party's well-practised 'mass-line' approach. By involving peasants in the seizure of land and in some cases in the killing of landlords, the Party ensured that a large part of the population gained a stake in the new

Box 1.5 Key dates in the history of the People's Republic of China (PRC)

1950   14 February – the PRC and the USSR sign Treaty of Friendship, Alliance and Mutual Assistance.

1950   October – the PRC enters the Korean War after US forces advance towards the Chinese frontier.

1957   May – the Hundred Flowers movement is followed in June by the Anti-Rightist campaign.

1958   5–23 May – Eighth Congress of the CCP launches the Great Leap Forward.

1960   16 July – the USSR withdraws all technical advisors from China.

1962   20 October – outbreak of border war between the PRC and India.

1963   20 May – Socialist Education Movement launched to combat rural corruption.

1966   16 May – Politburo sets up the Cultural Revolution Group. On 5 August Mao attacks Party rivals in a wall-poster entitled 'Bombard the Headquarters'.

1969   2 March – PRC and Soviet forces clash at the Ussuri river.

1971   13 September, Mao's deputy, Lin Biao, is killed in an air crash in Mongolia after an unsuccessful coup attempt.

1971   25 October – the PRC is admitted to the UN.

1972   21 February – US President Nixon arrives in Beijing.

1976   9 September, Mao Zedong dies. On 6 October, the Gang of Four are arrested.

1978   November – posters calling for political reform appear on 'Democracy Wall' in Beijing

1978   December – Deng Xiaoping initiates economic reform at the 3rd Plenum of the 11th Central Committee

1979   17 February – PRC forces invade Vietnam.

1979   29 March – 'Democracy Wall' activist Wei Jingsheng arrested and subsequently sentenced to 15 years jail.

1980   China joins the World Bank and the International Monetary Fund (IMF). The 'four great freedoms', including the right to put up wall posters, are removed from the Chinese constitution.

1989   4 June – Pro-democracy demonstrations in Beijing's Tian'anmen Square are brutally dispersed.

1997   19 February – Deng Xiaoping dies.

1997   1 July – Hong Kong reverts to China.

order and strong reasons to fear any restoration of the old regime. Tenant farmers were given title deeds to land they had previously rented, while poor and landless peasants received grants of land. In all, about 40 per cent of China's farmland was redistributed (Phillips, 1996: 166), but the holdings of 'middle' and rich peasants were largely left untouched, so there remained considerable inequality among the mass of small farmers. Meanwhile, the government soon began moves towards its long-term aim of collectivization.

The Korean War and its Consequences

The PRC was formed as the wartime alliance against Germany and Japan broke up, and the world polarized into two hostile camps led by the USA and the Soviet Union. The Cold War forced China to 'lean to one side' and declare for the socialist camp. When fighting broke out between US and Soviet proxies in neighbouring Korea, the Chinese found themselves faced with hostile UN forces led by the USA approaching the industrial area of Manchuria. When the UN ignored warnings not to continue their advance, PRC 'volunteers' entered Korea and drove them back to the 38th Parallel, where the war ended in stalemate. Despite heavy casualties, the success of the armed forces was a source of some pride domestically. Internationally, however, the Korean War had serious repercussions. Prior to the Korean War, it seemed only a matter of time before Taiwan fell; after the war, the Americans did everything in their power to build up Taiwan as a military and economic counterweight to Beijing. They were also able to ensure that the government in Taiwan, still known as the Republic of China, retained China's seat at the UN, maintaining the international isolation of the People's Republic until the 1970s.

First Five-year Plan and Socialization

Although 'New Democracy', in theory, allowed for a relatively long period of substantial private ownership and economic activity, the remaining private firms were in fact taken into state or collective ownership by the mid-1950s. (Many industries had already been nationalized by the GMD, often in post-war confiscation of Japanese property.) In the countryside the peasant farmers were organized into collectives in 1955–6. This was supposed to happen in stages, with each household's income initially depending partly on the amount of land it brought with it into the collective; in practice, the collectives often moved directly to a system of payment according to work carried out by household members.

In 1953, the government adopted a Five-year Plan on the Soviet model. A key component was the import from the USSR of entire industrial plants which were constructed and operated with the aid of Soviet technicians. The plan was overwhelmingly geared towards heavy industry, with half of total investment devoted to just 150 projects. In crude terms the plan was a great success, achieving an average annual growth rate of 9 per cent. However, given the emphasis on heavy industry, it must be doubted whether its value in terms of overall economic development was so impressive. Crucially, while wages of urban workers rose by a third over the five years, rural incomes grew by only a fifth, implying a long-term widening of the gap between town and country.

The Hundred Flowers Movement and the Anti-Rightist Campaign

By the mid-1950s Mao was becoming increasingly critical of the bureaucratic deformities that he believed Chinese socialism had inherited from the Soviet Union. In order to combat bureaucracy, Mao was prepared to allow forces outside the Party to criticize, and so contribute to the 'rectification' of, Party practice. He also saw limited public criticism of the regime as a useful safety valve to pre-empt the emergence of opposition groups. In 1949 China's intellectuals had for the most part either welcomed or remained neutral towards the new government. But following a series of heavy-handed thought-reform campaigns many, if not most, now resented and feared the regime. Mao was not blind to the dangers of a disaffected intelligentsia, a condition contributing to a deepening crisis of East European socialism that came to a head in the 1956 Hungarian uprising.

In May 1956 CCP propaganda chief Lu Dingyi signalled an easing of ideological controls when he raised the slogan 'Let a hundred flowers bloom and a hundred schools contend'. In February 1957 Mao delivered an address 'On the correct handling of contradictions amongst the people', in which he distinguished between 'antagonistic contradictions' – broadly speaking conflicts between classes to be resolved by force – and 'non-antagonistic contradictions' – conflicts within classes that should be solved by persuasion. He insisted that people outside the Party should be encouraged to take part in the process of rectification. Most of the leadership were opposed to allowing public criticism of the Party but Mao won their grudging acceptance by arguing that a period of free debate would inoculate the People's Republic against the Hungarian disease (Gray, 1990: 304).

Many people deeply mistrusted the authorities and responded hesitantly to the invitation to voice their opinions. Eventually, however, during May 1957, an avalanche of hostile criticism from students and intellectuals descended on the Party, coalescing around the demand for an end to its monopoly of political power. Mao, who had been convinced that his personal authority would allow him to guide the movement within acceptable limits, was placed on the defensive and fell in line with the party leaders who had opposed his initiative from the start. The Party's response to criticism was draconian. In June 1957 the Hundred Flowers Movement was superseded by an Anti-Rightist Campaign directed by Deng Xiaoping, during which over 500 000 people were removed from their jobs or imprisoned. If Mao had shown his willingness to invite the people to 'rectify' the Party, the Anti-Rightist Campaign demonstrated the dangers of accepting the invitation. The Hundred Flowers episode exemplified a pattern repeated several times during the history of the PRC, the Party relaxing its control, actively encouraging people to speak out, even mobilizing them in large numbers, only to return a policy of repression. Some observers saw in this no more than a cynical ploy to flush out oppositionists, but it is likely that in 1957 Mao simply underestimated the extent of hostility to the regime among intellectuals.

Overall it should be kept in mind that, apart from brief periods of relaxation, the CCP ruled over one of the world's most regimented states. The population was organized into structures that facilitated social and political control. The mass media served as propaganda instruments, cultural life was stultifying and dissent virtually impossible. A Chinese gulag was constructed into which millions disappeared, often for trivial reasons. Certainly the standard of living improved dramatically for most of the population, but the cost in social terms was excessive. Meanwhile, although most officials apart from the top leadership lived rather modestly, over time there was a significant growth in patronage and nepotism.

The Great Leap Forward

The Five-year Plan was rated a success, but Party leaders hankered after even higher rates of growth, and set China the task of over-taking the UK within fifteen years. Mao was also unhappy with the Plan's one-sided emphasis on urban industry and wanted a more balanced approach which would develop industry in rural areas – 'walking on two legs' as he put it. The dry and bureaucratic style of work encouraged by the first Plan sat uneasily with Party traditions. The CCP was accustomed to a 'mass-line' approach stressing the political motivation and mobilization of classes and communities. The experience of enthusiastic and often successful war-time im-provisation in the 'liberated areas' had convinced Mao that the rural workforce, under-employed on mainly seasonal tasks, was an un-tapped resource a poor country could use to pull itself up by its bootstraps. In 1957 these ideas gave birth to a new policy initiative which became known as the Great Leap Forward.

During the winter of 1957–8, tens of millions of peasants were mobilized in a great drive to improve irrigation and water-conser-vancy schemes. The peasants initially responded with enthusiasm and amid much banner-waving and drum-banging some important infrastructural improvements were achieved. But it was not long before ill-judged directives from the centre, inflexibly implemented by local cadres, began to send things badly wrong. In August 1958, the Central Committee called for the formation of People's Com-munes throughout China, each to be constructed from several lower-level collectives. In six months of frenzied activity the whole of rural China was organized into these radical new institutions. A typical commune might have 30 000 inhabitants organized into 16 brigades, each of which was divided into eight work-teams of about 250 people, the work-teams roughly corresponding to a small village or hamlet. The communes were supposed to organize production, distribution, and defence through the formation of militias. Suppo-sedly modelled on the new form of workers' state discerned by Marx in the Paris Commune, they were to supersede the centralized, bureaucratic, bourgeois state inherited by the revolution. Some CCP leaders began to talk of them as vehicles for China's transition from mere socialism to full-blown communism. The economic objectives of the Leap became inextricably intertwined with a massive utopian socialist experiment.

The 1957 harvest yielded 195 million tons of grain. In 1958, this was increased to 200 million tons, mainly because of excellent weather. But the drive to meet ever-higher production targets led to massive over-reporting by zealous local officials. The centre believed that production had reached 260 million tons and used this incorrect estimate as the basis for economic plans. The acreage set aside for planting was reduced while grain requisition targets were increased. Labour was diverted from agriculture to rural industries, including the now notorious 'backyard furnaces' which absorbed much effort but produced little usable steel. Disaster followed. In atrocious weather conditions the harvest fell to 170 million tons in 1959 and 144 million tons in 1960. As supplies of raw materials and food to cities dried up, industry halted and workers returned to the countryside to seek food. The human cost will probably never be known accurately, but inferences from population statistics suggest that between 10 and 30 million people may have died from malnutrition-related illnesses between 1959 and 1961. At the time, the Chinese media were strictly controlled, and victims were prevented from moving out of famine-stricken areas; many Chinese discovered the extent of the tragedy only in the 1980s.

Crisis in the Leadership

The failure of the Great Leap Forward caused a profound crisis in the leadership of the CCP. Defence minister Peng Dehuai presented Mao with a deeply critical private letter at the August 1959 Central Committee meeting in Lushan. Mao's response was to polarize opinion against Peng, publicizing the letter and threatening to resign all his posts if Peng was not denounced and dismissed. Presented with these alternatives, the Central Committee backed Mao, and Peng was duly disgraced, never to return to public life. In the heat of the anti-Peng campaign, all possibility of reassessing the Great Leap policy was lost despite the fact that, before the Central Committee met, a broad consensus, in which Mao shared, accepted that its excesses must be reined in. In destroying Peng, Mao had also destroyed the tradition of relatively open debate in the leading bodies of the party which until that time had acted as an important corrective mechanism. But suppressing debate did not suppress division. As the full consequences of the disaster emerged, previous supporters of the Great Leap Forward, such as Liu Shaoqi and

---

Box 1.6 Mao Zedong, 1893–1976

The son of a farmer, Mao entered revolutionary politics in his provincial capital, Changsha, in the May 4th period. He moved to Beijing and became a founder member of the CCP. Mao had become effective leader of the CCP by 1936, and he dominated the party until his death. He may be credited with leading vigorous guerrilla warfare against the Japanese from 1937 to 1945, with ousting the Guomindang government and with establishing a unified central government in 1949. Except for brief periods, Mao was undisputed leader of the PRC from 1949 to 1976. However, his reputation is deeply stained by disastrous policy decisions after 1949: he may be held responsible for millions of deaths in the Great Leap Forward and the Cultural Revolution.

Deng Xiaoping, drew back and espoused pragmatic policies which Mao was later to denounce as 'rightist'. No longer sure of his support in the Party, Mao ensured that Peng Dehuai was replaced as head of the armed forces by his political supporter, Lin Biao.

In the mid-1950s, Mao was perhaps at the height of his powers, and revered by many Chinese as a national saviour (Box 1.6). He had the credit of defeating the Japanese, the Nationalists, and the USA in Korea. He had united the country and regained its territorial integrity. There was an effective central government which had already adopted successful measures for economic reconstruction. However, the Great Leap Forward revealed that he had made disastrous errors of judgement which plunged the country into chaos and caused enormous suffering. Mao's vicious campaigns against supposed opponents, intolerance of debate, and incompetent economic policies contributed to an irretrievable decline in the Party's moral standing. His authoritarianism and monomania, and the personality cult built around him, led to a collapse of rationality in public life from which China has yet to fully recover. The conflict in the party leadership, between 'rightists' and the Maoist 'left', and Mao's drive to regain personal power, set the scene for the Cultural Revolution.

Trends in Chinese politics are often characterized by the terms 'left' and 'right', which derive from European political debate. It is important to understand that they may be misleading if used indiscriminately: issues in Chinese and European politics are not identical. Outside China, 'left' broadly refers to radical and egalitarian policies, deriving from Marxist, socialist, or anarchist ideas; 'right' to more traditional conservatism. After the 1917 revolution, the Soviet Union was therefore considered a cause of the 'left'; despite its degeneration into Stalinism, in many respects the antithesis of radicalism, the term 'left' was still widely used by its supporters, for example the European Communist parties.

In Communist China, 'left' usually refers to the line of Mao and his supporters, who pursued policies that were a mixture of idealistic radicalism, authoritarianism, and personal adulation of Mao. Consequently 'rightist' in China usually refers to those Communist leaders, like Deng Xiaoping, who espoused more pragmatic, although still Marxist, policies. But confusion may easily arise. For example, the vicious 1957 Anti-Rightist Campaign attacked a broad spectrum of the population who were considered potential enemies of the regime; the campaign was directed by Deng Xiaoping. And in the mid-1990s, Li Peng was called both 'leftist' and 'conservative', because he was thought to favour a command economy and the continuance of the Party dictatorship. The terms are used here and in many other texts as a shorthand, but the reader should elucidate their meaning in the particular circumstances of each controversy.

The Sino–Soviet Split

In the 1950s, Western Cold War propaganda portrayed a monolithic Communist bloc led by Moscow as the major threat to world peace. By the early 1960s it was clear that the two giants of world communism were at loggerheads and by the 1970s China had adopted an extreme anti-Soviet foreign policy which led it to form a bloc with the USA against the USSR. How did this turnaround take place, and what underlay it?

In 1960, as China's difficulties with the Great Leap Forward mounted, Khrushchev abruptly withdrew all Soviet technical assistance from China. This impetuous act, entirely in keeping with the Soviet leader's nature, soured relations between the two states. Yet the break between the two leaderships had been long maturing. The relationship between the Chinese and the Russian parties had never been easy. Mao, who unlike most other Communist leaders had not been appointed by Moscow, was keenly aware of how the Comintern had treated the CCP as a junior partner of the GMD during the 1920s. Even on the eve of the Party's victory in 1949 it appeared that the USSR was hedging its bets as the Soviet ambassador left Beijing with the retreating Nationalists.

The PRC's initial alliance with the Soviet Union followed from the leadership's ideology and it was on ideological issues that the alliance began to unravel. Stalin had left the Soviet leadership the poisonous inheritance of the gulag and Khrushchev attempted to lance the boil. He freed hundreds of thousands of prisoners and went on to denounce their jailer. But while the denunciation of Stalin was probably politically inescapable in Russia, it was an inconvenience and embarrassment to the Chinese, who had dutifully portrayed him in propaganda as a Communist icon, along with Marx, Engels, and Lenin. When removal of Stalin from the pantheon was followed by Russian theorizing about the possibility of peaceful coexistence with imperialism and parliamentary roads to socialism, the Chinese denounced the Russians for revising the fundamental tenets of Marxism–Leninism and abandoning class struggle in favour of class collaboration.

Ideological dispute was accompanied by regional conflicts of interest. In the 1950s, the Chinese resented Soviet indifference to their claims over Taiwan. In 1962, a border dispute between China and India resulted in a brief war, which China comprehensively won. The Soviet Union, however, maintained a strictly neutral attitude, if anything tending to support India, despite treaty obligations to China. In later years border disputes, hangovers from the 'unequal treaties' between Tsarist Russia and Imperial China, were revived, and a serious military clash took place between Soviet and Chinese forces at Ussuri in 1969.

Continuing Crisis – The Cultural Revolution

For some years following the trauma of the Great Leap Forward, Mao Zedong took a less active part in day-to-day affairs, leaving effective control in the hands of Liu Shaoqi and Deng Xiaoping, whose pragmatic approach allowed the battered economy to recover. Communes were reduced in size and increased in number. Management and accounting functions were decentralized to the brigades and teams. Peasants' private plots and sideline activities were revived and extended. The scale of the retreat from collective agriculture was remarkable; by 1962, in some areas, around half the land was being managed by private households and rural markets were flourishing. It was at this time that Deng made his famous remark, that it does not matter what colour a cat is, so long as it catches mice.

Mao, however, was reconciled neither to his reduced role nor to what he saw as rightist policies. Under his influence, in May 1963, the Party launched the Socialist Education Movement, with the aim of rebuilding collective agriculture and combating demoralization and corruption among rural cadres. The political struggle shifted to how the campaign should be conducted. Mao wanted to mobilize poor peasants against corrupt cadres and emerging rural capitalists. Deng Xiaoping was determined that rural production should not be disrupted, and tried to tone down Mao's approach. Liu Shaoqi took a much harder line against cadre corruption than Deng, but saw the crux of the campaign as a tightening of Party discipline. If Deng's line seemed to threaten a revival of private capitalism, Liu seemed to be following the bureaucratic approach that Mao found so repugnant in the Soviet system.

In 1966 Mao plunged China into turmoil once again, calling millions of Chinese into battle against the Liu and Deng clique whom he accused of attempting to steer China down the 'capitalist road'. To foreigners, the Cultural Revolution was a baffling phenomenon. The founder of the People's Republic was apparently inciting the masses to attack the institutions of the state he had created. Some analysts pondered whether the Cultural Revolution, given its massive scope, was the expression of genuine social tensions. Certainly Chinese society, while more equal than most, was not egalitarian, despite seventeen years of socialist government. Systemic inequalities persisted, between town and country, between the minority with higher education and the vast majority with only primary schooling and, most importantly, between the officials of the regime and the rest of the population. Mao claimed that the Communist bureaucracy was in danger of turning into a new exploiting class. No doubt there was genuine popular resentment at official privileges and high-handedness, but without Mao's intervention and campaigns orchestrated by powerful figures in his entourage, an explosion of this magnitude would not have occurred.

The first phase of the Cultural Revolution, the campaign against the Four Olds, (i.e. old ideas, old culture, old customs, and old habits) mainly targeted intellectuals. College students, organized into detachments of Red Guards, denounced and humiliated their teachers, or smashed religious artefacts, works of art or anything else which reminded them of the old society. Foreign influences of all sorts, especially Western fashions and haircuts, were denounced and suppressed, sometimes by intimidation and beatings which the police did nothing to prevent. The movement changed its character on 5 August, when Mao issued a call to 'Bombard the Head-quarters'. From this point on, the Red Guards began to direct their fire against Liu, Deng and their followers on the 'capitalist road'. The composition of the movement also changed. Most early Red Guards had been the children of cadres. Now wider layers were drawn in, including children of 'bad classes', who proved only too eager to attack the Party bureaucracy. Before long, fighting broke out between rival factions of Red Guards, with the children of officials coming to the defence of their parents.

Red Guards were given the right to travel free of charge on China's railways to 'exchange experiences', and millions did so, clogging up the transport system, often attending mass rallies in Beijing addressed by Mao. Industrial workers, especially in Shang-hai, were drawn into the movement and soon won huge pay increases with which they emptied the shops of goods. However, since many workers were instinctively distrustful of students, they were sometimes used by their managers as a counterweight to the radicals, leading to a number of bloody encounters. It should not be thought that all the victims of the Cultural Revolution were con-servative bureaucrats. On the contrary, threatened officials showed themselves capable of acting with extreme brutality towards the radicals. But as all factions proclaimed their allegiance to Mao and brandished the Little Red Book of his thoughts it became increas-ingly difficult for activists, let alone outsiders, to discern a pattern to the fighting.

After purging Liu and Deng, the central leadership remained divided and in crisis, with several factions competing for Mao's ear. The Cultural Revolution Group of the Central Committee, led by Mao's wife Jiang Qing, promoted radical policies. Lin Biao's clique controlled the PLA. Most official government bodies were con-trolled by premier Zhou Enlai who, while not openly opposing the Cultural Revolution, acted as a moderating influence and attempted to mitigate some of its worst excesses (Box 1.7). Zhou also main-tained links with foreign governments and ensured that certain areas – for example, China's nuclear and space programmes – were off-limits to political campaigning. Consequently, alone among the top leaders he emerged from the Cultural Revolution with his reputation amongst the people intact, even enhanced.

Box 1.7 Zhou Enlai, 1898-1976

Zhou studied in Paris, and worked in the underground section of the CCP in Shanghai in the 1920s. From the 1930s, he was in Yan'an, and rose to become effective second-in-command to Mao Zedong. Zhou was Premier of the PRC for most of the period between 1949 and 1976. Of all CCP leaders, he was perhaps the most loved by the public, perhaps for his calm, dignified bearing and for an alleged concern with the fate of ordinary citizens. Public commemoration of his death turned into a protest against 'leftists' then in power. However, he was also a skilful political operator, and there appears to be little reason to differentiate his policies from those of Mao. Li Peng, a leading political figure in the 1980s and 1990s, was an adopted son of Zhou's.

During 1967, fighting intensified as armed Red Guard units responded to calls from the Cultural Revolution Group to seize government and party headquarters around the country. Virtual civil war broke out in some places as rival factions deployed field guns and tanks, and PLA units were drawn into the fighting. Wuhan and Changsha saw particularly bloody clashes, while a guerrilla war raged for some months across Sichuan. Towards the end of the year even the instigators of the Cultural Revolution could discern no logic in the fighting and Mao agreed that the chaos must be brought to an end. During 1968, the PLA began to restore order across the country. Revolutionary committees, dominated by the army, were set up to replace the shattered party organizations. The Red Guards were unceremoniously disbanded by the army and dispatched in hundreds of thousands to the countryside to work in agriculture. The enhanced political role of the army was recognized when PLA leader Lin Biao was officially named as Mao's deputy and successor in 1968, replacing the 'number one traitor' Liu Shaoqi, who died in prison the following year.

Rapprochement with the USA and the Fall of Lin Biao

In the early 1970s dramatic changes in international relations were taking place. The USA was placed on the defensive by its difficulties in Vietnam, and sought negotiations with China and the Soviet Union. In 1972, following secret contacts, US President Nixon visited China to re-establish links broken in 1949. In the era of détente which followed, the Soviets and Chinese effectively competed with each other for the favours of Washington, each continuing to denounce the other in extravagant terms. By the late 1970s détente between the USA and the USSR was a dead letter, but China continued to follow a fiercely anti-Soviet foreign policy, and in 1979 fought a short, unsuccessful war against Russia's ally, Vietnam.

Despite years of propaganda against Soviet 'revisionism', forming a bloc with the chief 'imperialist' power against the land of the October Revolution must have severely tested the loyalty of many Chinese Communists. This may explain the sudden disappearance of Lin Biao from the Chinese political scene in 1971. The Chinese authorities eventually let it be known that Mao's deputy had been killed in an air crash while attempting to flee to the Soviet Union following a failed coup attempt. It was implied that Lin opposed the impending rapprochement with the USA. It remains possible that the story of a coup attempt was fabricated by Mao to justify liquidating a rival at the top of the Party, but most experts now believe the official account is well founded.

In the 1990s, further 'revelations' concerning the Lin Biao affair were made public, alleging that Lin Biao himself was basically a pawn of his ambitious wife, Ye Qun, and scheming son, Lin Liguo. The Lin family clique suspected Mao of being about to discard Lin, whose plan to resurrect, and occupy, the post of PRC Chairman was unacceptable to Mao. The Lins then planned an armed uprising known as 'Plot 571' while Lin Liguo personally intended to assassinate Mao during a train journey; the plot was however betrayed (perhaps by Lin's daughter) and crushed. This version of events may be closer to the truth, or it may serve to mask the involvement of senior military figures by identifying convenient scapegoats: a treacherous woman and a duped husband. Whatever the truth of the matter, the affair illustrates the Byzantine intricacies of CCP politics. Above all, the revelation that yet another second-ranking leader was a national traitor dealt a severe blow to Mao's and the Party's reputation.

Balance Sheet of the Cultural Revolution

Although the Cultural Revolution claimed fewer victims than the Great Leap Forward, their fate has been given greater prominence by historians. This is no doubt partly due to their different social

---

Box 1.8 Deng Xiaoping, 1904–97

Deng studied in Paris, where he joined the local cell of the CCP. On his return to China he joined the Red Army, and served, mainly as commissar for supplies, until the Communist victory. A senior leader in the 1950s, Deng implemented a vicious crackdown on intellectuals in the Anti-Rightist campaign of 1957. He opposed some of Mao's extreme 'red' policies in the early 1960s, which earned him spells in detention during the Cultural Revolution: Mao denounced him as a 'capitalist roader' and 'number two traitor'. Deng returned to power in 1978, and dominated political life for two decades. Regarded as the architect of the reform period, Deng steered China to economic success; nevertheless, he was ruthless in handling political dissent, as he showed in 1989.

---

origins. While the victims of the Leap were for the most part illiterate peasants, many of those repressed during the Cultural Revolution not only came from China's ruling elite but also lived to tell their tale and did so from regained positions of power. This is not to belittle their suffering – tens of thousands died and hundreds of thousands were imprisoned or exiled – but simply to place it into perspective beside the millions of victims of the Great Leap Forward. What of the utopian aims of the leftists? Almost nothing remains of the ambitious schemes to abolish the privileges of mental over manual labour; almost the only reform which seems to have been successful was the training of large numbers of paramedics, the famous 'barefoot doctors', whose efforts did improve rural health care. The millions of rusticated students for the most part merely kicked their heels in the countryside and were treated with contempt by the peasantry. As to Mao's determination to arrest China's progress down the 'capitalist road', China is today much further down that road than could have been conceived in 1966, having had 'number two traitor' Deng Xiaoping in the driving seat for some twenty years (Box 1.8).

The Death of Mao and the Return of the Right

The early 1970s saw a continuing factional battle between the left and right, with the latter gradually gaining the ascendancy. In 1973

Deng Xiaoping was rehabilitated and appointed vice-premier. In 1975 Zhou Enlai announced the Four Modernizations – of agriculture, industry, technology, and the armed forces – signalling an emphasis on pragmatic, economic goals over political campaigning. Zhou's death on 8 January 1976 provided the occasion for an outburst of popular anger against the leftists on 5 April when a massive demonstration in his honour in Tian'anmen square turned into a riot. The left were able to use the disorder as a pretext to briefly reassert their authority by dismissing Deng from office, but it was the last spasm of a spent political force. In July the city of Tangshan was devastated by an earthquake which killed a quarter of a million people and injured some hundreds of thousands. Such natural disasters were held to presage the collapse of a dynasty in traditional China, and it seemed fitting that on 9 September Mao Zedong himself died. Only his unchallengeable authority had stood between the left and the abyss, and, within a month, the chief leftists, now ridiculed as the Gang of Four, were in jail. An orthodox Maoist and political non-entity, Hua Guofeng, succeeded to both Zhou's and Mao's posts but, behind this facade, Deng and the rightists gradually established control. Deng declared that that in future the party should 'Seek truth from facts', the unspoken addendum being to distrust the word of allegedly infallible leaders such as Mao Zedong (see p. 108).

The Open-Door Policy and the Reform of Agriculture

Deng's power was confirmed in December 1978 at the 3rd Plenum of the 11th Central Committee which initiated the decollectivization of agriculture and declared an 'open door' to foreign investment. Under the 'responsibility system', households could obtain land from collectives in return for contracting to meet a minimum target of production for sale to the state at fixed prices, any surplus being saleable on the free market. Initially the contracts were renewable yearly but this was later extended to fifteen years (the standard contract duration is now thirty years). The results were rapid and spectacular. Within five years, almost all collective farms had been dismantled. Improved incentives and increased state procurement prices gave a major boost to agricultural output, and the annual grain harvest rose to 400 million tons. Agricultural prosperity generated investment funds which fuelled a boom in rural light industry, much of it owned and operated by local government bodies, as successful communities diversified into other sectors. Rural industry became the great success story of China's economy in the 1980s, generating nearly a quarter of China's total industrial production by 1984. Ironically, something approaching Mao's dream of a Great Leap Forward in agriculture and rural industry took place, just as the People's Communes – the institutions Mao founded as vehicles for the Leap – were being dismantled.

The opening up to foreign investment was initially implemented in designated pilot areas called Special Economic Zones (SEZs), for example the Shenzhen SEZ bordering on Hong Kong. The success of the zones soon spurred local governments to demand that restrictions on foreign investment be more widely relaxed. Over time, the relative importance of the SEZs as destinations for inward investment declined as other areas were allowed to compete for funds. Interestingly and ominously, however, the historical uneven pattern of foreign investment has been reproduced with the coastal regions, Guangdong province and the area around Shanghai receiving the lion's share. Some worried that the uneven economic growth generated by the reforms would generate political tensions between China's regions.

The Democracy Wall

From 1977 onwards some senior figures within the Party, notably Hu Yaobang, began to press for moderate political reforms. A limited amount of extra-party dissent was tolerated – and, indeed, encouraged by the right, since it allowed them to demonstrate the extreme unpopularity of the leftists. In November 1978 wall posters appeared in several cities, most notably on the perimeter of a bus depot in central Beijing, which became known as Democracy Wall. Many of the posters denounced the leftists and demanded the punishment of those responsible for suppressing the 1976 demonstration in Tian'anmen square. Democracy Wall was allowed to flourish for about a year under Deng Xiaoping's protection. As usual, however, the people refused to stick to the script prepared by their Party sponsors, and began to question the whole system of CCP rule. Wei Jingsheng, a former Red Guard, then working as an electrician at Beijing zoo, called for a Fifth Modernization: political democracy and an end to the Party's constitutionally guaranteed leading role. But with victory over their factional opponents now secure, the right felt that Democracy Wall had served its purpose and closed it down. Wei Jingsheng was sentenced to fifteen years jail on trumped-up charges, and Deng announced that four cardinal principles were sacrosanct: the socialist road, the dictatorship of the proletariat, the leading role of the Communist Party and Marxism–Leninism-Mao Zedong thought.

It remained for the right to institutionalize its victory. Some cosmetic democratic reforms were introduced, Hua Guofeng was removed from office, and the Gang of Four including Mao's widow, Jiang Qing, put on trial. Deng became head of the key Military Affairs Committee of the CCP, Hu Yaobang became Party General Secretary and Zhao Ziyang, who had risen to prominence by successfully reforming agriculture in Sichuan, became Premier. In 1987 Hu was dismissed for excessive liberalism and replaced by Zhao, whose post as premier was taken over by the adoptive son of Zhou Enlai, Li Peng.

Problems of Reform

The agricultural reforms boosted farm production and rural industry, but the leadership faced much graver problems with ailing, state-owned urban industries, many built up with Soviet aid in the 1950s. The urban working class was a relatively privileged group within Chinese society, guaranteed a job for life which provided an assured, if modest, income with housing, health care and social welfare provided by their employers. Furthermore, many former Red Guards had taken jobs in industry, providing an educated and politicized leaven within the class. To break the workers' 'Iron Rice Bowl' by allowing inefficient factories to close was a political risk the Party was reluctant to take. Nevertheless, certain changes were introduced in the 1980s which themselves gave rise to new problems. Under central planning, state industries returned all profits to the centre which likewise covered all enterprise losses. This system was replaced by a tax on profits to give managers an incentive to improve efficiency. At the same time some price controls were lifted. These changes resulted in serious inflation as de-controlled prices soared and the state covered the fall in its income from enterprise profits by printing money.

The price rises created discontent, sharpened by the fact that a small minority were making fortunes. Since many basic prices, especially for fuel, some raw materials and foodstuffs, remained fixed by the state, it was possible to make easy money by buying inputs at low prices and selling the resultant product on the free market, best of all by exporting it. The ability to engage in this sort of arbitrage was usually restricted to the already privileged managerial and official class and to those with 'connections'. Growing corruption, often involving the children of top leaders, led to widespread popular disgust.

Meanwhile the collapse of collective farms in the countryside transformed the massive rural under-employment they had disguised into actual unemployment. Not all the displaced workforce could be absorbed by rural industry and many ex-members of collectives drifted into the cities where they formed a new urban underclass of part-time workers, petty entrepreneurs, and unemployed. Outside the traditional control mechanisms of the work-unit and often residing in the cities without official permission, this new phenomenon was viewed by the Party, and by many established urbanites, with some alarm.

Explosion in Tian'anmen Square

In 1989 as the CCP prepared to celebrate the fortieth anniversary of the founding of the PRC, what achievements could it point to? National unity had been achieved and the economy was growing at an unprecedented rate. But the people, weary of incessant political campaigning and policy switches, were largely contemptuous of the Party, prepared to tolerate its continuing rule on condition that it leave them alone. It was no longer possible for the Party to mobilize masses of people and, more fundamentally, it was not easy to imagine a goal for which it would wish to do so. Perhaps Deng and his aging contemporaries in the leadership may have felt their greatest achievement was simply to have remained in power.

They would certainly have remembered that 1989 was also the seventieth anniversary of the great May 4th movement which had inspired so many of them to devote their lives to the cause. Anniversaries are potent symbols in Chinese politics. When the popular Hu Yaobang died in April 1989, students from Beijing University gathered in Tian'anmen square to honour his memory and to demonstrate their anger at inflation and official corruption. Demonstrations continued throughout May (the May 4th anniversary was explicitly commemorated) and, as the students' protest drew support from all social classes, crowds of up to a million people in central Beijing disrupted a visit by Soviet president

Gorbachev. Similar demonstrations took place in most other cities. The movement developed rapidly into the greatest challenge to CCP power since 1949. Initially the leadership was divided. Party General Secretary Zhao Ziyang favoured conciliation while Premier Li Peng argued for repression; but as the students' demands crystallized into a call for political democracy symbolized by their makeshift 'statue of liberty', Deng Xiaoping decided to disperse the demonstration. Army units cleared the centre of Beijing in a brutal and clumsy manner, reflecting the leadership's state of panic, and some hundreds of demonstrators were killed.

Taiwan and Hong Kong

Meanwhile, how had Taiwan and Hong Kong fared? In 1949, after defeat in the civil war, some 1.5 million mainlanders moved to the island of Taiwan. Most of them were GMD soldiers or officials and their families; some brought substantial wealth, usually looted during their years of power. For most of the Qing dynasty, Taiwan had been a prefecture of Fujian province; considered almost barbarian, it had only slowly been Sinified. From 1895 to 1945 the island was occupied by the Japanese, who made some improvements to its infrastructure and also exploited its resources. The Japanese retreated in 1945 and were replaced by predatory units of GMD officials and soldiers. They compounded irretrievable corruption with extreme brutality. In the most notorious incident, on 28 February 1947, an unknown number of Taiwanese, perhaps from ten to twenty thousand, were murdered by GMD troops. Such actions prepared the island for Chiang Kaishek's relocation.

Throughout the 1950s, the Republic of China (ROC) government, heavily reliant on US aid, introduced economic and social reforms. In the next three decades, the island achieved an economic 'miracle', recording some of the fastest growth rates in the world. From a poor agricultural economy, Taiwan moved to become a world leader in machine tools, electrical appliances, textiles, and computers. The island became an industrial, urban and, to some extent, Westernized society. Politically there was a gradual improvement, especially under the leadership of Chiang Kaishek's son, Chiang Ching-kuo after 1978; martial law was finally repealed in 1987, and by the 1990s Taiwan was probably the most democratic territory in the Chinese world. Still an economic power-house, its international position deteriorated after US recognition of Beijing in 1972. Relations with the mainland remain an important regional issue, which is examined in Chapter 7.

In the same period, Hong Kong prospered under British rule, building up first a light manufacturing base and then achieving great prosperity in the 1980s as an entrepôt for trade with China and as a centre for financial services. The PRC chose not to interfere with the governance of Hong Kong, and finally negotiated a settlement with the British government in the mid-1980s for retrocession of the territory in 1997.

China in the 1990s

In 1989, the Chinese government responded viciously to the challenge of the democracy movement. Internally, it mounted an effective security operation against activists, and appeared to assert its control by a combination of detentions, summary executions, expulsions, and bullying. The international community at first expressed its outrage, but the criticism soon mollified under the attraction of doing business in 'the world's largest market'.

As we explore in later chapters, China in the 1990s has been undergoing a rapid and profound transformation. China has become a major economic force in the world, and its power in the Asia Pacific region is growing rapidly. It regained control over Hong Kong in 1997, and is moving to a gradual, if stormy, rapprochement

---

Box 1.9 Jiang Zemin, born 1926

Jiang is President of the PRC, General Secretary of the CCP, and chairman of both the state Central Military Commission (CMC) and the Military Affairs Commission (MAC) of the Communist Party. He was born in Yangzhou in the lower Yangzi to an intellectual family, and studied engineering at Shanghai Jiaotong University and in Moscow. He joined the CCP in 1946. As mayor of Shanghai in the 1980s he presided over a major investment and modernization programme. He succeeded Zhao Ziyang as CCP General Secretary after the suppression of the pro-democracy movement of 1989. Jiang dominated the 15th Party Congress of 1997 that opened the door to widespread privatization of China's state industries.

with Taiwan. A new political leadership that crystallized around Jiang Zemin (Box 1.9) managed to achieve a smooth transition of power during the senescence of elder statesman Deng Xiaoping. There has been massive investment, especially from overseas Chinese, leading to a boom in manufacturing. Its economy runs increasingly on market lines, and new social groups are emerging. Regional disparities are increasing, and the cultural monolith is giving away to a new wave of Chinese culture, heavily influenced by Hong Kong and Taiwan. The government, despite occasional expressions of concern, has stimulated consumerism to an unprecedented extent. The population seems willing to postpone settling accounts with the Party, as long as it can continue to deliver economic growth – sensing, perhaps, that China is set to become a leading power in Asia and a major force in the world.

2

Land and People

As this chapter will make clear, there are many Chinas. A first distinction may be drawn between the core or heartland and the peripheries of the PRC. The core provinces are heavily populated by the majority ethnic group, the Han Chinese. Here, the landscape reflects intensive human activity over dozens of centuries. One can still see many tracts of land cultivated as they were hundreds of years ago, but if one gets a little closer to village life one will also discover a surprising responsiveness to new ideas and new technologies. The Chinese countryside is always buzzing with movement, to and from market towns and farming villages. Because of difficulties with transport, accommodation, and language, foreign visitors would be well advised to make prior arrangements, for example through an academic institution or specialist tour company, for visits to rural areas.

Cities are in many respects drab, with countless suburban housing blocks built in grey concrete slabs according to Stalinist Russian design principles. True, the centres have recently started to resemble those of other Asian states, where one can enjoy shops, restaurants, public transport, nightclubs, museums and so on. But it adds much to know something of the city's history: was it a former national capital (Nanjing), a 'paradise of adventurers' (Shanghai), the centre of classical culture (Xi'an) or a wartime stronghold (Chongqing)? English is increasingly widely spoken, as is Japanese. This can be somewhat disconcerting as foreigners may find themselves often used as a kind of target for language practice by large groups of friendly, curious passers-by. But it also means one can have interesting conversations, and Chinese are often very quick to respond in a positive, generous way to anyone who shows an interest in their history or culture. And, hidden beneath dull facades, one can still find rich treasures of the cultural heritage.

45

Box 2.1   Key facts about China

Official name	Zhonghua Renmin Gongheguo (People's Republic of China).
Type of government	Socialist Republic.
Capital	Beijing.
Currency	Renminbi (Yuan).
Area	9,632,922 sq. kilometres.
Land border	22,800 kilometres
Common borders with (NE to SW)	Korea, Russia, Mongolia, Kazakhstan, Kyrgyzstan, Tajikistan, Afghanistan, Pakistan, India, Nepal, Bhutan, Myanmar, Laos, Vietnam.
Highest point	Qomolangma (Mount Everest), 8848 metres.
Major rivers	Changjiang (Yangzi), 6,300 kilometres, Huanghe (Yellow River), 5,464 kilometres.
Land and mineral resources	95 million hectares of arable land, 400 million hectares of prairie, 129 million hectares of forest, coal reserves 1,000 billion tons, iron ore 49 billion tons, significant reserves of tungsten, tin, antinomy, zinc, molybdenum, lead and mercury.
Population	1,221,462,000 (annual rate of growth 1.3%; proportion under 15: 26.3%).
Life expectancy	Men 68.2 years; women 71.7 years.
Principal national groups	Han Chinese (over 90 per cent); Zhuang 15.6 million, Manchu 9.8 million, Hui 8.6 million, Miao 7.4 million, Uighur 7.2 million, Yi 6.6 million, Tujia 5.7 million, Mongolian 4.8 million, Tibetan 4.6 million, Bouyei 2.5 million, Dong 2.5 million, Yao 2.1 million, Korean 1.9 million, Bai 1.6 million, Hani 1.3 million, Li 1.1 million, Kazakh 1.1 million, Dai 1 million (figures from 1990 census).
Major cities	Shanghai 9.2 million, Beijing 7 million, Hong Kong 5.4 million, Tianjin 5 million, Shenyang 4.2 million, Wuhan 4 million, Chongqing 4 million, Guangzhou 4 million, Harbin 3.2 million, Chengdu 3 million, Changchun 2.6 million, Nanjing 2.6 million, Xi'an 2.6 million, Dalian 2.5 million, Qingdao 2.5 million, Jinan 2.2 million (figures do not include suburban agricultural population).

Beyond the Han heartland, there are vast tracts of country that are often dramatic, sparsely populated, remote, exotic, and demanding. The far northeast borders Siberia, and has recently started a fledgling tourist industry based on hunting and trekking in almost virgin territory. The Tibetan plateau attracts a trickle of hardy travellers, prepared to tolerate the cold, poor diet, high altitude and difficult transport in order to see the lunar landscape, the mountain ranges, and the monasteries – or what remains of them. And it is still possible to see traditional ways of life in the jungles of southwest China, bordering on Myanmar (Burma), as well as getting a glimpse of what will probably become important trade routes in the twenty-first century, overland from China into southeast Asia.

Foreigners, especially Westerners, may feel that China is inaccessible or truly 'foreign', perhaps partly because of immediately noticeable characteristics like the use of chopsticks or the non-alphabetic script. These differences are of course real, but they are not insurmountable, and even without a knowledge of the Chinese language one can make a real effort at understanding this remarkable country. The information in this chapter introduces the contours of the land and its population; readers will find further details about Chinese social life and customs in Chapters 5 and 6.

The Making of the Land

Topography

Physical location and topography have had a profound effect on China's history. Imperial China was isolated from other comparable civilizations by great distances and the natural barriers of the Pacific Ocean, the jungles of Myanmar, the Tibetan highlands, and the steppes of Mongolia and central Asia. Apart from limited sea-trade carried on by coastal enclaves of merchants and the silk route to Damascus through central Asia, there was relatively little contact with Europe or the Islamic world. When foreign influences such as Buddhism took root, they did so in a modified, Sinicized form. China's relative isolation helps explain both the extraordinary longevity of the imperial system, and its inability to meet the challenge of foreign power in the nineteenth century. The extraordinarily rugged and mountainous terrain also determined two important constants of Chinese history: (1) the population, mainly peasants, was concentrated in the river basins and plains of the maritime east; (2) the major regions have until recently been only poorly integrated economically and have consequently developed relatively separately.

The Chinese landmass is dominated by the Tibetan–Qinghai plateau, the greatest highland region in the world. The plateau consists of a series of parallel mountain ranges running from west to east, bounded by the Himalayas in the south and the Kunlun Shan in the north. Geologists believe that the Tibetan plateau was created by the collision of the Indian subcontinent with Eurasia around 45 million years ago and that the mountains are still rising. These highlands alone occupy around one-fifth of the land area of the People's Republic. All China's major rivers, including the Yellow, the Yangzi, and the West rivers, run out through gorges on the fringes of the plateau – as, indeed, do all the major rivers of the Indian subcontinent and Indochina, including the Ganges, the Brahmaputra, the Mekong, and the Red River.

Chinese geological literature often describes the country as descending from west to east in four giant steps. The Tibetan plateau lies, on average, 4000 metres above sea level: to the north and east is a fringe of plateaux and basins lying at elevations between 1000 and 2000 metres. Moving further east are the coastal lowlands, including the Manchurian Plain, the North China Plain, and the lower Yangzi region. Finally, there is a broad continental shelf stretching into the East and South China Seas, lying at an average depth of 200 metres below sea level. The metaphor of giant steps is a useful simplification of China's landscape, although, admittedly, the step-like pattern is more easily discerned in northern China than in the hilly southeast.

Another useful generalization is that in the western half of the country, mountain ranges run, broadly speaking, from west to east, while in the eastern half, the prevailing direction is from northeast to southwest. Where these features intersect in central China, they accentuate another general feature of the Chinese landscape: sharply defined basins, plateaux, and plains lie separated from each other by intervening highlands, and form a pattern like the squares on an irregular chessboard or a patchwork quilt. Some of the best-defined squares on the chessboard are the Tarim and Junggar basins in the northwest, the Loess plateau in the north-central region, the Manchurian and North China plains in the northeast, the lower and middle Yangzi regions, and the Sichuan basin in central China.

Climate

China's weather pattern is highly seasonal, being largely determined by the annual monsoon cycle, although China's mountainous topography modifies its action to produce very different regional conditions. Apart from the southern fringes of Tibet, the west of China lies in the rain shadow of the Himalayas, and receives little moisture from the summer monsoon. Large areas receive less than 5 inches of rainfall per annum; agriculture is impossible outside oases and irrigated areas. Eastern China generally receives rainfall adequate for arable farming, but the Qinling mountain range marks a climatic divide. South of the Qinling, there is a surplus of water, while the north, apart from Manchuria suffers, although not usually disastrously, from a general shortage (Tuan, 1970: 19–23). It is important to note that the summer monsoon is unreliable and rainfall varies greatly from year to year. As a result, droughts and floods have punctuated Chinese history, and the management of water resources has always been a major concern of farmers and the authorities.

Regional temperature variation is much greater in winter than in summer. In the far northeast, January temperatures can be as low as minus 30°C. Beijing has a January average of minus 5°C while the corresponding figure for Guangzhou is plus 15°C. Again the Qinling mountain range forms a dividing line in eastern China, north of which average January temperatures are below freezing. However, all parts of China have winters that are colder than the average for their latitudes. Summers are uniformly hot over China, except for the Tibetan–Qinghai plateau, large sections of which are permanently frozen. Average July temperatures are over 25°C in the east, with the Beijing figure only 2°C below that of Guangzhou (Hook, 1992: 19).

Vegetation and Wildlife

Eastern China has been so extensively re-shaped by thousands of years of agriculture that we can give only broad hypotheses as to its natural state. However, it is most likely that it was once heavily forested, with conifers in the north giving way to deciduous forest, and finally to evergreens in the south (Tuan, 1970: 33). Tropical rain forest, pockets of which survive today, covered the south coast. Slash and burn agriculture must have accounted for large areas of forest in prehistoric times. In historic times, the demand for fuel, and the fact that the Chinese constructed their villages and cities out of wood, led to further clearances. Nevertheless, there remains enough wilderness in China to support a varied wildlife, including many reptile species, elephants, tigers, monkeys and, most famously, the giant panda. Many species are now confined to relatively small areas: elephants are found only in southern Yunnan and pandas mainly in a few remote highland areas of Sichuan, although a few species, such as bears and wild boar, are distributed more widely.

In the dry interior of the north and west, steppe and desert conditions prevail, and the sparse natural vegetation has been much less affected by the small human populations that live there. Tibet has large areas of meadow and alpine vegetation. China's border regions include some of the most inhospitable regions on earth, yet the steppe is home to considerable populations of wild goats, horses, antelope, yak, and camel, that, in turn, support a variety of predators, including wolves and eagles (Hook, 1992: 32).

Traditional Farming and Population Distribution

In imperial times the overwhelming majority of the population lived in peasant households cultivating small-holdings. Some owned their land, others rented, and both were often in debt to merchants and landowners. It was difficult for households to produce a surplus over and above their consumption needs and most of their efforts concentrated on grain production, supplemented by the produce of vegetable plots. It was rare for a Chinese peasant to eat meat. For the most part they reared only small, farmyard livestock such as pigs, dogs, and chickens, and these mainly for sale rather than home consumption. With little land available for pasture, there were few herds of grazing animals outside peripheral regions of the far north and northwest.

North of the Qinling mountain range, the main activity was dry-field cultivation of wheat and millet and the staple foods were millet porridge, noodles, and steamed bread. In the wetter conditions of the Yangzi region, rice was the main crop, cultivated in flooded paddy fields. In the subtropical regions of the far south, rice cultivation was combined with hunting, gathering, and fishing, on a pattern found throughout southeast Asia. In all cases the predominance of grain in the Chinese diet meant that the bulk of the population was concentrated in areas suitable for arable farming – principally the river basins and alluvial plains of China's maritime east and south. This striking pattern of distribution has persisted up to the present: most of China's huge population lives in the eastern half of the country and large areas of the west and north are virtually deserted.

Better-off farmers marketed their surplus grain and livestock and cultivated a number of other crops for sale. Silkworms were reared from very early times, painstakingly hand-fed with mulberry leaves: it took nearly a ton of mulberry leaves to produce ten pounds of raw silk. Tea was cultivated on the hillsides of south and central China. Cotton and tobacco later became important cash crops. But given the limitations of the transport system, most trade was conducted on a local or regional basis. While gentry and merchants might trade over large areas, the social horizon of the peasant was usually limited to his village or, at best, a local market town.

Only around 10 per cent of China's land is suitable for agriculture (Figure 2.1) and the growing population was forced to make ever-more intensive use of existing farmland and to extend cultivation to marginal areas of swamp and hillside. Given such imperatives, agricultural techniques in traditional China became highly advanced within the limits of the pre-scientific age. Irrigation and land drainage were well developed from early times, and machinery such as pumps and watermills became quite sophisticated. Terracing extended the available land to hillsides, and contributed to soil and water conservation. Fields were intensively fertilized, mainly with human excrement, with the consequence that farmland close to towns and cities was especially productive. New crop varieties and field-rotation systems were introduced. Fast-growing varieties of rice allowed two or even three crops to be grown each year. When crops from the Americas, such as potatoes, peanuts, and maize became available they allowed whole new areas in the southeast and southwest to be opened up. Nevertheless, it seemed that each gain in productivity was matched by a rise in population, and most farmers remained desperately poor.

Regions and Peoples

Origins and Development of the Chinese state

The earliest Chinese states were a cluster of small, bronze-age kingdoms situated on the North China plain and the adjacent Wei river valley. The first great push towards unification came from the

Figure 2.1   Agriculture

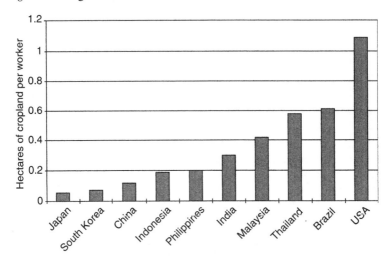

Although a largely agrarian country, China is extraordinarily poor in agricultural land *per capita*. Of the countries listed, only Korea and Japan are worse off in this respect.

Source: Data from World Bank, 1997g: 3.

Wei valley state of Qin: its ruler Shi Huangdi is famous for conquering neighbouring kingdoms, building the first version of the Great Wall, and for the terracotta army that guards his tomb. He was a particularly ruthless leader, who destroyed private libraries and massacred several hundred scholars. Although the dynasty barely outlasted him, it was the precursor of the first genuine imperial dynasty, the Han (202 BCE–220 CE). Han military success against the Xiongnu (Hun) nomads extended Chinese rule into modern Xinjiang and established control over the silk road to western Asia. Colonies and military outposts also reached as far as the southern coast. For the first time, the Chinese state bore some relation to its modern shape and dimensions and its population reached around 60 million.

Throughout history the Chinese state has tended to perceive its northern frontier as a threat, while viewing the south as an opportunity. In the north lived nomad herders, expert horsemen with fearsome cavalry, who regularly raided Chinese settlements.

Confederations of nomad tribes were capable of fielding massive armies: indeed the imperial throne was captured on several occasions, most notably by the Mongols and the Manchu. Military operations against the nomads were expensive, risky and had, at best, a temporary, punitive effect. The enemy could simply retreat into its vast hinterland while the Chinese could not occupy nomad territory permanently because neither land nor climate were suitable for settlement by farmers. The empire adopted a permanent defensive posture, symbolized by the Great Wall. In periods of military weakness it would resort to paying protection money. Nomad chiefs in the Chinese capital to pay tribute to the emperor were showered with lavish gifts in return for what was often a purely formal act of obeisance.

In contrast to the north, the south consisted of river basins, valleys, and plains suitable for agriculture. The existing, non-Chinese population consisted of farming communities, who were militarily no threat to Chinese settlers. They could be either assimilated or, if they resisted, could be driven into marginal areas by imperial troops. Over the centuries, the empire expanded fundamentally from north to south, consolidating its grip on the best agricultural land. As it did so, those indigenous peoples who resisted acculturation retreated to the hills. Even today, national minorities in the south are separated from the Chinese population more often by height above sea-level than by lateral distance. In parts of south-west China it is common for several nationalities to inhabit successive altitude zones in the same area.

China was by no means the most ancient of the world's early civilizations; by the time of the earliest Chinese records, the major achievements of ancient Egypt were already in the past. But from the Han dynasty until the fall of the empire in 1911, the Chinese state showed a virtually unparalleled degree of political continuity. In periods of unity, the structure of government remained more or less constant over 2000 years. Threats to the Empire came from peasant rebellions, military *coups d'état*, or foreign invasion. The net political effect of a victorious, million-strong revolt was usually equivalent to that of a military putsch: the foundation of a new dynasty, which was obliged to rule through the old apparatus. Even foreign conquerors made few lasting changes; on the contrary, foreign rulers risked assimilation. Tellingly, although there are officially around 9 million Manchu in the PRC, descendants of the previous ruling caste, their language is virtually extinct.

The PRC inherited borders that were, for the most part, defined in treaties between the failing Qing empire and western powers. Prior to the nineteenth century, imperial China did not operate with modern concepts of state sovereignty and precisely delimited frontiers. China considered itself the centre of the civilized world, and the emperor to be the ruler of 'all under heaven'. His authority was theoretically unlimited, even if there were geographical limits to his power. Naturally, the empire was aware of the existence of other states, but it declined to deal with them on an equal basis: their rulers were expected to recognize the emperor's authority and pay tribute to him. For long periods this reflected the reality of Chinese hegemony over east Asia. Vietnam and Korea recognized Chinese suzerainty for much of their history, while Chinese culture profoundly influenced countries outside its political sphere of influence – most notably Japan. Both Republican and Communist China denounced treaties signed by the Qing as unequal, which in many respects they were. But in respect of territory, the treaties recognized Chinese sovereignty over large areas where the empire had exercised only intermittent and partial control. The economic base of the Chinese state had always been arable farming and the core areas of empire were those areas that were able to sustain a large farming population. In practice, this meant the river basins of central and eastern China. In the sparsely inhabited northern and western border regions the empire maintained control only with difficulty. It is important to bear in mind the continuing contrast between core and peripheral areas, and the continued contestation of Chinese rule in Tibet and Xinjiang.

Regions of China

Over 90 per cent of the population of the PRC belong to the majority nationality, who call themselves 'Han' Chinese after the first great imperial dynasty. However, this bald statistic over-states the homogeneity of the population, since the Han themselves are differentiated in important respects. One striking difference is that Han Chinese from different regions often speak mutually unintelligible dialects, although the great majority of people with some education can and do use modern standard Chinese, known outside China as Mandarin. Mandarin was formally defined only in the 1920s, and is based on the language spoken around Beijing: since 1949 it has been vigorously promoted, in schools and by the media, as a national language. Nevertheless, a third of the population, mainly in the south-east, use a dialect for much of their daily social life. The principal dialects are Wu, spoken mainly in the region around Shanghai; Xiang, spoken in Hunan; Gan, in Jiangxi; the various Min dialects spoken in Fujian; Yue, more usually known as Cantonese; finally there are communities of Hakka speakers scattered across south China. On the other hand, characteristics of the Chinese script allow it to serve as a shared writing system for people who speak different dialects. It differs sharply from alphabetic scripts, notably in that every character, as a rule, corresponds to a semantic unit. Thus the written culture of China is far more integrated than the spoken language.

Linguistic differences are compounded by variations in religious affiliations, popular festivals, styles of cooking and so on. Many Chinese feel more comfortable with friends from their own part of the country and have stereotypical images of those from other parts. It is common for colleagues in business or politics to form cliques based on regional affiliations.

The striking regional differences among the Han Chinese can be explained by a combination of history and topography. As the state extended and consolidated its power, Chinese settlers successively occupied the fertile river basins of eastern China, displacing or assimilating the existing inhabitants. We have already noted that China's rugged terrain meant that settled lowland regions were relatively isolated from each other. Travel between regions involved an expensive and hazardous trek through highlands. Within regions, transport – often via natural or man-made waterways – was relatively cheap and convenient. For these reasons trade tended to develop on a regional basis, and inter-regional contact was relatively restricted.

China's transport network is still very poor: the railway system is a skeleton, connecting major centres only, and nearly a quarter of the track is in the northeast, the site of original investments by the Russians and Japanese. Waterways carry about 20 per cent of freight traffic but are largely unmodernized and concentrated mainly around the Yangzi river. Before 1949, China had few roads, and even today around 2000 towns and nearly 200 000 villages have no road access at all. The government recognizes that unless the transport infrastructure is radically improved, present economic growth rates will be unsustainable; as a result there is currently an unprecedented zeal in road-building over much of China.

In the 1930s, the Chinese scholar Chi Ch'ao-ting put forward the concept of 'key economic regions' as an aid to understanding China's development. More recently, in several very influential works, the anthropologist G. William Skinner has proposed that the core, eastern area of China can be divided into eight or nine 'macro-regions', each based on a major river drainage basin. According to Skinner, each macro-region should be thought of as comprising a fertile, densely populated core, surrounded by a less fertile periphery. The towns and cities of each macro-region form a distinct urban system that evolved to 'perform the region's central functions'. Skinner also points out that major historical events – for example, invasions, rebellions and famines – were often regional rather than national in scope and reinforce the case for treating the regions separately (Skinner, 1977).

Northwest and north China are the oldest settled regions in the country; both have dense populations and some of China's worst poverty problems. The basis of agriculture in both regions is the light, easily worked loess soil that geologists believe was deposited on the hills of north China by high winds after the last ice age. The loess forms a blanket several hundred feet thick in places. It is loose and very prone to erosion and gulleying. Soil carried downstream by the Yellow river over millennia has built up the surface of the North China plain. Silt deposits have raised the river bed above the level of the plain and despite centuries of dyke construction and maintenance, serious floods still occur.

The lower and middle Yangzi regions have soil that is heavier and more water-retentive, suitable for growing rice in paddy fields. Although the soil is less naturally fertile than loess, the more favourable climate meant these regions became China's rice basket during the Tang (618–907 CE) and Song (960–1279) dynasties. The core of the upper Yangzi region is the Sichuan basin, one of China's most prosperous agricultural areas. The mountains that surround the basin force the summer monsoon to deposit its rains, while in the winter the mountains to the north act as a barrier to icy northerly winds and protect crops from frost.

The southwest was settled relatively late by Han Chinese, and although they are the majority in the core area, the region is home to many national minorities. Yunnan province alone has more than twenty distinct national groups. Many of the minorities speak languages related to Thai, and some groups straddle the borders with neighbouring states.

The core of the Cantonese-speaking southern coastal region is the Pearl River delta. In the past twenty years this has become one of China's most dynamic economic regions, fuelled by investment from Hong Kong. Readers can find a fuller description in Chapter 3.

The mountainous southeast has traditionally looked to the sea because of the paucity of agricultural land. Fishing and coastal trading were common occupations in this region. Most of the Han colonists who settled in Taiwan from the seventeenth century onwards came from here, as did many of the emigrants who founded present overseas Chinese communities in Asia. The relationship with overseas Chinese has resulted in an investment boom in recent years based on family ties.

National Minorities

The PRC defines itself as a unitary, multinational state. The CCP followed a nationalities policy that, with some important differences, was modelled on the Soviet example. National minorities are officially recognized, their languages and national customs are, within limits, encouraged, and they enjoy certain privileges, such as less rigorous application of population control. There are fifty-six different national groups officially recognized by the government, selected from a larger number that responded to the government's invitation to register. A number of province-level governments have the status of 'autonomous regions', although the Chinese stopped short of the Soviet practice of setting up republics with the right of secession.

Although national minorities make up only a small percentage of the population, a few live in border provinces where they are the majority. In some areas, Chinese rule is fiercely contested, most famously in Tibet, which retains a strong national identity, based around Lamaist Buddhism. After the 1911 revolution, Tibet declared itself an independent state, and remained so, *de facto*, until the PLA re-established Chinese rule in 1950–1. An attempted uprising was crushed in 1959 and the Dalai Lama fled to India. Tibet suffered badly during the Cultural Revolution and was closed to foreigners from 1963 to 1971. Repression was relaxed somewhat in the early 1980s, but serious street fighting took place in Lhasa in the late 1980s, since when Chinese rule has been uncompromising and heavy-handed. In 1996, the Dalai Lama accused China of

committing 'cultural genocide' in Tibet by promoting Han immigration and suppressing Tibetan Buddhism.

While Tibet receives a good deal of international publicity, a less
well known but potentially very serious situation is developing in
Xinjiang where the 7 million-strong Uighur are the largest ethnic
group. The Uighur are an Islamic, Central Asian people, racially
distinct from the Han Chinese. They have made periodic attempts to
throw off Chinese rule, and in the 1990s, perhaps inspired by the
example of the ex-Soviet Central Asian republics, nationalists have
stepped up their activities. In 1997, Uighur nationalists attacked
Chinese troops and detonated bombs in Beijing and the provincial
capital, Urumqi. Riots broke out in several towns but were heavily
repressed, and the Chinese authorities carried out a number of
executions.

There is insufficient space here to deal with all fifty-six national
groups, but we can offer a brief overview based on linguistic
groupings. Minority languages are an important element in preserving national identities, and since 1949 scripts have been devised for
many languages that had no previous written form. Nevertheless, all
PRC citizens have to learn Chinese if they want to progress in
education or find employment outside village farming. Among
speakers of *Altaic* languages, who live mainly in the north and west,
we have already mentioned the Uighur. The 1 million Kazaks are
also followers of Islam, while the 4.8 million Mongolians are mainly
Lamaist Buddhists. Manchu is also classified as an Altaic language
although, as already mentioned, very few of the 9.8 million Manchu
nationals speak it. Speakers of *Dai/Tai* languages live mainly in the
south-west, and include China's largest national minority, the
Zhuang, who live mainly in the Guanxi autonomous region. The
Zhuang have largely assimilated to a Han way of life. *Tibetan*
belongs to a language group that includes Chinese and Burmese.
Among minorities who speak related languages are the Bai of
Yunnan, and the Tujia of Hunan and Hubei. Speakers of *Miao-
Yao* and *Mon-Khmer* language groups are mainly mountain dwellers
in south-west China, closely related to groups in Myanmar, Laos
and Vietnam. In Taiwan there are three to four hundred thousand
indigenous inhabitants who speak languages of the *Malay-Polyne-
sian* group, related to Filippino. They are known by the Chinese as
Gaoshan, 'high-mountain people', although they inhabited the
plains until driven into the hills by Han colonists.

One group that deserves special mention are the 8.6 million Sinified Muslims known as the Hui, who live in pockets throughout China, though mainly in the northwest. Thought to be partly descended from Arab traders and soldiers, the Hui have long since become physically indistinguishable from Han Chinese, speak Mandarin, and apart from religion and related dietary laws, are culturally very close to the Han. Nevertheless, they have the status of a national minority (Hook, 1991: 77–78).

Population and Policy

In the late 1990s, China's 1.2 billion population was growing at a rate of around 1 per cent per year, the equivalent of adding the population of a large European country every five years. The population had more than doubled since the formation of the PRC in 1949. But China's population explosion can be traced back much further, to the sixteenth and seventeenth centuries, when it was perhaps partly stimulated by the introduction of new crop varieties from the Americas (Figure 2.2). Population pressure has arguably contributed to poverty and social crisis since the early nineteenth century. According to the present government it is one of

Figure 2.2   Population, 2 CE–1997 CE

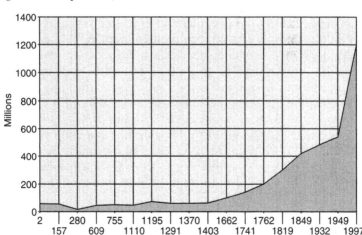

China's population began to grow strongly from around the end of the sixteenth century. Under the CCP regime it has more than doubled.

China's most intractable problems. Since the early 1970s the authorities have made a sustained effort to reduce the birth rate; campaigns to popularize contraceptives have raised usage rates to those prevalent in developed countries. In 1980 regulations were announced to restrict families, with some exceptions, to a single child.

The one-child policy is the most ambitious and draconian population policy ever introduced by a state. Although the government claims it is implemented by a combination of persuasion and economic incentives, there is no doubt that more or less coercive measures are employed, ranging from intense social pressure to enforced abortion and sterilization in extreme cases. The policy has been heavily criticized abroad for its infringement of personal freedom. It has other negative side-effects. Traditional attitudes mean that many people want a son to carry on the family name. If a woman discovers she is carrying a female child, she may seek an abortion. By the late 1990s private clinics were offering ultrasound scans to determine the sex of foetuses. Cruder and crueller methods were sometimes used and there were many highly publicized cases of female infanticide during the early 1980s.

The one-child policy has been much more successful in urban then in rural areas. Many city dwellers are still dependent on their workplace organizations for housing and welfare and, therefore, subject to a high degree of social control (see Chapter 5). Peasants have less to lose in social benefits, and if well-to-do, may decide to have extra children despite financial penalties. The government accepts that the policy cannot be strictly enforced in the countryside, but the logic of its economic reforms is to reduce state control over the urban population. The growing urban middle class may soon find that it can defy the one-child policy with impunity. Nevertheless, despite all its shortcomings, the policy defused what might otherwise have been an uncontrolled and destabilizing population explosion in the 1980s and 1990s. Urbanization and improved living standards in other countries have been accompanied by a sharp drop in the birth rate. In the longer term, this phenomenon may offer China the best hope of avoiding a demographic disaster.

Urban China

Chinese towns and cities developed at different times and according to different imperatives. Han dynasty cities were fortified outposts of the empire as much as centres of trade and commerce. They were inhabited by large numbers of officials and soldiers, as well as craftsmen and merchants. The city walls usually formed a rectangle, oriented to the main points of the compass, and administrative buildings, markets, and residential areas were laid out on a grid pattern. Inner walls around the residential areas were locked and guarded at night: it seems that political control of citizens was as high a priority as their military protection. Many northern towns and cities retained a traditional rectangular appearance well into the twentieth century. During the Tang and Song dynasties, China's economic centre of gravity shifted from the Yellow river to the Yangzi. Merchant–landowners built large-scale commercial operations shipping rice surpluses north from the Yangzi along the Grand Canal. Large commercial towns and cities grew up, some with populations of over 1 million. The dynamism of these commercial cities could no longer be contained by the grid-like structure of earlier, administrative centres.

In the late nineteenth century, the designation of many urban centres as treaty ports provided another face of the Chinese city. Small towns were transformed into bustling centres of commerce and industry with railway stations, docks, and passenger shipping. In Beijing, Shanghai, Tianjin and other cities, a cosmopolitan way of life developed amongst a section of the middle class. Universities, newspapers, cinemas, and publishing houses opened. There was some opposition to such 'foreign', and 'corrupt' developments, mixed with resentment at wealthy and, allegedly, arrogant foreigners. But urbanization proceeded steadily. By 1938 around 5 per cent of the population lived in cities.

In the early years of the CCP regime, rural migration to the cities was encouraged, especially during the first Five-year Plan (1953–7, see chapter 1). Millions of peasants moved to urban areas to work in industry or on construction sites. Migration into the cities reached a peak during the Great Leap Forward, but in the economic catastrophe that followed, many of the most recent migrants were sent back to the countryside. From around 1960 onwards, migration was regulated by a strictly enforced system of residence permits and ration cards. China won praise for avoiding the unplanned growth of shanty-towns, that was a feature of so many developing countries, although this success came at the expense of severe restriction of personal freedom. A striking aspect of policy, that caused much misery, was the rustication of millions of urban youth during the 1970s.

During the 1980s, the growing role of the market in the economy undermined the controls on residency. Most significant was the end of rationing. No longer needing ration cards, hundreds of thousands of peasants began flooding into the major cities in search of work. By the 1990s, economic migrants were numbered in millions. They were initially resented by the existing residents and harassed by the authorities but by the late 1990s it was clear that they had become permanent features of the urban scene. It became quite common for migrants from a particular regional, linguistic or ethnic background to settle in a single district of the city, supporting each other through community organizations and personal networks.

Under Mao, there was relatively little investment in housing although from the 1950s the authorities began to address needs by building utilitarian apartment blocks; important elements of the architectural heritage were lost in the process. In the 1990s there was a boom in commercial property. In Beijing, traditional courtyard-style houses were demolished to make way for skyscraper offices and international-style hotels. Urban sprawl ate into farmland surrounding towns and cities, a worrying development since some of the most fertile land immediately surrounds the cities. New high-rise cities and business districts such as Shenzhen and Pudong were constructed. In another respect, however, a more traditional face of the Chinese city was revived by the market reforms. Small enterprises had suffered badly under Mao: for example, the number of restaurants in Beijing declined from over 10 000 to fewer than 700 between 1949 and 1980 (Croll, 1983: 49). Now, hawkers and all sorts of small businesses are bringing back life to the streets as well as providing much-needed goods and services.

Overall under CCP rule, the urban population has increased roughly threefold in percentage terms. In 1949 the urban population was around 9 per cent of the total. In 1996, the State Statistics Bureau estimated that 28.85 per cent of China's population lived in urban areas (Xinhua News Agency, 11 April 1996). These bare statistics hide the problem of defining who qualifies as an 'urban dweller'. The official estimate may under-state the urban population, since it excludes people in rapidly industrializing small towns. On the other hand, it includes all resident in urban areas for six months or more, including seasonal workers with permanent homes in the countryside.

Location of Industry

When the monarchy was overthrown in 1911, China had virtually no factories in the modern sense of the word, apart from a few weapons factories and shipyards built during the 'self-strengthening' movement of the late nineteenth century (see Chapter 1). In the early twentieth century, however, light industry developed quite rapidly in the treaty ports, and Shanghai became an important centre of textile manufacturing. Although financed by foreign investment, a good deal of this light industry was Chinese-owned and managed. Meanwhile in Manchuria, Japan, who dominated the area after defeating Russia in 1904, was building up a complex of heavy industries, mainly coal, steel and chemicals.

These components, together with industries the Nationalists had relocated to Sichuan during the Second World War (see Chapter 1), constituted the industrial inheritance of the CCP government. The CCP recognized that industrial development had been extremely uneven, and the first Five-year Plan attempted to address this issue by directing investment inland. Fear of attack from the USA provided a further motivation for switching production away from coastal areas. After the Sino–Soviet split, industrial location policy switched again. For about ten years from the mid-1960s, around half of national investment was directed to regions designated as the 'third front', mainly in Sichuan and the southwest (Cannon, 1990: 39).

The open-door policy of the 1980s, and especially the setting up of Special Economic Zones (SEZs) with incentives for foreign investors, favoured the development of coastal regions. In effect, a version of the old treaty-port pattern of development began to re-assert itself. The aim of policy appeared to be to increase regional inequality in the short term. The authorities hoped that, in the longer term, the wealth of the maritime east would trickle west. It has, however, proved difficult to tempt foreign investment into inland areas where the transport and telecommunications infra-structure is often very poor.

A key feature of the reform period of the 1980s and 1990s has been the explosive growth of rural industry. There are now around 20 million rural firms, known as Township and Village Enterprises (TVEs). The development of TVEs *ipso facto* means the dispersal of industry from urban areas. But in practice this often means from city to suburb. Areas with a skilled labour force, competent managers, and easy access to urban markets have shown the most impressive growth. Again this tends to favour the the east and south coasts with Shandong and the areas around Shanghai and Guangdong in the forefront.

Problems of Twenty-First-Century China

Resource Exhaustion

Water has been a major concern of China's people and rulers for centuries, but perhaps never more so than now. Urban water supply *per capita* in China as a whole is about half that of advanced countries, and demand from industry and households is increasing rapidly. Since 1949 the main strategy for coping with the situation has been to construct new storage reservoirs or underground aquifers. Cities such as Beijing, Tianjin, Taiyuan, Xi'an and others are critically dependent on groundwater for domestic, industrial, and suburban farming usage, and this has led to serious depletion in local watertables. Furthermore these sources of water often contain dangerous levels of pollutants.

Two characteristics of the socialist state make the water shortage worse. The general trend of Chinese government response to problems such as this is to go in for grandiose projects – for example, the diversion of entire rivers from south to north – rather than less spectacular, 'good housekeeping' programmes. Second, consumers – and especially state consumers such as the vast industrial complexes – with few exceptions, pay very low, subsidized prices for water and have little incentive to avoid wastage. The question of applying market disciplines, or some other form of effective regulation, to the use of resources such as water, is topical in many countries, and in China it is particularly urgent.

Some analysts believe a rapidly industrializing China will soon face an energy crisis. At first sight this seems unlikely; China's coal reserves are the third greatest in the world, after the former Soviet Union and the USA, and coal output was the highest in the world in the 1990s. Most of the coal is of high quality and accessible. But demand is growing fast and, as with water, there is a major problem of wastage, while low coal prices give consumers little incentive to invest in efficient energy use. Transport is another serious problem.

Coal reserves are concentrated in the north and northeast, and the rail network cannot cope with demand.

China's oil reserves are much less significant than its coal, and the country has been a net oil importer since 1993. The government has high hopes that the South China Sea hides vast reserves, but to date there has been no oil bonanza. There are proven reserves of 5 billion tonnes which, at projected consumption rates will be exhausted in twenty years. Chinese estimates of undiscovered reserves range from 20 to 70 billion tonnes, but these figures are highly speculative. Like coal, known oil reserves are highly localized. The Daqing field in the northeast produces 40 per cent of China's total.

If energy demand continues to increase on present trends, China will be forced either to import huge quantities of oil, or switch much of its power generation to other sources, such as nuclear or hydro-electric. Fortunately, China's topography makes it one of the most favourable regions in the world for the generation of hydro-electricity. With its emphasis on self-reliant, local development, Maoist China constructed many small-scale hydro-electric plants, but large-scale schemes were limited, mainly due to the lack of an adequate transmission infrastructure. In the late 1990s this was set to change, as the government began implementing the controversial Three Gorges project, to dam the upper Yangzi to generate 18 000 mega-watts of electricity per annum. The project has been fiercely criticised, inside and outside China, because it involves relocating over 1 million people, and will flood an area of great natural beauty. In 1992 a third of the delegates to the National People's Congress (NPC) voted against the scheme. But the dam is something of a political sacred cow, as it was advocated many decades ago by China's first president, Sun Yatsen. Its grandiose scale also fits it with the approach of the Soviet-trained technocrats in China's leadership.

Pollution

It is a modern orthodoxy that industrial development in communist command economies leads to serious pollution. Under Mao, however, China was one of the cleanest countries in the world. Households generated very little waste since consumption of packaged goods was very low. Private cars were virtually unknown, and urban traffic mostly consisted of bicycles. Farms used natural waste as fertilizer, rather than chemicals. Until the late 1970s, industry remained confined to a few areas. Admittedly, many plants were pouring out dangerous emissions, but the problems were localized.

During the 1980s and 1990s, consumerism arrived with a vengeance and discarded trash can now be seen everywhere. A more affluent and concentrated population is making increasing demands on the transport system, and traffic in cities is leading to levels of congestion rivalling Los Angeles or Tokyo. The use of chemical fertilizers has more than quadrupled since the introduction of household farming; carcinogenic nitrates are polluting drinking water and fresh vegetables (Smil, 1993: 170–5). Industry has mushroomed in small towns and rural areas; unregulated factories pollute agricultural land and groundwater with oil and chemicals. Power stations pump out ever-increasing levels of greenhouse gases and sulphur dioxide. Combined with domestic coal-burning and increased motor traffic, this is causing catastrophic air pollution in some northern cities. Chinese government statistics implicated air pollution in the deaths of 3 million people from bronchial diseases between 1994 and 1996.

The government has made efforts to address the problems. Environmental regulations were introduced as far back as 1956. Following the first UN Conference on the Human Environment in 1972, China set up a National Environmental Protection Agency (NEPA), and during the early 1970s there was a major campaign to encourage recycling of industrial waste. In the 1990s the NEPA carried out occasional high-profile crackdowns on polluters, but there is a suspicion that corruption allows large-scale pollution to go unpunished. Environmentalists charge that, in practice, protecting the environment is given a low priority. The government, for its part, admits that it lags behind in environmental protection, but requests technical and economic assistance from richer countries. In the five years to 2002 environmental spending was budgeted as US$23 billion, of which two-thirds was to be provided by foreign governments and international agencies.

Some environmentalists fear that China's industrialisation could have a disastrous effect on a regional, or even a world scale. The argument runs like this: Chinese consumption of energy per capita is around a quarter of the average for the developed world, but is growing rapidly, and the absolute numbers involved are staggering. Over 300 million Chinese are expected to move into cities by 2010; demand for electricity is expected to soar as households acquire washing machines and refrigerators; in the near future, the private car market will take off. The effect on climate alone through global warming alarms many analysts. The fundamental question is: can the environment support Western levels of consumption by China's 1.2 billion people? Chinese officials dismiss such concerns as hypocritical and point to the pollution generated by the USA and other developed countries. But it is undeniable that China's economic growth raises serious environmental issues, and disputes with the international community are likely to become increasingly acute.

3

The Chinese Economy

As we saw in Chapter 1, reforms introduced by Deng Xiaoping in 1978 were the prelude to a period of extraordinary growth in the economy. According to official statistics, China's gross domestic product (GDP) more than quadrupled between 1978 and 1994 (PRC Year Book, 1995: 281). GDP per capita, again according to the official record, grew at an average rate of 8 per cent over the same period (adjusted figures calculated by the World Bank give a lower growth rate of 6.8 per cent) (World Bank, 1997: 3). If we accept the official figures, then China was the fastest-growing economy in the world from the late 1970s until the mid-1990s; the World Bank places it in second place, marginally behind South Korea. In either case, the point is made that China in the 1980s and 1990s experienced a remarkable economic boom – given China's great size and huge population, possibly the most significant boom in history (Figure 3.1).

A key feature of the period was that China abandoned the previous, Maoist policy of economic self-reliance and aggressively entered the world market as an exporter of industrial goods. Between 1980 and 1993 the annual volume of China's foreign trade grew from US$ 38.1 billion to US$ 195.8 (Lardy, 1994: 30). The proportion of manufactured goods in China's exports grew from under 50 per cent to over 80 per cent over the same period. From 1982 onwards China built up a large and growing trade surplus with the USA that became a symbol of its success in penetrating overseas markets. It also helped fuel debate about the long-term consequences of China's boom, in particular, whether China would at some time 'overtake' the USA. A new perception of China as an economic giant and a vast potential market gradually displaced the

Figure 3.1   Gross domestic product, 1980–94

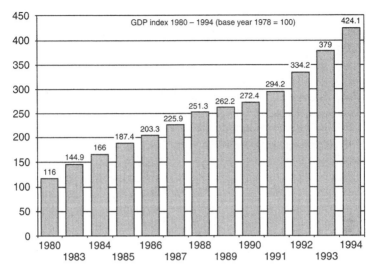

Source: *PRC Yearbook*, 1995: 281.

old picture of a communist monolith. As China opened up its economy, firms owned by overseas Chinese based in Taiwan, Singapore and throughout southeast Asia became the biggest inward investors. Some commentators discerned in these deepening ties the emergence of a Greater Chinese economy of enormous size and growth potential.

Some qualification of the optimistic picture is necessary: the PRC is growing from a very low starting point and remains a very poor country in per capita terms. Productivity in the mid-1990s was probably still less than 20 per cent of Western levels. China's market size and dynamism are offset by poor infrastructure, appalling environmental problems, and undeveloped financial and political institutions. Furthermore, estimates of the overall size of China's economy vary greatly, so assertions that China has 'overtaken' Germany or Japan are not easily verified. In general it is easier to determine the rate at which an economy is growing than its absolute size; this is because price levels vary greatly between countries. Chinese domestic prices are extremely low by world standards, so if we simply convert the GDP figure from renminbi to its US dollar equivalent, we get a figure that severely under-estimates the size of

---

Box 3.1   Key facts about China's economy (1995 figures)

GDP	US$ 745 billion
GDP per capita	US$ 610
GDP, by sector	Agriculture 20.5%, industry 49.2%, services 30.3%
Total workforce	689 million
Workforce, by sector	Agriculture 54%, industry 23%, services 23%

Output of major commodities (million tons unless otherwise stated)

Coal	1361	Grain	466.62
Crude Oil	150	Oil-bearing crops	22.50
Steel	185	Cotton	4.77
Cement	476	Sugarcane	65.42
Fertilizer	26	Sugar beet	13.98
Electricity (billion kwh)	1008	Tobacco	2.07

---

the economy. Furthermore, a significant proportion of China's agricultural produce is consumed directly by its producers and so is not included in official statistics. A more realistic estimate can be derived using a method known as Purchasing Power Parity (PPP). This involves using notional international prices for the purpose of calculating GDP. However, PPP calculations of GDP are complex and controversial and estimates of GDP consequently vary considerably. The World Bank estimated China's GDP for 1990 to be US$ 2.2 trillion; other estimates were as low as US$ 1.14 trillion and as high as US$ 2.9 trillion (Lardy, 1994: 15).

The expansion of the economy over the 1980s and early 1990s was anything but smooth. Growth rates fluctuated considerably, with inflationary boom periods and slow-downs alternating on a 4–5-year cycle. The stop–go cycles contributed to social unrest and were accompanied by corresponding political cycles of liberalization and repression. The whole process was extremely destabilizing, and contributed to the 1989 Tian'anmen crisis that nearly brought the entire reform process to a halt. By the late 1990s, however, it was generally agreed that the government had become more adept at managing the economy, and that inflation had been brought under control.

The Maoist Legacy

Prior to the economic reforms, China operated a command economy on the Soviet model. Almost all industry was state-owned, and agriculture organized into collectives. As in the Soviet Union, the command economy was bound up with a particular strategy for national development based on the rapid development of heavy industry. Production was directed by a central authority known as the State Planning Commission, that drew up plans for the current year based on longer term Five-year Plans (see Chapter 1 for the first Five-year Plan). The aim was to catch up with and overtake the West. The method was self-reliant development, in accordance with Stalin's dictum of building socialism in one country, with domestic industry protected from foreign competition by a state monopoly of foreign trade. The planning authorities were able to secure the enormous investment funds they required because they set the level of prices and wages and determined the key relationship between the prices of industrial goods and agricultural procurement prices. In effect, a large surplus was extracted from the peasantry for investment in industry and, despite Maoist rhetoric, the gap between town and country widened.

It is important to note that the economy inherited in 1978 by Deng Xiaoping had registered some successes. Overall, the economy grew at an annual rate of 6 per cent between 1952 and 1978, around 4 per cent in per capita terms. (Wong, 1993: 42). The Great Leap Forward led to a disastrous fall in output in the years 1958–61, but the economy recovered rapidly in the early 1960s and continued to grow despite the political chaos of the Cultural Revolution. Government finances were sound, inflation was virtually zero, and the country had low external debt. In the politically chaotic first half of the twentieth century per capita income fell, and the initial period of communist rule was in many ways one of recovery and reconstruction. The command economy transformed China from an essentially agrarian country into a considerable industrial power, with powerful productive sectors in chemicals, engineering, and textiles; it is probable that even without fundamental economic reform, respectable rates of growth would have continued for some time (Figure 3.2).

A major problem was that the welfare content of the growth in the command economy was relatively low. Much of the output of heavy industry was destined for military use, and key investment decisions

Figure 3.2   Employment, by major sectors, 1952–95

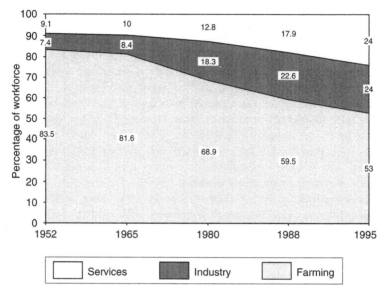

The shift of workers from agriculture to industry began well before the reforms of the 1980s; recently there has has been strong growth in service-sector employment.

were taken for defence reasons. For example, in the late 1960s, fearing attack from the Soviet Union, the CCP ordered the relocation of strategic industries to remote parts of western China (see Chapter 2). Investment was often wasteful and irrational. Protected from foreign competition, industry had fallen well behind world standards in terms of technology, product quality was low, and factories carried large inventories of unsaleable goods. Many major projects were started but never finished. In agriculture, obsession with self-sufficiency led to an insistence on the production of a few strategic crops, particularly grain, even where local conditions were inappropriate. As a result, although basic food, health care, and education were generally assured (except during the disaster of the Great Leap Forward) thanks to the relatively equitable distribution system in rural areas, the standard of living remained low. Most consumption goods, including food, were rationed, and the government used its control of ration coupons to impose restrictions on internal migration, effectively confining three-quarters of the population to village life.

From Plan to Market

The Gradual Character of the Economic Reforms

The overall effect of the economic reforms was to transfer economic decision-making from state planners to households and firms operating within the marketplace. While this trend could be discerned from the early 1980s, it was not made explicit until 1992, when the 14th congress of the CCP endorsed the concept of a Socialist Market Economy. Overall, the reform process was largely one of trial and error. Typically, change was introduced in a particular location or sector of the economy. If it worked, it was extended and generalized; if it did not, it was reversed. The most celebrated examples of this experimental approach are the Special Economic Zones (SEZs) of south China. The zones were areas set aside for foreign investment and the operation of market forces, and acted as testbeds for measures later applied nationally.

Opinions differ about the extent to which the Chinese government oversaw the process like some kind of master planner, or whether it was more reactive, driven by events and crises and generally rather incompetent. Some argue that the reforms worked despite, and not because of, the government. On the whole, the evidence appears to support the theory that the government stumbled into the reforms. Following the death of Mao Zedong, the leadership initially moved to strengthen the central planning apparatus, and announced a strategic, Ten-year Plan to build up heavy industry, among the main aims being to massively increase the production of chemical fertilizers and agricultural machinery. The plan turned out to be over-ambitious, and during the subsequent period of retrenchment, Deng and his colleagues introduced the initial measures that set China on the path to reform. The basic thrust of these initial measures was to cut investment, especially in heavy industry, to increase household incomes and consumption, especially in rural areas and to give priority to agriculture, light industry, and the production of consumer goods.

Perhaps the lack of an overall blueprint for reform turned out to be an advantage. Chinese reforms seem remarkably successful when compared with the experiences of successor states of the Former Soviet Union (FSU) and many of its former Eastern European allies. In these countries, in contrast to the gradualist approach of the Chinese, so-called 'Big-Bang' reforms were adopted on the advice of Western economists. With the partial exceptions of Poland and the Czech Republic, the consequences were dramatic and disastrous. The GDP of the Soviet Union's successor states fell by over 30 per cent from 1990 to 1995, and in 1996, despite many predictions of imminent recovery, the economy of the Russian Federation shrank by a further 6 per cent.

The Agricultural Reforms

Deng and his supporters began their economic reform in agriculture. In the late 1970s collective farm output was stagnant and rural incomes were lagging ever-further behind those of city dwellers. The new leadership group was looking for methods to increase food production and raise the standard of living in the countryside, partly in order to secure political support. Their first step was to increase agricultural procurement prices, by 20 per cent in 1979 and by a further 13 per cent over the next two years.

Meanwhile, with the support of Party leaders, local authorities in some poorer regions, notably Anhui, had begun to experiment by handing over management of land to individual households. The experiments succeeded in increasing yields and, over the next few years, variations on what became known as the household responsibility system (*baochan daohu*) were adopted on a national scale. Land, agricultural buildings, machinery, and draught animals which had formerly been managed by the People's Communes, were contracted to individual households. The terms of the contract provided for a fixed amount of output to be delivered to state procurement agencies at controlled prices; the remainder could be sold on the free market. Although contracts were initially of short duration, fairly soon some localities were leasing land for periods of up to thirty years. In 1982 the People's Communes were officially abolished and were replaced by township governments. By the end of 1983, in terms of management, Chinese agriculture had effectively been decollectivized. Land remained state or collective property, however.

Under the Commune system, about 5 per cent of the land had been set aside for peasants' private plots and a network of more than 30 000 rural markets already existed. These markets rapidly expanded in numbers and turnover as household farming spread.

Over time, procurement quotas declined as a proportion of total output and wholesale produce traders have taken over much of the distribution of agricultural output, although the state still controls the bulk of some key commodities.

One of the most important aspects of the agricultural reform was not, strictly speaking, an economic measure at all. This was the decision to abolish the 'bad-class' labels which had been applied to landlords and rich peasants during the land reform. The economic significance of this act was that people now felt they would not be punished if they became rich and successful. Confidence in the market economy was reinforced by the government slogan 'to get rich is glorious' and by media campaigns highlighting the achievements of successful entrepreneurs.

The initial results of agricultural reforms were very positive. Grain production grew from less than 300 million tons in 1978 to 414 million tons in 1985, sugar from 856 to 1760 million tons, cotton from 521 to 1578 million tons. Freed from the rigid cropping patterns imposed by the Communes, farmers soon diversified their output. Animal husbandry, especially pig production, increased considerably. Some farmers became extremely prosperous and diversified into handicraft industry, food processing, or running local transport firms. Areas within reach of urban markets became particularly prosperous.

However, not all the results of the household responsibility system were positive, and not all positive developments could be attributed to it. Since the collapse of the Communes, less attention has been paid to public works, especially in the field of irrigation and flood control. There is evidence of soil degradation, and the boom in housebuilding and rural industry has eaten into prime agricultural land. A portion of the increase in farm production in the 1980s can be attributed to a huge increase in the application of nitrogen-based fertilizers. To some extent, improved yields achieved by household farmers in the 1980s are the result of decisions by 1970s' central planners to increase fertilizer production. By the mid-1980s the initial boom in farm output had run its course and agricultural output began to stagnate. One major problem is that many farms are too small to be economically viable. Some economists have called for the land to be privatized so that less efficient producers will be gradually bought out, and their small-holdings consolidated into larger farms.

The Growth of Rural Industry

For most of the 1950s and 1960s, CCP policy stifled the development of handicrafts and small-scale industry in rural areas. State procurement policy obliged first the cooperatives, and later the People's Communes, to concentrate on crop production. As a result, traditional rural industries declined. However from about 1970 the authorities began to encourage the Communes to diversify into industrial ventures and, specifically, to concentrate on the so-called 'five small rural industries' of steel, cement, fertilizers, farm implements, and hydro-electric power. From a low starting point, 'Commune and Brigade' enterprises grew quite rapidly during the 1970s. When the Communes were abolished, responsibility for these firms was transferred to township governments.

Since economic reforms began, the 'township and village' (TVE) sector of Chinese industry has grown explosively and has become one of the main driving forces of the national economy. Numbers of enterprises, numbers of employees, and share of industrial output have all soared. In 1978, less than 2 million rural industries employed 28 million people. There are currently well over 20 million such firms employing more than 125 million people, around 40 per cent of the industrial workforce. They have entered all sectors of the economy, from textiles to consumer durables, engineering, building materials, and mining. Annual growth in the sector reached 30 per cent in the early 1990s; rural enterprises produce around 25 per cent of national industrial output and around the same proportion of its exports. The most spectacular growth has taken place along the coast and in areas close to major cities.

The principal characteristic of TVEs is that they operate on a commercial basis, outside the state plan. Competition is fierce and thousands of firms have gone bankrupt. But it is important to note that only around 5 per cent of township firms are privately-owned. The large majority are owned by local authorities; their profits may be used to fund road-building, schools, and welfare provision. Many other firms are cooperatives, although in some cases this is a cover for private ownership. There are also many hybrid forms of ownership. Increasingly, state industries have begun to form close relationships with TVEs, taking advantage of their low costs, flexibility, and broad product range, and in some cases subcontracting production.

Despite the enormous contribution of TVEs to overall growth, the picture is not entirely positive. In some sectors product quality is low even by Chinese standards. Most rural enterprises rely on cheap labour rather than on efficient use of modern machinery and many operate at even lower levels of productivity than state-owned industry. There is widespread neglect of workplace safety and pollution control. Industries in rural areas can also have a negative impact on food production, by diverting land and labour power from agriculture.

The Growth of Domestic Private Enterprise

According to official statistics, in June 1996 there were 709 000 private firms employing 10.14 million people. Additionally, there were approximately 25 million individual or household traders (*getihu*), defined as private firms with fewer than eight workers, employing around 45 million people (Xinhua News Agency, September 1996). Many private firms and traders operate in the service sector, running small retail businesses, bus and taxi firms, restaurants and small hotels, hairdressers, vehicle repair shops and so on. But quite large numbers are involved in manufacturing, for example small-scale engineering or the production of building materials.

The leadership encouraged the growth of the private sector – for example, by offering bank credit on concessionary terms and by ordering state firms to set aside a proportion of their goods for sale to private firms (Figure 3.3). They did this for several reasons. Originally, the main aim was to provide employment for increasing numbers of jobless youth and for rural workers displaced by the dissolution of the Communes. They also hoped to encourage existing state employees to 'jump into the sea' (*xiahai*) of private enterprise, and so reduce the over-manning of state firms. More generally, it was recognized that the command economy had left the service sector undeveloped, and private enterprise was called on to fill the gap. Not only individuals but also state firms now rely on private firms to provide goods and services that the state sector finds it difficult to provide.

The official statistics probably under-estimate the extent of private enterprise because an unknown number of firms officially classified as collectives are, in reality, privately-owned. In the early period of reform collectives were subject to less restrictions than

Figure 3.3   A socialist market economy or nascent capitalism, 1985–95?

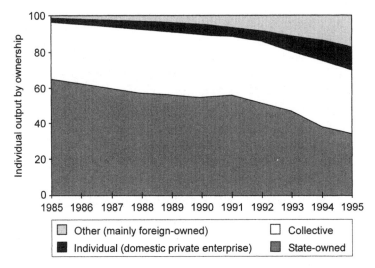

Growth of domestic and foreign private enterprise has eroded the position of state industry, but around 70 per cent of industry remained in public (state or collective) hands in the late 1990s.

Source: Data from World Bank, 1997a: 146 (authors have slightly adjusted some figures to add up to 100%).

private firms and this encouraged a certain amount of subterfuge. As explained earlier there is a wide variety of ownership structures in Chinese industry. For all these reasons, official figures on private enterprise should be treated as a minimum.

Reforming State Industry

State-owned enterprises were by far the most important component of the command economy, and in the late 1990s still formed the core of China's industrial system. State factories produced about half of China's industrial output in the mid-1990s, down from four fifths in 1978. The relative decline is due mainly to the explosive growth in the collective sector, particularly of TVEs, described above. There are some 360 000 state firms of which around 6 500 large units, with more than 500 employees each, produce 60 per cent of state firm output. Around 40 per cent of state firms run at a loss and many are technically bankrupt. Firms have huge debts which they have no realistic hope of repaying, not least because they are owed money by other state firms, and are often locked in a paralyzing deadlock known as 'triangle debt'(*A* owes *B* who owes *C* who owes *A*). Under the command economy, managers were in practice unable to sack staff (a system known as the 'Iron Rice Bowl') and most enterprises were grossly over-staffed. They still carry huge inventories of poor-quality, unsaleable goods, officially admitted as amounting to around 5 per cent of GDP: in 1996, it was claimed that a confidential World Bank document estimated them at an astonishing 17 per cent of GDP (*South China Morning Post*, 6 October 1996). Machinery is antiquated, much of it imported from the Soviet Union in the 1950s.

Reform of state industry is probably the most difficult economic problem China faces. Throughout the 1980s and early 1990s the leadership proceeded cautiously. They reduced the power of Party officials in enterprises in favour of professional managers. Firms were allowed to retain a proportion of their profits and to sell above plan output on the open market. From the mid-1980s, the level of output covered by the plan was frozen. Over time, therefore, as the economy grew, the proportion of output produced for the market increased. Ministries have gradually withdrawn from active planning and adopted a more regulatory role. The principal control mechanism at their disposal is a form of the responsibility system under which factory managers are appointed after a competitive tendering process, and sign contracts to deliver a certain level of profits. The contract specifies the proportion of profit that can be retained by the enterprise and also defines the managers' remuneration, which can be considerable by Chinese standards. But managers face financial penalties if they fail to meet profit targets, and some have to pay a bond before taking up their posts.

The government sees breaking the workers' 'Iron Rice Bowl' as the key to industrial reform. Under the old system as well as providing life-time employment, state-owned firms provided a wide range of subsidies and benefits, including housing, education and health care. Strongly entrenched interests protected this state of affairs, and only in 1986 did the State Council begin to announce radical changes. While existing employees were not affected by the changes, new employees would be taken on the basis of fixed-term contracts. Contracts gradually penetrated some sectors of the economy, more in some provinces. The process was more thorough in sectors where foreign companies operated, and in Special Economic Zones. A 1994 labour law calls for all relations between workers and employers to be governed by a written contract stipulating the duration of employment, length of the working week, pay, health and safety and so on. Less progress has been made in separating welfare provision from enterprise costs although, in 1996, China obtained a US$ 350 million loan from the World Bank to develop pilot projects in housing and social security.

The long-term aim of government policy is to create firms with sufficient resources to compete on the world market. Around 1000 major companies have been selected, from among the more profit-able and efficient firms in various sectors, including banking, transport and telecommunications, high technology, and defence. The plan is to concentrate financial support on these firms and encourage them to acquire subsidiaries and merge with other firms to form the backbone of a modernized industrial sector. This approach, reaffirmed at the 15th Party Congress in 1997, is explicitly based on the success of the South Korean government in supporting selected domestic conglomerates (known as *chaebols* in Korea) with cheap finance and tariff barriers. The Korean strategy, pursued over several decades, helped create a number of world-class firms, such as Hyundai and Samsung. The difference in the Chinese case is that the selected firms will remain state property.

Western experts, on the whole, believe that Chinese reforms of state industry have been too cautious, and have long been advising the government to privatize enterprises and let bankrupt firms fail (see for example World Bank, 1996). There are signs that the Chinese leadership is beginning to heed this advice. At the 15th Party Congress, Jiang Zemin announced that the majority of China's state firms were to be converted into shareholding concerns. The Congress shied away from calling this a process of privatization and insisted that public ownership would continue to predominate. Officials indicated that strategic enterprises, including China's fledg-ling '*chaebols*' mentioned above, would remain state-owned. But it is clear that the state wants to rid itself of the burden of its loss-making small and medium-sized enterprises, and is prepared to risk worker discontent to do so. Jiang recognized that the policy would cause 'temporary difficulties to part of the workers'. How the privatization process will work in practice remained unclear. There is a danger that, as happened so often in Russia and Eastern Europe, hasty, badly managed, or rigged privatizations will amount to little more than asset-stripping by managers.

Price Reform

The introduction of price reform is a good example of how the government's experimental, evolutionary approach resulted in radical change over time. We saw above how, under the responsibility system in agriculture, households agreed to sell a certain proportion of their output to state procurement agencies at fixed prices; the surplus could then be sold at free-market prices (or sometimes within a percentage band of a state 'guidance price'). This gave rise to a system of dual prices for agricultural produce. During the 1980s dual pricing was extended at varying paces to additional sectors of the economy. Its introduction into industry was more complex, and much slower than it had been in the case of agriculture. It proved especially difficult to introduce market prices into the distribution of major capital items, especially energy and freight transport. Despite these qualifications, the dual-price system turned out to be one of the fundamental motors of the economic reforms. In all sectors, the tendency was to reduce, or hold constant the 'planned', fixed-price segment of output so that, as the economy grew, an increasing proportion of output was produced for sale at market prices. By the mid-1990s, only a small minority of all categories of goods were still being delivered at state-fixed prices (World Bank, 1993a: 49–50, cited in Lardy, 1994: 11). Effectively, under the dual-price system, the natural process of growth was gradually creating a market economy (Naughton, 1995: 8–9).

Contract Law

A well defined law of contract between legal entities is a fundamental aspect of a market economy and one that is still far from perfect in China. Under the command economy, the aim of economic activity was to fulfil state planning demands: the main function of regulations was to demonstrate that the state had the power to enforce purchases and supplies. Even in the 1980s there was a very mixed and chaotic perception of the boundaries between the rights of the central planners and the rights of individual enterprises. An Economic Contract Law was enacted in 1981, as a first step towards codification of principles and practice. It was subsequently refined and added to by the Foreign Economic Contracts Law (1985), the Technology Contracts Law (1988), the

Industrial Enterprise Regulations (1992), a new Economic Contract Law (1993) and others.

The purpose of revising the law in 1993 was to make it more appropriate to the concept of a 'socialist market economy'. As regards dealings with foreign companies, it was also supposed to reflect the relevant provisions of the UN Convention on Contracts for the International Sale of Goods (1 January 1988). Its objectives include protecting the interests of parties to contracts between Chinese and foreigners, and promoting foreign economic relations (Wang, 1993: 43–44). Many references to the rights of the state planning system are deleted in the new version; for example Article 1 no longer states that the purpose of the law is to 'guarantee fulfilment of State plans' but now is 'to ensure the healthy development of the socialist market economy'. The role of the bureaucracy in monitoring contracts between enterprises has also been reduced, and parties to a contract are free to arbitrate disputes between themselves, or resort to litigation.

However, although China now has contract laws which are reasonable in theory, their implementation is not yet satisfactory. Chinese state power has never been subject to the rule of law as understood in the West. As one commentator points out, Chinese *rules* traditionally did not imply *rights*. The issuing authority may follow rules for the sake of consistency and stability, but a rule can be violated, 'whenever the circumstances of administrative efficiency that led to its adoption point the other way'. There are countless examples of higher political authorities overturning contracts, as in the famous instance when a McDonalds' burger concession was removed from its prime site in central Beijing. Together with serious problems in the legal infrastructure – in the courts, the legal profession and in the judiciary – arbitrary actions by power-holders mean that, despite definite progress, China still lacks a robust legal framework for its economic life.

Financial Reform

Reform of banking and taxation lies at the heart of the transition from a command economy to a market economy. In a planned economy, profits of state-owned industry finance government spending as well as investment. In market economies, by contrast, investment is funded from private savings channelled through the banking system and securities' markets; government spending is financed by taxation, supplemented by borrowing. A centrally planned economy has no need for capital markets or a sophisticated tax-collection system, so economies making the transition from plan to market face the task of creating these institutions from scratch. This can pose enormous problems, not least because of the lack of qualified personnel.

The lack of a modern taxation system can be an obstacle to reforming inefficient state-owned industry. In a command economy state firms are profitable, but as a result of trading at prices fixed by government fiat. Once prices are allowed to move to market-determined levels, the inefficiency of a large part of state industry is exposed, and many firms begin to run at a loss. They are often extremely over-staffed, and are, additionally, responsible for welfare services that in a market economy would be provided by the state and financed out of taxation. The work-unit system in China is a highly developed form of this type of welfare provision (see Chapter 5). Price reforms attack the profits of state industry, and so threaten the 'Iron Rice-Bowl' of urban workers. But simultaneously, since the state budget is largely financed from the same profits, the reforms reduce funds available for replacement, state-run welfare schemes.

In order to attack this problem, China announced a major reform of taxation in 1993–4. A 17 per cent value-added tax replaced remittances from state firms as the main source of revenue. Profit taxes were standardized at 33 per cent for state, collective, and private firms. At the same time, responsibility for tax collection was largely shifted from local to central government. Overall, the reform aimed to provide adequate central government revenue in the context of a market economy.

In 1978, China had only one bank – the People's Bank of China (PBC) – with branches all over the country (Box 3.2). In 1983, the PBC was designated the central bank with responsibility for regulating credit and controlling the money supply and its commercial banking functions were hived off to six state-owned commercial banks. A third tier of banking institutions was formed from local banks and credit cooperatives, which were given greater freedom to operate commercially. During the reform period the commercial banks lent huge sums to state-owned industries, and by the 1990s it had become clear that they had no realistic chance of recovering a large proportion of the outstanding debts. Many of their 'assets'

Box 3.2   Principal financial institutions

Central bank	People's Bank of China.
Major banks	Bank of China, Industrial and Commercial Bank of China, Agricultural Bank of China, People's Construction Bank, China Investment Bank, Bank of Communications, China International Trust and Investment Corporation.
Stock exchanges	Hong Kong, Shanghai, Shenzhen.

---

were effectively valueless and by international standards some banks were technically bankrupt. The consequences of a banking collapse would be disastrous, and the government has attempted to gradually restructure the sector by transferring non-performing loans to new, specialized 'policy' banks. By channelling what is effectively government development aid ('policy' lending), through the policy banks, the authorities aim, over time, to clean up the balance sheets of the remaining commercial banks.

Capital markets were slower to take shape, mainly due to the slow pace of privatization of state industry; although given the decision of the 1997 15th Party Congress to convert large numbers of state firms into share-holding corporations, this may well change. Stock markets were established in Shenzhen and Shanghai in 1990, but by the mid-1990s relatively few companies were quoted on the exchanges. Many more companies sold shares directly to their own workforces. Bonds, and especially government bonds, form the bulk of securities issued to date. The reincorporation of Hong Kong is expected to provide a major boost to the development of capital markets in China, but at the time of writing it is too early to tell exactly how this will take place.

The Open Door

Foreign Trade

Maoist China aspired to economic self-sufficiency. The CCP leadership believed that China's natural resources and huge labour force would permit a development strategy based on minimal participation in world markets. Free trade, according to their world view, would imply handing over China's industry to foreigners. Instead, domestic industry was protected from foreign competition by a state monopoly of foreign trade. The Party was determined to avoid trade deficits and the accumulation of foreign debts, either of which might imply handing to trading partners or creditors an unwelcome degree of political leverage. The overall result was that during the 1950s and 1960s foreign trade grew at a slower rate than the economy as a whole.

China's principal imports, in the pre-reform era, were capital goods and industrial raw materials. Like other developing countries, in the 1950s China exported mainly primary goods, principally coal, oil, and agricultural products. However, the share of industrial products in Chinese exports rose steadily to about a fifth of the total by 1970, a process which reflected the country's growing industrialization. In the 1950s, 70 per cent of China's trade took place with the Soviet Union and other socialist countries. This figure dropped rapidly during the 1960s, following the Sino–Soviet split. Trade with Western countries began to expand in the 1970s following US President Nixon's visit to Beijing in 1972. In the mid-1970s, after adopting the slogan of the 'Four Modernizations', China imported large quantities of Western industrial plant, often on a turnkey basis. This was especially pronounced during the short interregnum of Hua Guofeng, who proposed to revitalize central planning after the chaos of the Cultural Revolution.

Since 1978, China's trade has grown at a rate of approximately 16 per cent annually, twice as fast as world trade over the same period, so that by the mid-1990s China's total trade was ten times its 1978 level (Table 3.1). From 1978 until the mid-1980s China expanded her exports of raw materials, taking advantage of high world oil prices to earn extra foreign exchange. The massive increase in agricultural productivity that followed the introduction of the household responsibility system also boosted exports of primary products, and for a short time in the mid-1980s the proportion of manufactured goods in China's exports actually fell marginally. As market reforms deepened, however, higher domestic prices reduced oil exports, while the share of manufactured goods in total exports rose dramatically, from approximately 50 per cent in the mid-1980s to more than 80 per cent in the mid-1990s. Over the same period, the share of industrial goods, mainly machinery, in China's total imports grew from around two thirds to four fifths. In approximate

Table 3.1 China's foreign trade, by major categories, 1996 ($US million)

Classification	Exports	Imports
Miscellaneous manufactured goods	56 426	8 484
Machines and transport equipment	35 313	54 771
Basic manufactures	28 511	31 391
Food and livestock	10 232	5 672
Chemicals	8 879	18 106
Fuels	5 928	6 877
Crude materials excluding fuels	4 047	10 697
Beverages including tobacco	1 342	497
Animal and vegetable oil and fats	376	1 697
Unclassified	12	646
Total	151 066	138 838

Source: China State Statistical Bureau.

order of importance China's main trading partners are Japan, the
USA, Taiwan, Germany, Russia, South Korea, and Singapore.

A large proportion of China's manufactured exports is from
labour-intensive, light industries, principally clothing, textiles and
footwear (Table 3.2). Electrical goods and household appliances are
another important sector. The growth in exports is intimately
connected with foreign investment. Over a quarter of China's
exports originate from foreign firms and joint ventures and the
share of such firms in total exports is growing rapidly. A common
pattern of trade is to import components for assembly and re-
export. This is predominant in the electrical goods sector and
accounts for many of China's exports of relatively high-technology
items such as telephones, televisions and so on. One fast growing
area is so-called 'contract manufacturing', often of branded goods
such as sports shoes, where China-based companies are paid to
process imported materials while marketing and sale of the finished
goods remain in the hands of the foreign partner. In such cases, the
share of the final selling price accruing to the Chinese partner, and
especially to the workforce, is often extremely low. Technology
transfer in the case of assembly processes is minimal.

Despite her strong export performance, China's trade balance has
been in deficit for most of the reform period. Although the cumu-
lative trade deficit is, therefore, quite large, this is not necessarily a
severe problem for China. In effect, the current account deficit is

financed by longer-term funds from foreign investors. These investments, as well as development aid and remittances from overseas Chinese, mean that the trade deficit is manageable. On the other hand, China has a well publicized trade surplus with the USA that has led to friction between the two countries. The US accuses China of protecting its domestic industries from American competition, of dumping goods on the US market and of tolerating the widespread production of counterfeit goods. Despite US accusations of unfair trading practices, it is China which suffers most from protectionist policies. Tariffs imposed by developed countries on Chinese goods can be extraordinarily high. Australia imposes duties of nearly 50 per cent on some items (World Bank, 1993c: 146, cited in Lardy, 1994: 42). It is in China's interest that both tariff and non-tariff barriers are kept low on a world scale, and its leadership has expended considerable effort to secure China's membership of the World Trade Organization (WTO), formerly known as the General Agreement on Tariffs and Trade (GATT).

The growth of foreign trade led to the breakdown of old systems for managing the exchange rate of the renminbi. Under Mao, only a handful of Foreign Trade Corporations were allowed to engage in overseas trade, and the exchange rate was fixed by the PBC. As many more exporting firms began to handle foreign currency during the 1980s, the government allowed an internal currency market to develop. The market rate of the renminbi coexisted with an official rate until 1 January 1994, when the official rate was brought into line. By the mid-1990s, then, the renminbi had achieved internal convertibility. At the time of writing, however, the government had set no definite date for a move to full convertibility.

Foreign Investment

During the 1980s and 1990s vast quantities of foreign capital flowed into China. These funds played an enormous role in the development of the economy. As well as the amount of investment, it is important to distinguish between the various forms it takes. Multilateral or bilateral aid in the form of grants or 'soft' loans results from public policy decisions. Private investment can take various forms, from bank lending and bond purchase to both direct and indirect equity investment. The particular mix has profound influence on a country's financial stability.

Table 3.2 China's principal exports and imports by commodity

Exports	US$ millions	Imports	US$ millions
Garments	19 950	Rolled steel	6670
Cotton cloth and yarn	4000	Petroleum	4420
Petroleum	3030	Chemical fertilizer	3740
Aquatic products	2090	Grain	3580
Vegetables	1570	Motor vehicles,	
Electric fans, bicycles,		ships, aircraft	3260
sewing machines	1510	Vegetable oil	2430
Coal	1010	Paper pulp, paper	
Raw silk, silk and		and paperboard	2410
satin products	960	Machine tools	2200
Live hogs and pork	650	Synthetic fibre	1320
Machine tools and bearings	570	Iron ore	1230
Porcelain and pottery	550	Wool	940
Medicinal materials	440	Logs and plywood	930
Tea	270	Aluminium, Copper	920
Peanuts	260	Sugar	900

Source: *PRC Yearbook*, 1996–7: 433–4.

The World Bank has been by far the biggest single source of foreign investment. Between 1980 and 1996, it committed over US$ 25 billion to 175 development projects in China. A third of this sum was channelled through its 'soft' loan department, the International Development Association (IDA). IDA loans are repaid over thirty-five years at an annual interest rate of less than 1 per cent. China was the largest borrower from the World Bank in the 1990s, and in 1993 received 15 per cent of all IDA lending for that year. The bulk of World Bank funds are designated for infrastructural development and social welfare programmes. Much of the investment has been directed to the less-developed western regions of China. Examples include agricultural development and road building in Xinjiang, drinking water projects in Gansu, and poverty alleviation projects in Guizhou.

Developed countries have provided large amounts of development aid. While most countries suspended new loan approvals after the Tian'anmen incident in 1989, they continued to deliver tranches of loans already agreed. Consequently, the amount of money actually received by the Chinese rose in 1990. By 1991, economic sanctions had been lifted and the growth in bilateral aid programmes resumed. The sums involved are considerable. Between 1979 and 1995 Japan, the biggest contributor, made official development loans to China totalling around US$ 10 billion.

China has raised large amounts of finance on commercial terms, either via syndicated loans from foreign banks, or by issuing bonds on international markets. Political uncertainty following the 1989 crisis led to a downgrading of China's international credit rating and a collapse in bond sales. But as with the suspension of bilateral aid, this proved to be a temporary setback. As strong economic growth resumed in the 1990s, political risk ceased to be a major factor for foreign investors. China's previous credit rating was restored and foreign investors bought heavily into Chinese bond issues.

Privatization of China's state-owned industry, banks and utilities is, potentially, a major source of foreign capital. Since 1992, foreigners have been allowed to buy so-called 'B' shares in companies listed on the Shenzhen and Shanghai stock exchanges. Around two dozen Chinese corporations are listed on the Hong Kong stock market, and a few are listed in Europe and the USA. However, portfolio investment in China forms a small proportion of total foreign investment when compared with, for example, the former Soviet bloc or Latin America. Mexico raised over US$ 27 billion from privatizations between 1988 and 1994; over the same period China raised just over US$ 6 billion.

By contrast with countries that relied heavily on privatization to raise foreign capital, China has encouraged long-term, direct investment by foreign firms. Since 1986, foreign firms have been allowed to run wholly-owned subsidiaries in China and have qualified for many tax concessions and other incentives. Results have been spectacular. Foreign direct investment (FDI) has been the principal source of foreign finance in China, over the reform period, dwarfing even receipts from the World Bank. Between 1979 and 1993 more than US$ 60 billion was invested by foreign firms in joint ventures and other direct investments. In the early 1990s, China was the destination of nearly a quarter of total FDI in developing countries. Probably the majority of these funds came from Hong Kong, Taiwan, and overseas Chinese investors throughout southeast Asia. But huge amounts were also invested by European and US firms. Significantly, most large investment projects were undertaken by the multinationals.

One consequence of the preponderance of direct investment over portfolio investment is that China was not subject to periodic crises of confidence in emerging markets that caused the Mexican peso crisis of 1994, and the collapse of Asian currencies and stock markets in 1997–8. While securities can be bought and sold rapidly for speculative reasons, a directly managed investment project involves a long-term commitment of funds and expertise. In this respect, the government's caution over privatization has had some beneficial, unforeseen results.

The overall impact of foreign investment is hard to assess. Despite its importance, it is not the only motor of China's economic success. Growth has been almost as strong in the domestic sector (Naughton, 1995: 21–22), where it is the result of market reforms and buoyant domestic demand. Technology transfer and skills development have been slower than the leadership hoped; the biggest growth area has been routine assembly operations. High-technology components are often imported rather than manufactured locally, while technical research, product design, and marketing have tended to remain the preserve of foreign partners. The impact of private foreign invest-ment, moreover, has so far been mainly on the capital and coastal regions such as the Pearl river delta, the Shanghai region, and the Shandong peninsula. A corollary of investment is increased indebt-edness: China's foreign debt increased a hundredfold from US\$ 623 million to US\$ 69 321 million between 1978 and 1992 (World Bank, 1993b, vol. 2: 90, cited in Lardy, 1994: 50). While foreign reserves are currently high, China must at least maintain current levels of exports in order to preserve a manageable debt-service ratio.

Despite these qualifications, the net impact of foreign investment has been positive (Figure 3.4). While not easily quantifiable, ex-posure to modern management techniques will undoubtedly im-prove the performance of the economy over time and technology transfer, while taking longer than hoped, will surely occur if China follows the examples of Japan and South Korea, both of which graduated from light manufacturing to high-technology industries.

In future, China can expect stiffer competition for investment funds from other developing countries. Its own economic success means that from 1999 it no longer qualifies for IDA assistance. Direct investment is also likely to slacken off. The major untapped source is a mass privatization programme. At the 15th Communist Party congress in 1997 it seemed that the leadership was preparing to bite the bullet of privatization, despite its profound ideological and social implications.

Figure 3.4   Foreign direct investment, 1991–5

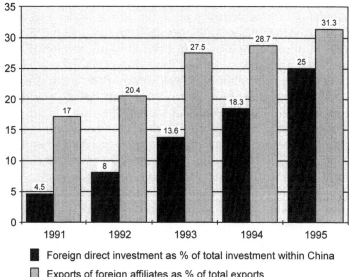

■ Foreign direct investment as % of total investment within China
□ Exports of foreign affiliates as % of total exports

Foreign direct investment has contributed a growing proportion of total domestic investment and has boosted China's exporting industries.

Source: World Bank, 1997g: 22.

Achievements and Problems

Growth Regions: Guangdong and Shanghai

Guangdong province was the power-house of the Chinese economy in the 1980s and early 1990s. The engine room was the Shenzhen SEZ in the Pearl river delta between Guangzhou and Hong Kong. In the 1980s Guangdong was the source for 25 per cent of China's total exports and attracted more than 40 per cent of the FDI into China. In 1993, when the national economy grew by 13.4 per cent, Guangdong outperformed it by nine points, and in 1995, the province's growth of 15 per cent was five points above the national rate. Guangdong's success was such that some analysts wondered whether, not for the first time this century, it might become a political rival to the capital.

However in 1996 the engine began to falter: growth in GDP, exports and foreign investment fell short of the national average. Guangdong's initial success had owed much to a once-for-all transfer of Hong Kong's light manufacturing industry over the border to Shenzhen. Much of the investment was in low-skill, low-added-value assembly operations. But by the mid-1990s, the investment incentives offered in Shenzhen were available in most parts of the country and rising wage costs and property prices were driving investors away. The province can no longer compete in simple export-processing, and urgently needs to develop more advanced, capital-intensive industries. Unfortunately, there is a marked shortage of qualified workers and the provincial government will be obliged to step up investment in training and education.

Shanghai, by contrast has a highly educated labour force and is attracting more high-tech and capital-intensive investment. Although it lagged behind the south coast in the 1980s, by 1997 FDI into Shanghai and the surrounding Yangzi delta had risen to Guangdong levels. Furthermore, the average size of projects was much greater, and the principal players were not overseas Chinese, but European, American, and Japanese multinationals. Both the central and city governments are spending enormous sums on infrastructural development. The public investment effort is symbolized by the transformation of Pudong, a previously derelict area east of Shanghai, into a massive new business district. Reform of state industry has proceeded further here than anywhere else in China, and Shanghai's over-staffed textile industry has been drastically downsized. If, as planned, the renminbi becomes a fully convertible currency, the Shanghai financial services industry may come to rival that of Hong Kong. With Shanghai politicians Jiang Zemin and Zhu Rongji holding the key posts in Beijing, the city seems set to rival and even overtake the south-coast growth regions.

Corruption

In recent years, commentators have become concerned about the levels of nepotism and corruption in China: as with many developing economies, what are politely referred to as the 'transaction costs' of doing business are quite high. This is not always a matter of straightforward financial corruption. Businessmen, anecdotally, stress the importance of developing 'connections' (*guanxi* in Chinese) as a prerequisite to concluding deals. The notion of *guanxi* is dwelt on in countless business guides and seminars for novice investors: for some foreign businessmen it has become a sort of mystical explanation for the success or failure of their ventures. The term covers a broad range of activities and stratagems held to be widespread in Chinese business, from advancing the interests of friends and family, or performing services in return for past or future favours, to outright bribe-taking.

Some see *guanxi* as a cultural phenomenon specific to China and profess to find parallels in the behaviour of overseas Chinese businessmen (see Chapter 6 for further discussion of 'national psychology'). But many of the social practices it refers to were common to all state socialist economies, and the term *guanxi* is quite similar in application to the Soviet term *blat*. All command economies suffered notoriously from shortages and bottlenecks: obtaining goods sometimes required hours of queueing, which might be avoided if one knew the right people. It is easy to see how complex chains of obligation can be created by the exchange of such favours (for some interesting examples, see Christiansen and Rai, 1996: 246–7). Such practices are not confined to individual purchases, but were at the heart of the operation of 'planned' economies. State firms were often unable to obtain critical supplies through the plan, and employed teams of fixers to negotiate deliveries from other firms (Szego, 1990: 56). Without such improvisation the economy would have simply ground to a halt.

During the 1980s there was a massive increase in corruption in all planned economies as they attempted market reforms. The reason everywhere was the differential pricing of goods. When a commodity is sold at different categories of prices, 'in the broad cracks between these categories, all kinds of speculation, favoritism, parasitism, and other vices find room, and this rather as the rule than the exception' (Trotsky, 1989: 75–6). The Chinese dual-price system was especially open to abuse. Goods obtained at fixed state prices were often immediately resold at the higher, market price. When carried out on a large scale involving commodities such as oil, simple arbitrage can lead to enormous fortunes being made.

Corruption has not, on the whole, been a great deterrent to foreign investors as anticipated profits offset excess transaction costs. A more serious risk is that public disgust will lead to further political unrest or disillusionment with the reform process. The government insists that it is tackling corruption and occasionally imposes exemplary punishment, up to and including execution, on high-profile offenders. But even the heaviest punishments are not realistic deterrents if detection rates remain low, and observers question how committed the authorities are to the elimination of abuses in which many leading officials are themselves implicated.

Uneven Development and Poverty

During the initial period of reforms, rural incomes grew by around 150 per cent in real terms, narrowing the gap between town and country and thereby reducing social inequality. This improvement, however, was due to increases in farm procurement prices administratively decreed by the government, as well as the operation of market forces, and in retrospect it seems to have been once-and-for-all boost to rural earnings. Since 1985, agricultural production growth has slowed and farm incomes have stagnated. The old problem of a growing differential between agricultural and industrial prices has reappeared.

In 1978, according to a Party document released in 1996, 260 million of the rural population lived below the poverty line, despite the relative egalitarianism of the collectivized agricultural system. By 1996, the figure was still 65 million, some 5.5 per cent of the national population. If this figure seems to represent a reasonable achievement, one should remember that the Chinese state definition of the poverty-line is an income of around US$ 36 a year, a mere 10 per cent of the international standard of US$ 370. Given recent inflation in China, this figure is below subsistence level.

The great majority of rural poor live in remote mountain or hinterland areas in central and western China. The situation is continuously exacerbated by differential investment patterns in both state and non-state sectors, both of which heavily favour the eastern coastal provinces. Official Chinese economists admitted that there was little prospect of improvement in the poorer regions, given 'capital shortage, inadequate investments, financial drainage and weak development' (State Council of China, 1996). The income differential between coastal and inland provinces is greater than 1:15, and more than 90 per cent of FDI is in the south and east coastal provinces (Prybla, 1997: 19).

The reforms have also led to increasing urban poverty, alongside greatly increased affluence. There is no comprehensive social security network in China (despite the good social benefits granted to many employees in large enterprises). The new urban poor are mainly those who have no secure income and no access to work-unit benefits: the unemployed or semi-unemployed; migrants; retirees; and the handicapped or invalid. Of these, the largest group is the unemployed. According to recent estimates, which are inevitably very approximate, there were some 50 to 70 million rural labourers who had left the countryside to seek work in urban areas in 1995–6. These people are not included in official statements and policies on unemployment and are classified as a 'floating' population which inhabits the slums and shanty-towns of the boom cities. Of true urban residents, the State Statistical Bureau reported in 1994 an unemployment rate of 3.5 per cent, affecting some 7 million people (Jiang *et al.*, 1996: 125–37). Since 1995, redundancies have increased. Reports in 1996 and 1997 calculated that some 40 million people had been laid off due to the closure of factories and other enterprises, and the increasing rate of bankruptcies was expected to continue. These unemployed, and the other categories of urban poor, usually receive no state support at all and rely on personal or family resources.

Income differential between regions has already been noted; it is also very marked between individuals. There is undoubtedly a large class of newly rich in China, whose precise contours have yet to be mapped. It includes those who have made lucrative pickings out of the dual-track economy; those who have thrived through nepotism; private entrepreneurs; managers and technocrats, often linked with foreign businesses. Many of their assets are located in overseas banks and will never figure in accounts. Nevertheless, even official sources report that there are over 2 million Chinese millionaires, and that 3 per cent of the population hold total savings of 290 billion renminbi, a figure that is in excess of the entire savings of 800 million peasants (Prybla, 1997: 18).

The CCP itself has acknowledged the potential for conflict arising from extreme differences in wealth, and has expressed concern about threats to social stability arising from gaps in development. It is particularly worried by any signs of resistance to Party and government organized by workers threatened with unemployment. Any outbreak of unrest would destabilize the current optimistic economic climate. Poverty is a major humanitarian problem which demands the reallocation of resources; equally, it could easily become a social and political issue.

Summary and Prospects

Following Deng Xiaoping's 1992 trip to the south to re-launch the stalled reform process, there was an outbreak of 'China fever' among foreign businessmen and economic commentators. Enthusiasm for the Chinese economy mingled with general optimism about seemingly unstoppable growth in the 'tiger' economies of east and southeast Asia. Popular social commentaries attributed the region's economic success to a specific, Asian model of development: although details varied, it was usually said to involve a high savings rate, export-led growth, low wages, strict labour discipline and an authoritarian, pro-business government. For many, inside and outside China, this seemed a fair description of 'socialism with Chinese characteristics'.

To add to its reputation for ruthlessness, the Chinese leadership was acquiring one for sound economic management. The 1990s were much less of a roller-coaster ride for the Chinese economy than the 1980s, and this was attributed to the competent management of China's 'economic Tsar', Zhu Rongji. While praising the government's commitment to reforms, foreign economists urged it to take bolder action, in particular to speed up reform and privatization of China's ailing state industries. At the 15th Party Congress in 1997, President Jiang Zemin announced the leadership's intention of doing precisely this, stating that all but a few thousand strategic enterprises would be left to sink or swim in the marketplace. In March 1998, Zhu Rongji was appointed state Premier in a move that symbolized the domination of pro-reform leaders.

But in 1997 and 1998, a profound crisis swept through the economies of China's neighbours and placed a question mark over the whole region. The crisis broke with the collapse of the Thai currency and stock market in July 1997 and quickly spread to Indonesia, Malaysia, and the Philippines, who were all forced to seek emergency loans from the IMF. By November, problems had spread to South Korea some of whose giant *chaebol* conglomerates were revealed as bankrupt. All over Asia thousands of companies, whose dollar-denominated debt had previously been manageable, were bankrupted by the collapse of local currencies. In May 1998, demonstrations led to the fall of the Suharto regime in Indonesia. Meanwhile in the background the Japanese economy, which had shown no significant growth since 1992, went into recession. In the space of a few months, the 'Asian miracle' was being repackaged by media commentators as an Asian disaster.

Although the Hong Kong stock market suffered a severe setback, China's economy was not immediately affected by the crisis. Taiwan also, although forced to devalue its currency, escaped the worst. But there were reasons to believe that China might not remain unscathed in the medium to long term. The devaluation of southeast Asia's currencies cheapened exports from the region and posed a competitive threat to China's. A flood of cheap exports from the region might also strengthen the hand of protectionist politicians in the USA and Europe. There was the risk that 'Asian flu' might spread and cause a global downturn. In any event it seemed China's export sector was bound to suffer, at a time when its domestic sector was already slowing down fast. The crisis seemed bound to have a negative effect on inward investment into China. Apart from a general reduction in confidence, China may suffer particularly due to severe financial losses suffered by the overseas Chinese of southeast Asia.

Looking to the longer term, the crisis placed a question mark over an economic model that inspired major aspects of China's policy. In many ways the Korean crisis was especially worrying, since China seems to have based its industrial strategy on state sponsorship of a few chosen conglomerates, as the South Korean state systematically routed investment to the *chaebols*. The crisis has also placed under the spotlight many of the aspects of China's economy that resemble those of the failed tigers: the non-performing 'policy loans' to favoured industries, hidden insolvency of banks and major corporations, and all-pervasive corruption.

No doubt, more conservative elements in China are using the crisis to retard the pace of opening up the economy. The leadership must surely have reflected that if the economic reforms been more advanced, the renminbi would have been fully convertible and foreign investors would have had free access to China's securities markets. China might then have suffered along with the rest. Almost certainly this scenario will give them pause for thought before pursuing further financial reform. But it may not require a panic by foreign investors to bring down China's shaky financial structures. Market reforms mean that the millions of Chinese small savers have the power to bring about a home-grown financial collapse should they lose confidence the banking system.

None of this implies that China's economic miracle has come to an end, or even that Asia as a whole has suffered a permanent setback. The problems of 1997–8 have a cyclical aspect and many commentators believe that the fundamentals point to continuing strong growth in both China and the rest of Asia. At the least, however, the downturn provides a corrective to some of the more outlandishly optimistic projections for China's twenty-first century (see Chapter 8).

4
Political Life

Two events sum up political developments in China in the last decade: the massacre of 4 June 1989 following anti-government demonstrations in Tian'anmen Square; and the reintegration of Hong Kong on 1 July 1997. The first was a disaster that revealed a government in disarray and was thought by many to presage the collapse of Communist rule. The second was a triumph that seemed to reflect both government stability and a new sense of international power and prestige. The triumph in Hong Kong was all the more complete as the leadership was able to build a solid base of support within the former colony, especially from business interests, for its policy of 'one country, two systems', and for the annulment of the limited and belated democratic reforms introduced by British colonial governor Patten. The Party approached the end of the century with a confident, secure leadership presiding over a booming economy, and with a major foreign policy success under its belt.

There had been much speculation in the foreign press about a succession crisis that might follow the death of Deng Xiaoping. In the event, Deng's death on 19 February 1997 was handled almost as business as usual. The contrast between the political calm of 1997 Beijing, and the the palace intrigues and arrests that followed the death of Mao Zedong in 1976, could not have been sharper. The subsequent 15th Party Congress in September 1997 was a triumph for Party General Secretary Jiang Zemin. The congress sealed Deng's canonization by raising 'Deng Xiaoping Theory' to the same level as 'Mao Zedong Thought' in the Party's constitution. In the process, Jiang secured the demotion of a number of political rivals, and was able to present himself as Deng's successor.

In contrast to the political calm of the 1990s, the previous decade was turbulent. In 1978, Deng Xiaoping struggled for power as head of the generation of cadres purged during the Cultural Revolution. The defeat of the hard-line Maoists, and the rehabilitation of their opponents, created widespread hopes of a more general political reform. These hopes inspired the democratic movement of 1978–9 and, while the movement was suppressed, the ensuing repression was relatively selective and left the majority of activists untouched. There was an outbreak of student demonstrations in late 1986, following which conservatives within the Party were able to secure the dismissal of its relatively liberal General Secretary, Hu Yaobang. Despite such setbacks, and government campaigns against 'spiritual pollution' and 'bourgeois liberalization', a broad, unorganized movement for democratic reform grew in strength through the 1980s. The Tian'anmen Square demonstrations in 1989 marked the climax of popular opposition to the Party.

The pro-democracy forces were decisively defeated by massive repression, starting with the Beijing massacre; most activists subsequently were either imprisoned or fled the country. The Tian'anmen events, and the collapse of Eastern European Communism, removed political reform from the CCP agenda. Throughout the 1990s, the Party combined a drive to a market economy with a political freeze. Outside the Party, there were few signs of a revival of the mass movement, and many dissidents and activists remained in jail, or subject to restrictions. There were potential political problems on the horizon, however. Having swallowed Hong Kong, the leadership was obliged to digest a powerful and undefeated democratic movement. In Xinjiang, Islamic rebels, inspired by the example of the newly independent former Soviet republics of Central Asia, began to take militant action to secure independence from Beijing. Perhaps most importantly, at the 15th Party Congress, the leadership decided it could no longer shy away from the task of rationalizing state industry and the civil service, a course that risks both confrontation with China's working class and conflict within the government apparatus.

The Chinese State

China's leaders mostly live and work in a huge area known as 'Zhongnanhai', in the centre of Beijing. Their decisions may be influenced by personal loyalties, lines of authority, connections with the military and business sectors, advice from specialists, discussions with provincial leaders, and dozens of other factors. Some journalists watch Zhongnanhai, like an earlier generation of Kremlinologists, and academics produce analyses of the system, but nobody can really claim insight into the heart of decision-making. On the whole, foreign analysts and Chinese citizens alike have proved incapable of predicting power shifts and new policies among the political elite. Events that shook the entire nation, like the Great Leap Forward, the Sino–Soviet split, the Cultural Revolution, the Deng reforms, and the response to the Beijing 1989 movement seem to have taken everyone by surprise. Perhaps Chinese leaders themselves are often uncertain about where power actually lies on any given issue. Specialists may have a good grasp of the contours of Chinese politics, but one should be chary of accepting precise explanations and predictions.

The Leading Role of the Party

The defining characteristic of the Chinese political system since 1949 has been the leading role played by the CCP. Since its inception, the government of the PRC has operated under the Party's centralized, unified direction. The Party's role is not confined to government or politics as narrowly defined in liberal democracies. Its ideological and administrative roles extend into almost all aspects of life, including education, industry, commerce and the military. There are Party branches in almost all institutions, including factories, offices, shops, schools, colleges and army units. In the early years of the PRC, the leadership envisaged that the Party would determine policy, and government officials would carry it out. However, the distinction between Party and state quickly collapsed. Roughly speaking, every element within the Chinese government is shadowed by a corresponding Party organization. The Party controls all major appointments to state bodies, and most leading state officials are also Party members. Furthermore, for many years, it was the practice for Party members within an organization to caucus separately before policy-making meetings, to ensure that each member followed the correct 'line'. For these reasons we may say that the Party is not *parallel to*, but *interlocked with* the state apparatus.

The leading role of the Party is a key feature of all communist systems, but in the Chinese context should be qualified by the unusually important part the military has played in political affairs.

From 1927 until 1949 the CCP was engaged in an almost continuous armed struggle for power (see Chapter 1). Most leaders, including Mao Zedong, Deng Xiaoping, and Lin Biao were also military figures. Mao insisted on a politicized military, and to this day the PLA swears allegiance to the CCP rather than to the Chinese state. The other side of the coin was the militarization of politics. Military and political structures in communist China were from the start enmeshed, unlike in the Soviet Union, where the Red Army was created after the revolution with ex-Tsarist officers at its core. The political influence of the PLA reached its height in 1969 towards the end of the Cultural Revolution, when nearly half of the Central Committee of the CCP were military personnel. Although the army's influence waned after the return to power of Deng and other rehabilitated victims of the Cultural Revolution, it returned to centre stage in 1989 to save the regime.

China's political system has been described as totalitarian, but this is not an adequate characterization of its practical operation. Divisions within the leadership have often created space for the expression of popular resistance to Party policies – for example, the demonstrations around the time of Zhou Enlai's death in 1976, or the democracy movement of 1978–9. Provincial and local governments also have their own spheres of influence. If the 'totalitarian' tag had any validity it would have been in Mao Zedong's time. More recently, economic reforms have created social groups, such as well-to-do peasants and private entrepreneurs who are, for many practical purposes, outside the Party's sphere of influence. By the late 1990s many provincial and local Party leaders were in charge of considerable business empires, and had their own agendas, quite separate from that of the leadership in Beijing.

Party Organization

The organization of the CCP is theoretically based on the principle of 'democratic centralism', defined by Lenin as allowing Party members freedom of discussion but insisting on unity in action once a decision has been reached. It was supposed to provide balance between grass-roots' input and executive power; but in practice, the centralism was stressed far more than the democracy. In its early years, under the leadership of Chen Duxiu, the Party had tolerated a variety of opinion. Mao later recalled that 'when Lenin was still alive . . . and before Stalin had come to power . . . generally speaking, there was no dogmatism' (cited in Benton and Hunter, 1995: 5). However, in the mid-to-late 1920s, the Comintern began a program of 'Bolshevization' of foreign communist parties. In practice, this meant the imposition of 'iron discipline, blind obedience, doglike loyalty, and extreme centralism'. Thus even before it conquered power, the Chinese Party had adopted heavily bureaucratized forms of organization that developed in the Russian Party only after the October Revolution. Twenty years of operating under military discipline in rural areas, the enormous cultural gap between urban CCP leaders and peasant recruits, and the personality cult of Mao Zedong all intensified authoritarianism in the Party.

The formal structure of the Party is at first sight democratic. Basic-level congresses, usually representing a small district or a workplace, elect delegates to county congresses. The counties elect provincial delegates who, in turn, elect the National Party Congress. The Party Congress elects the Central Committee. Finally the Central Committee elects the Politburo and the Standing Committee of the Politburo. In theory, the lower bodies determine the composition of higher bodies; in practice, the opposite is the case. The results of most elections are predetermined by caucuses of leading members. At all levels, small committees made up of key leaders meet much more frequently than congresses and are able to dominate the larger assemblies. Party members are not allowed to freely publish their views or form internal groupings, so no effective political opposition to the leadership can grow from the grass roots (although this does not preclude cadres forming 'factions' based on cronyism for the purpose of mutual advancement). The main qualities required for election to Party bodies are length of service and unquestioning loyalty to sponsors in the leadership.

Real power is in the hands of those individuals who sit on a small number of key Party bodies. The main policy-making body for the whole of China is the Standing Committee of the Politburo (Figure 4.1). This body comprises about six to eight key political leaders, selected from the twenty or so who sit on the full Politburo. While the Standing Committee of the Politburo makes policy, day-to-day administration is handled by the Secretariat of the Central Committee. The key individual on both bodies is the General Secretary, who convenes the meetings of both the Standing Committee and the Secretariat. At the time of writing, this post is held by Jiang Zemin. Another crucially important body is the Military Affairs Commission (MAC). Deng Xiaoping held the key role of chairman of the

Figure 4.1   Structure of the Chinese Communist Party

```
┌──────────────────┐  ┌──────────────────┐  ┌────────────────────────────────┐
│ Politburo Standing│  │ General Secretary│  │ The post of General Secretary is│
│    Committee      │  └──────────────────┘  │ key in the CCP hierarchy.       │
│   c. 6 members    │           ⇑            │ The General Secretary           │
└──────────────────┘                        │ convenes the meetings of both tho│
                       ┌──────────────────┐  │ Politburo and its Standing Committee,│
┌──────────────────┐  │   Secretariat    │  │ and supervises the Secretariat  │
│     Politburo     │  │   c. 5 members   │  │                                 │
│   c. 20 members   │  └──────────────────┘  │ KEY   ⇒   = elects.             │
└──────────────────┘           ⇑            └────────────────────────────────┘
        ┌──────────────────────────────┐
        │   Central Committee of the    │
        │   Chinese Communist Party     │
        │  Approximately 320 members    │
        │  (full members and alternates)│
        └──────────────────────────────┘
                      ⇑
┌────────────────────────┐  ┌─────────────────────────┐  ┌─────────────────────────┐
│ Military Affairs Commission│⇐│    National Party Congress │⇒│ Central Commission for   │
└────────────────────────┘  │    Held every five years  │  │  Inspecting Discipline   │
                            │  Approximately 2000 delegates,│  └─────────────────────────┘
┌────────────────────────┐  │ representing 58 million members (1997)│
│Central Advisory Commission│⇐└─────────────────────────┘
└────────────────────────┘
```

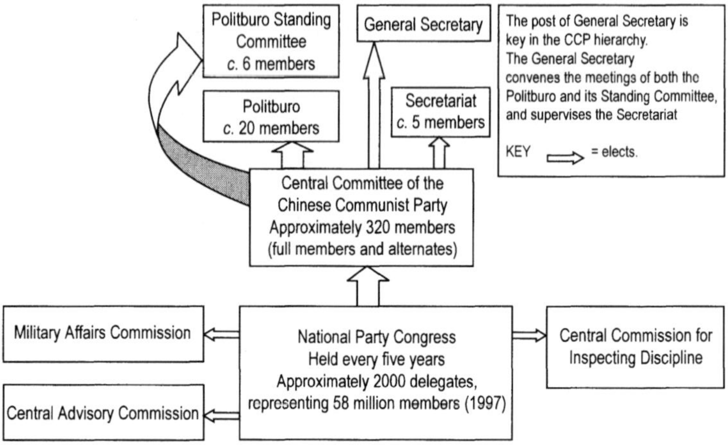

MAC from 1978 until October 1989, when he ceded it to Jiang
Zemin. The MAC controls the PLA and is, therefore, the ultimate
guarantee of power against a military coup or civilian unrest.

The CCP Organization Department is another key element in
China's political system. This body is responsible for assessing and
evaluating candidates for appointment to both Party and State
posts. The CCP maintains lists of reliable cadres and corresponding
lists of posts, together with the level of vetting required for each
appointment. Senior appointments require the approval of the
Central Committee or the Politburo. Lower-level appointments
are dealt with by Party committees further down the hierarchy.
The term *nomenklatura* was coined in the Soviet Union to refer to
the Party's system for vetting all key appointments, and is often
applied to the very similar system which operates in China. The
Chinese term *renshi zhidu* is roughly equivalent (Christiansen and
Rai, 1996: 13).

Organization of the Government

In imperial times there were four tiers of government bodies, at
central, provincial, county and town levels, and the same basic
structure continues to function today. There are twenty-three provinces, many of them the size of major European countries. The

largest, Sichuan, has a population of 120 million. Five autonomous regions (Guanxi, Inner Mongolia, Ningxia, Tibet, and Xinjiang) and four municipalities (Beijing, Chongqing, Shanghai, and Tianjin) are equivalent in status to provinces. China's internal administrative boundaries have remained relatively stable over a long period, and many provinces and counties have existed in roughly their present form for over 2000 years. Until recently, urban work-units effectively functioned as a fifth level of government (see Chapter 5); in the countryside this level was represented by the People's Communes until their functions were transferred to township authorities around 1982.

In theory, the Chinese government is democratically elected by a system of People's Congresses that meet at each level (Figure 4.2). County-level congresses elect provincial level congresses. The provinces, autonomous regions and province-level municipalities elect delegates to the National People's Congress (NPC) which is formally the highest government organ of the PRC. The National People's Congress elects the State Council, headed by the Premier. As well as the CCP, several small, legal parties are allowed to contest elections. Although the structure is apparently democratic, manipulation by the CCP has turned it into a sham; the handful of legal parties all recognize the leading role of the Communist Party, so the electorate is offered no genuine political choice.

Although the State Council is officially the government of China, the Standing Committee of the Communist Party Politburo corresponds more closely to a European-style Cabinet. This is not to say that the State Council is powerless. It includes very senior figures in the Chinese leadership: Zhou Enlai, for example, occupied the post of Premier for many years. The State Council also controls key appointments at provincial level and in those cities which have provincial rank. But like all other state bodies in the PRC, it is enmeshed with, and subordinate to, the Party apparatus.

Formal and Informal Power

Students of politics should bear in mind that power is not always in the hands of formal office-holders as they appear on organization charts. Real power-holders may occupy apparently trivial offices or no offices at all. Some mismatch between office and power is a feature of all political systems, but it has been especially pronounced

106

Figure 4.2   Government of the People's Republic of China

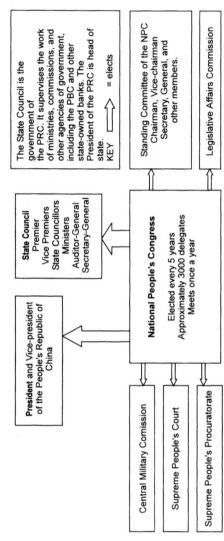

in the PRC. The handling of the 1989 student demonstrations was a notorious example. As the crisis reached its climax, the formal lines of command within the Chinese state and the CCP ceased to function. Neither the standing committee of the Politburo nor the State Council ordered the suppression of the demonstrations. The mayor of Beijing announced that the decision to impose martial law had been taken at a meeting 'of cadres from the Party, government and military institutions' (Christiansen and Rai, 1996: 160). China's official leader, state Premier and CCP General Secretary, Zhao Ziyang, refused to attend the meeting and was arrested, apparently indicted with revealing to Mikhail Gorbachev, the 'state secret' that Deng Xiaoping retained a veto on all important issues.

In practice, all major decisions during the Tian'anmen crisis were taken by Deng Xiaoping, backed up by Party veterans from the Central Advisory Commission (ironically a body set up by Deng for the purpose of removing the elderly from the centre of power). Deng's only formal office was chairmanship of the MAC; the other members of the Central Advisory Commission held no executive offices. It was their prestige as leaders of the revolution that enabled the elders to assume control of events. However there are signs that things may be changing. Biology is steadily thinning out the ranks of the veterans. Deng is dead, and there is no candidate likely to inherit his role as a behind-the-scenes leader. The generation that made the revolution was necessarily unique, and successive generations of retired leaders will not share their prestige and authority. It is likely that in the future formal office and real power will coincide more closely.

By the late 1990s most of the old revolutionaries had been replaced by cadres who had played no part in the Party's struggle for power. Their educational background is also different from previous leaders. Many early CCP members, for example Chen Duxiu, Zhou Enlai, and Deng Xiaoping either studied in the West or were strongly influenced by Western culture; some say that Mao, who was steeped in Chinese culture and spoke no foreign languages, was relatively free of Western influence. Many of the current top leadership, including Jiang Zemin and Li Peng, were educated in the Soviet Union, a fact that may explain their somewhat pedestrian style of work, while many middle-ranking or senior cadres are products of Chinese universities of the 1950s and 1960s, which were strongly influenced by Soviet-style Marxism. However, when the current leadership retires, some power at least will be inherited by cadres educated outside China during the reform period. It has been argued that the large numbers of Taiwanese who received overseas, especially US, education contributed to the democratization of Taiwan when they returned home to take up managerial or administrative positions. A parallel development may be a factor in mainland politics in the next generation.

Political Thought

The Critique of Maoism

Over the last twenty years China has moved from a centrally planned economy under an ideology-driven regime to a dynamic market economy with a political leadership largely made up of technocrats. Who were the architects of this reform process and from where did they derive their ideas? What were the parameters of the debate? Have the reforms reached an impasse? However one finally answers these questions, the first impetus of the reforms was clearly the repudiation, intellectual and practical, of Maoism.

In 1977, Deng Xiaoping, who was not then rehabilitated from political disgrace, launched the slogan 'seek truth from facts'. (The slogan, *shishi qiushi* in Chinese, had in fact been advocated by Mao, quoting a classical Chinese historian, in 1942 (Schram, 1989: 201–2): Deng used a Maoist slogan to attack the essence of Maoism.) This call appears a simplistic proposition, but its implication was shattering: that the Chinese political elite should drop its uncritical acceptance of Maoism, and instead adopt a pragmatic, reasoned approach to policy-making and government. This was, of course, diametrically opposed to the politics of the Cultural Revolution. Senior Party figures supported Deng against Mao's immediate successors, and towards the end of 1977 the media began to carry articles on the subjects of science, democracy and the personality cult. Hu Yaobang, then head of the Central Party School, formalized the attack by proposing a re-evaluation of Mao's policies and the use of empirical criteria, instead of ideological purity, to determine policy.

The slogan 'seek truth from facts' eventually led to a wholesale re-thinking of socialism. One political scientist regards the rejection of Maoism as the key to understanding the entire reform process: within a few years almost the whole political spectrum (with the exception of die-hard Maoists) shared the analysis that 'a basic mistake in the past Chinese socialist experience has been to under-estimate the unique difficulties of building socialism in an undeveloped country' (Sun, 1995: 264). According to the new critique, the Maoist leadership had been engaged in an impossible undertaking, namely to implement communism in a country where the material resources were totally inadequate for it; the Maoists mistakenly believed that mass mobilization and class struggle could compensate for the lack of modern economic structures, of which they were mostly ignorant. Their fundamentalist interpretation of socialism led to dogmatic anti-capitalism; their unachievable programme could be enforced only by an irrational state structure, the personality cult and abuses of power which discredited the regime and indeed the idea of socialism itself.

Soon, intellectuals working in state research institutions began to question the validity of Marxism itself. For example, as early as 1979 Su Shaozhi (director of the Marxism–Leninism Research Institute at the Chinese Academy of Social Sciences until his removal in 1987) proposed the then shocking idea that socioeconomic conditions in China did not permit the implementation of socialism. He argued that China faced a paradox, having a relatively advanced social system (rule by a communist party) but a backward economy. In 1983, Su published the startling argument that Marxism had only limited applicability to Chinese reality, that particular 'Chinese characteristics' were of great importance, and that China should not be obsessed with dated theories developed in the context of different societies. Until he was obliged to flee China in 1989, Su addressed the issues of 'humanizing' socialism, alienation, social justice and political freedom. His work illustrates that far from being mindless oppressors, there were many in the CCP who were dedicated to finding humane political solutions within the socialist framework.

In place of ideological purity, pragmatism was enshrined as a guiding principle, epitomized by Deng's frequently-quoted remark that either a black cat or a white cat is fine, as long as it catches the mouse, and Zhou Enlai's that China would proceed by 'crossing the river feeling for stepping-stones' – i.e. undertake incremental, practical reforms. In short, *revolution* was rejected by almost all Chinese political thinkers in favour of *material prosperity*. Deng Xiaoping himself explained that poverty, even if shared relatively equably, is not socialism:

The primary task of socialism is to develop production forces and to elevate the standard of the material and cultural life of the people. Our twenty years of experience from 1958 to 1976 have told us: poverty is not socialism, [the purpose of] socialism is to eliminate poverty. (Deng Xiaoping in 1984, cited in Sun, 1995: 203)

The main slogan of the early reform period, still much-promoted today, was the Four Modernizations of agriculture, industry, defence, and science and technology. The objective was to turn China into a powerful, rich, modern state governed by the CCP; the free market and other reforms were instrumental to this objective, not ends in themselves. The ground of political debate thus shifted almost entirely to issues of how prosperity could be attained most efficiently.

At this point it may be helpful to distinguish between moderate reform within the system, more extensive reform, still within the system but challenging some of its basic features and radical opposition calling for overthrow of the entire regime. We should also mention leftists or conservatives who were basically opposed to reform. The above categories are not watertight: some ideas were common to all groups and some thinkers changed their views over time. The arguments of the 'conservatives' do not require much attention here. Briefly, they opposed many aspects of the reform process, although tolerating its broad thrust. In the 1980s they were often on the defensive, as radical reformists appeared to hold central stage politically. The conservatives upheld the Four Fundamental Principles (the leadership of the Party, supremacy of Marxism–Leninism and Mao Zedong thought, the socialist road and the people's democratic dictatorship, in effect code-words for monolithic Party rule), and were extremely suspicious of moves towards a market economy and popular freedoms. They were more important for their political power than for their intellectual energy. Their great opportunity to recover lost ground came in the aftermath of the Tian'anmen crackdown, when the apparatus united to fight the popular challenge. Despite this most promising environment, the return to hard-line leftism was limited, and had evaporated by 1992. Nevertheless, the conservative-leaning Li Peng held the number two position in the leadership hierarchy into the late 1990s.

Deng Xiaoping himself was of course the most outstanding moderate reformer. To summarize his political and economic project: government policy should be pragmatic, always aiming at a stronger, richer, more powerful China. Policies which promote economic growth should be encouraged, even where they are heterodox by orthodox Marxist standards – for example, encouraging the free market, personal acquisitiveness and private ownership. Socialist ideas should be adapted to Chinese circumstances and updated to deal with contemporary society. A limited re-evaluation of Party history should be permitted. Trade with the West should be encouraged, especially to facilitate the transfer of technology; cultural contacts, while not ruled out, were less welcome. Above all, during the chaotic process of economic modernization, the Party should retain power by all necessary means, guaranteeing a return to a purer form of socialism at some unspecified date in the future. Deng and his supporters were far from democrats, nor did they advocate an uncontrolled capitalist revival. The critique of Maoism was widely accepted; threat to Party rule was not. Deng made it plain that there would be no relaxation of political control in 1979, when he cracked down on democracy activists; he repeated the lesson in 1989. This line represented the consensus among political leaders throughout the period and was, broadly speaking, operational into the late 1990s.

Two politicians in particular, Hu Yaobang and Zhao Ziyang, represented the trend for more extensive political reform within the context of the CCP regime. Both had close contacts with networks of younger intellectuals in think-tanks and research institutes, for whom they afforded political protection. Reform proposals from these groups included granting freedom of speech and assembly, the regulation of CCP power, freedom of debate, political pluralism, and privatization of the economy. They also proposed reducing the size of the Party to diminish its all-pervasive presence in Chinese life, and allowing factions to operate freely within the CCP. Neither Hu nor Zhao shared all the ideas that were put forward by their followers, but they helped to created the space within which they could be discussed.

By the mid-1980s, reformist ideas were breaking new ground to the extent that the very fundamentals of the socialist economy were being challenged. Until then, commodity exchange had been tolerated as a more rational way to circulate goods within the confines of a socialist system; now the very system itself came under question. China began to move towards a quasi-capitalist economy with private ownership of property, including enterprises, encouragement of private accumulation and trade on the world market. In less than a decade the reformists had arrived at a full-scale legitimization of a 'market economy'. In fact, despite the political hiatus after 1989, in broad terms the economic reforms proposed by the 'radicals' of the mid-1980s were being implemented in the 1990s by Party leaders: Jiang Zemin and his group accepted that the planned economy had failed in many ways and needed ever-increasing doses of free-market medicine.

One of the best-known reformist establishment intellectuals was Yan Jiaqi, director of the Political Institute of the Chinese Academy of Social Sciences and an adviser to Zhao Ziyang. Among the issues he and his group addressed were the scope of state and Party power: the state was to assume control for the constitution, laws, education and culture, in place of the CCP; the Party was to become more democratic and to lead by example rather than by force. By 1988 they were calling for democratization, pluralization and privatization. Yan took a rather passive role in the 1989 democracy movement until as late as May, and he was probably regarded by most of its participants as part of the state apparatus, albeit of the reformist wing, rather than as a rebel. However, he did eventually come out in whole-hearted support of the student movement and was one of the most senior cadres to escape overseas. Once in the West, he further developed his critique of the Chinese state, and became a vigorous spokesperson for 'wholesale Westernization' and a leading figure of the exile democracy movement.

New Marxism, New Authoritarianism

Many of the above reformers tended to favour a 'new Marxism', some of it deriving from, or running parallel to, the 'Eurocommunist' ideas that had developed inside West European communist parties. Starting in the late 1980s, but with increasing clout after 1989, there surfaced a new stream in Chinese political thinking, that strayed even further from traditional socialist ideals. By 1988 it had become apparent that, despite some successes, the economic reforms were creating serious discontent among the general population. One problem was inflation which, coupled with growing income disparity, led to acute problems, especially for the many millions on fixed state incomes. The other major issue was corruption, which had reached massive proportions by the late 1980s. Conservatives in the Party leadership used evidence of public discontent to call for an end to the reforms and for Zhao's dismissal. Zhao responded by legitimating the reforms with a new ideology which became known as 'new authoritarianism'. In late 1988 and early 1989 members of think-tanks associated with Zhao Ziyang were prepared to drop democracy altogether from their political programme in an attempt to forestall, by stealing half their clothes, the conservatives' plans to bring both the economy and society back under greater state control. The theory of 'new authoritarianism' was loosely derived from the American political scientist Samuel Huntington, who argued in the 1960s that, in developing countries, a strong government capable of keeping society orderly and stable is an essential condition for modernization. The sort of government China's new authoritarians had in mind was one modelled on autocratic free-market regimes like that of South Korea.

The theory points to a key concept which distinguished the Chinese reform process from the Russian one: it was vital to retain strong political leadership during the period of transition to a market economy. It was therefore a defence against conservative criticism that the reforms had gone too far; it was also a denial of calls for greater democracy. For the latter reason, it was opposed even by some in Zhao's circle, like Yan Jiaqi. For them, democratic safeguards and participation were far more likely to reduce social tensions than a strict re-imposition of state controls. Not surprisingly, the theory became increasingly acceptable to Chinese politicians after 1989, when they were no longer prepared to tolerate even limited democracy. It gained new credibility from the increasingly close ties of the Asia Pacific economies, and the explicit defence of authoritarianism by regional political leaders figures such as Lee Kuan Yew of Singapore and the Malaysian leader, Dr Mahathir Bin Mohamad.

Opponents of the Regime

The intellectuals and ideas discussed above were, for the most part, either attached to the political elite itself, or not explicitly opposed to it. But from 1978 China also witnessed the spread of ideas about democracy and human rights that directly confronted CCP power itself, demanding an end to dictatorship, corruption, and illegal governance. Those we mentioned earlier as radical challengers launched a critique of the entire CCP project. Despite different strands of opinion within the opposition groups, most of them condemned the Party for its brutality in the Maoist era and lack of honesty in acknowledging its failures. Most also disagreed with the planned economy and wanted a free market. All wanted an end to Party rule, its ideological monopoly, its corruption, the bureaucratic oppression and the gulag system. Perhaps a minority of the radicals wanted a democratic socialist alternative to CCP rule; some were explicitly in favour of a free-market economy, multi-party parliamentary democracy, and 'wholesale Westernization'; many were stronger on criticism than envisioning a workable future.

The 1978 democracy movement sprang up at the same time as Deng and his supporters were taking power within the CCP. While Deng argued for a more pragmatic policy, and for limited re-evaluation of the Party's record, the democratic movement went much further: many of its proponents argued that the Party was irretrievably discredited and that superficial reforms were impossible. Others, while accepting that the Party should hold political leadership, demanded elections and procedural politics in place of rule by police and diktat. The movement's centre was in Beijing, specifically on the perimeter wall of a large bus depot on which activists would stick posters, and where they met to debate and distribute pamphlets (see Chapter 1). Groups were also in regular contact with dissidents in Shanghai and other cities. For a period, it suited Deng and his political allies to allow this wild card to survive, probably in order to pressurize remaining Maoists to leave their posts.

The movement had mixed intellectual and social backgrounds. Many of its members were factory workers, others were nonconformist painters, poets and writers. Students, and young people who had been sent to the countryside in the Cultural Revolution, also participated. The ideological mix was also quite varied, calling on East European dissent (Tito, Solidarity), Trotsky and the young Marx on the one hand, anarchism, Dada and liberalism on the other. Some were strongly sympathetic to revolutionary socialism, arguing chiefly for the radical deconstruction of the CCP bureaucracy. Others argued for a Western-style capitalist democracy. The movement's most famous spokesperson, and perhaps greatest martyr, is Wei Jingsheng, who was imprisoned in a 1979 clampdown and kept in the most appalling conditions often suffering torture and solitary confinement. Wei was editor of the dissident journal *Tansuo* (Explorations) and the author of well known articles such as 'Democracy, the Fifth Modernization' and 'Democracy or a New

Dictatorship?'. The latter, which was cited as evidence against him in his trial, attacked Deng Xiaoping directly, even though Deng was, at the time, apparently a champion of progress:

> Does Deng Xiaoping want democracy? No, he does not. He is unwilling to comprehend the misery of the people. He is unwilling to allow the people to regain those powers usurped by ambitious careerists . . . We can only trust those representatives who are supervised by us and responsible to us. Such representatives should be chosen by us and not thrust upon us. Only a genuine general election can create a government and leaders ready to serve the interests of the electorate. (Wei Jingsheng, cited in Benton and Hunter, 1995: 182–4)

The movement was suppressed by force in the winter of 1979–80, and many of its leading members imprisoned. Nevertheless they left a legacy of moral integrity and some of them, and their ideas, resurfaced through the 1980s.

Somewhat different issues inspired a series of student protests from the mid-1980s. University students were, for the most part, children of the elite; at the same time, many of them had grievances: they were forced to subsist on low grants and were over-controlled by the university authorities. As such, they were fertile ground for persuasive orators who could easily stir them to political action. One of the best-known of Chinese oppositionists in the West, Fang Lizhi, came from an academic background. Himself a physicist, he was a talented university administrator and in touch with student opinion. From the mid-1980s he used this base to launch a series of scathing attacks on the Party bureaucracy; like Wei, he demanded radical democratic reforms, arguing that wholesale Westernization of China's social, political, and economic systems was needed. However, Fang certainly had a traditional elitist view of China's rural population:

> I feel those uneducated peasants, living under traditional influences, have a psychological consciousness that is very deficient. It is very difficult to instil a democratic consciousness in them. (Fang in 1986, cited in Kraus, 1989: 299)

Kraus argues that Fang 'links a very Confucian conception of moral responsibility to some notions from Western pop sociology', but his ideas were attractive to some Western commentators and he became promoted as 'China's Sakharov'. In 1989, Fang displayed considerable courage in demanding the release of political prisoners and respect for human rights; after the demonstrations he took refuge overseas.

Such were the immediate precedents of the 1989 democracy movement. It is important to note that, despite its massive popular support, its ideological foundations were actually quite limited. The 1979 democrats were hardly known, and Fang Lizhi only to a tiny number of students and intellectuals. Thinkers like Yan Jiaqi and Su Shaozhi had been making radical proposals in government circles but they fell far short of demanding an overthrow of the CCP and, besides, they reached only a restricted audience. In hindsight, the 1989 movement appears to have been a popular protest without a clear political programme. Its immediate causes were widespread disgust with cadre corruption and CCP bullying; the reformists in government had allowed enough free space for intellectuals to start agitating against abuses of power; and economic instability created the conditions for turmoil in the capital. Coupled with a volatile situation on campuses and a couple of random events (the seventieth anniversary of the May 4th movement, and Gorbachev's visit to Beijing), the movement escalated.

What ideas did it promote? The simple answer is, very few. Certainly most participants wanted to control corruption and they wanted greater freedom of speech. For most of the course of the movement, they probably assumed that the CCP could be pressurized into at least promising some improvement in these areas. Some of the student demands were simply for greater academic freedoms, better employment prospects, more autonomy and higher grants. All these aspirations were diverted onto, and summarized by, the gigantic notion of 'democracy' symbolically embodied in the statue on Tian'anmen Square. (Indeed a recent study argues that the notion of naming the student demonstrations a 'pro-democracy movement' can be attributed to the Voice of America, which first used the term on 20 April (He, 1996).) As the movement developed, more sophisticated tactics gradually emerged–for example, the need to liaise with workers in factories. The students also took up the call for a free press. But as a whole, the movement was not about laying the intellectual foundations of a new system of government: it was a blind cry for an end to oppression and corruption, mixed with rather naive, populist and inexperienced notions about democracy.

One shortcoming of the movement was its failure to engage seriously with the industrial workers of the city, although many thousands of workers were in Tian'anmen by the end of the movement. One reason was the students' elitism, which led them to envisage a 'pure' movement similar perhaps to their May 4th precursor. It was also relevant that industrial workers in the late 1980s had not yet felt the brunt of retrenchments and redundancies. By the late 1990s this had changed dramatically as grossly overstaffed state-owned enterprises began firing large numbers of workers, usually without prospects of alternative employment or of adequate social security. There were reports of of strikes, lockouts, underground activism and even sabotage in many parts of China, including the communist heartland, the industrial areas of the north and northeast. Interestingly there was also evidence of labour militancy in southern factories, often owned by overseas Chinese or other foreign investors. It remains to be seen whether the Chinese working class is preparing to enter a new phase of radicalism. If it does, it will be interesting to see whether it will appeal to traditional socialist symbols of working-class struggle, or whether, these having been totally discredited, it will turn to pro-Western models.

Political Forces in China Today

Crisis of Legitimacy

In the Maoist period all political issues were represented and debated in strongly ideological terms. During red 'high tides' such as the Cultural Revolution, Mao Zedong Thought was applied, often ludicrously, even to straightforwardly technical issues. Millions of citizens were mobilized in mass campaigns, and took part in compulsory political meetings. As late as the mid-1970s, it seems that most Chinese took CCP study sessions and campaigns quite seriously (Schell, 1995: 242). By the 1990s however, campaigns against 'bourgeois liberalization', 'peaceful evolution' and other alleged evils were regarded as a joke or minor irritant by most people.

The decline of ideology is partly the result of a conscious decision by the Deng leadership to demote the 'red' and promote the 'expert'. It also reflects broad social developments caused by the reforms, changing technology and China's increasing openness to the outside world. Party propagandists have lost their captive audience. Alternative points of view are no longer easily suppressed since the Party has forfeited monopoly control over the media and communications. Tens of thousands of Chinese are now connected to the Internet, while hundreds of thousands have satellite televisions and mobile telephones, and travel abroad. Private publishers print magazines and books that would never have seen the light of day under Mao, and the Party's often turgid propaganda has to compete for attention with imported music, films, videos, and literature.

The official ideology, Marxism, has not only lost its grip on ordinary citizens, but has a radically reduced role in policy-making. Leaders know that the CCP can stay in power only if it delivers sustained economic growth and improved living standards, so in practice it has to continue its pragmatic approach by deepening market reforms. Furthermore, the Party now contains vast numbers of cadres who, whether or not they are politically committed to a market economy, personally profit from it. It is unlikely that a leftist tendency within the Party will recover influence in these circumstances. Although the left still exists (indeed in the present climate, many even of the early supporters of reform are now considered impossibly leftist) it is politically marginalized. Debate within the Party centres almost exclusively on technical issues, within the framework of a broadly right-wing consensus.

The lack of ideological debate, in many ways, suits the Soviet-trained bureaucrats who now dominate the leadership. But because since 1949 the Party justified its right to rule in terms of Marxism–Leninism, the collapse of the official ideology is contributing to a long-term crisis of legitimacy for the regime. Forced to re-define its political mission, the Party is doing so in increasingly nationalist terms, emphasizing building a strong and prosperous China, the return of Hong Kong, and eventual re-unification with Taiwan. Official pronouncements cling to the threadbare formula of 'socialism with Chinese characteristics', but cannot disguise the fact that the Party has effectively abandoned its original goals.

The ideological bankruptcy of the regime was amply illustrated by the late 1990s' campaign for Spiritual Civilization, apparently inspired by Jiang Zemin. Following months of propaganda on the theme, in May 1997 the CCP Central Committee set up the 'Central Guidance Committee for Spiritual Civilization Construction'. Jiang Zemin, in an almost impenetrable address to this body, explained that Spiritual Civilization involved patriotism, socialism, collectivism, reform, opening up, modernization, material wealth and spiritual well-being. In the finest traditions of CCP campaigns, model work-units and townships were held up as exemplars of spiritual civilization. The PLA was urged to 'go to the forefront' of the campaign. There are faint, rather absurd echoes of the Cultural Revolution in the Spiritual Civilization campaign. The foundation of the Central Guidance Committee mirrored the foundation of the Cultural Revolution Group in May 1966, and there appeared to be an attempt to generate a personality cult of Jiang. But the sheer emptiness and dullness of the campaign, and the inability of the leadership to generate the smallest enthusiasm, ensured that Spiritual Civilization would scarcely qualify as even a farcical reprise of Mao's tragic folly.

Paradoxically, the decline of ideology has also adversely affected the dissident movement. Many intellectuals are now so busy making a living in the new market economy that they have little time or inclination for politics. Furthermore, the framework of political debate has moved so far to the right that critiques of the regime couched in terms of a humanist version of Marxism now appear out of date and irrelevant; while the liberal opposition finds that most of its ideas in the economic sphere are being implemented by the government. Current forces in Chinese politics therefore operate in a rather strange environment, where the ruling Party hardly believes in its own fundamental ideas, yet tries to impose them on a recalcitrant public; and where dissidents see many of their outlawed proposals being implemented by their persecutors.

Political Tendencies within the CCP

The CCP never equalled its parent Soviet Party in imposing orthodoxy. Stalin systematically killed his opponents, and would almost certainly have executed such a formidable adversary as Deng Xiaoping. Mao Zedong, although he used terror as a political weapon, was vain enough to believe he could re-educate his enemies. Consequently, while all opposition within the Soviet Party was crushed by 1930, the CCP has always contained distinct political tendencies. Divisions were often acute, and sections of the leadership sometimes mobilized public support for their position. During the Cultural Revolution, the Party almost destroyed itself in factional fighting. In the late 1990s, political divisions within the Party appeared more muted than in the past, but the issues facing the

Party were, perhaps, more acute than ever, placing in question its *raison d'être* and very existence. It would be foolish to exclude the possibility of further factional battles.

Overseas, the line-up of forces within the Party in the 1990s was usually seen as a struggle between reformers and conservatives. (Slightly confusingly, the conservatives are also described being on the left; see our remarks in Chapter 1). The leftist, conservative wing was made up of two main, overlapping, groups: those who, harking back to the 1950s, favour various degrees of Soviet-style central planning, and those who joined the Party during the Cultural Revolution. The left was in a minority at the highest levels but it had considerable support in the Party apparatus and could not be ignored by the leadership. One of its major supporters was the veteran head of the Organization Department, Song Ping. The left's ideological leader was Deng Liqun, a former central committee member and political secretary to Liu Shaoqi: Deng Liqun consistently criticized the market reforms and Deng Xiaoping's open-door policy. Some observers suggest that Jiang Zemin has insufficient support within the apparatus to ensure that his policies are implemented, and that the left will be able to 'make the emperor a mere figurehead'. This seems far-fetched but the left's real opportunity might come if urban workers act against threats to their job security.

In 1998 Chinese politics was dominated by the triumvirate of President Jiang Zemin, NPC Chairman Li Peng, and Premier Zhu Rongji. All are in favour of market reforms but oppose any moves to compromise the leading role of the Party. Within the core leadership, Zhu Rongji is regarded overseas as leaning to the right, and therefore, by many Western commentators, as the most progressive. Zhu was once denounced by leftists as 'China's Boris Yeltsin', but his competent management of the economy has won respect even from former opponents. Li Peng is regarded as having conservative leanings towards central-planning solutions, while Jiang Zemin, who shares Li's Soviet education, is thought to take a centrist position within the leading group.

Further to the right, still in political disgrace, is Zhao Ziyang. Zhao has recently been allowed to travel within China and reports of his political views are sometimes published abroad. Following Deng Xiaoping's death, Zhao is said to have expressed his support for Jiang Zemin. This may have been a gesture to secure his own rehabilitation. Or it may be that he genuinely agrees with Jiang's policy, which in many ways could be described as new authoritarian, in that it combines market reforms with a dictatorial state committed to national development. Although his views are of interest, by the late 1990s Zhao looked very much like yesterday's man. One obstacle in the way of a return to public life is that he and his family were, in the past, regarded as among the most corrupt members of the elite.

Forces outside the CCP

Outside the Party, although many oppositionists started from a position of rethinking Marxism and reforming socialism (see p. 109 above), over the past ten years a broad consensus has emerged in favour of capitalism and liberal democracy. The students of 1989 appear to have been initially motivated by disgust at profiteering and corruption and their radical tactics were viewed with alarm by the liberal opposition. Some oppositionist intellectuals blamed the students' intransigence for the bloody outcome of the protest movement; but the student leaders developed no independent political ideas, and in exile have gravitated to the liberal-democratic consensus of the opposition. Simultaneously, they seem to have moderated their tactical approach to political struggle. In June 1997, Wu'er Kaixi, a leader of the Tian'anmen demonstrations, expressed the view that China needs a market economy and to develop the institutions of civil society. He predicted that 'newly emerging entrepreneurs' would soon form political parties to contest local elections, and that China would follow the Taiwanese path to gradual democratization (*Southeast Asian Business Times*, 4 October 1997).

Should a credible, home-grown alternative to the CCP fail to appear, it is conceivable that the Guomindang may yet play a role in mainland politics. Taiwan is an attractive political model for many reasons. Most ordinary Chinese can only dream of the standard of living of the average Taiwanese. For liberal intellectuals, it is proof that a Chinese society can be modern, pluralistic and democratic, and also deliver a high level of economic welfare to its people. Even Party bureaucrats admire the island's efficient administration and economic management. The Taiwanese authorities are well aware of their potential political strength on the mainland and have cultivated potential supporters among the opposition. But they are likely to be wary of taking major initiatives for fear of provoking a military confrontation or jeopardizing Taiwan's considerable economic interests on the mainland.

Another regional force that may play a national role is the Hong Kong democratic movement. Hong Kong residents have staged mass vigils on 4 June each year since the 1989 Beijing massacre. In 1997, less than a month before the handover of Hong Kong to China, the demonstration attracted 50,000 people. In the only democratic elections ever held to the colonial assembly, pro-democracy candidates, mainly from the Democratic Party led by Martin Lee, decisively defeated pro-Beijing candidates. Shortly before the handover, the assembly granted collective bargaining rights to trade unions, and allowed them to maintain political funds. After 1 July Beijing disbanded the assembly and replaced it with an appointed body, many of whose members were defeated candidates in the recent elections. The shipping magnate Tung Chee-hwa was appointed chief executive of the Special Administrative Region (SAR).

Within days of taking office, the new authorities suspended the recently passed labour laws. The leader of the Hong Kong federation of trades unions, Lee Cheuk-yan, began a hunger strike, denouncing the new assembly as 'rule by tycoons'. The line-up of political forces in Hong Kong is extremely interesting. Beijing has formed a close alliance with big-business interests who are happy to combine capitalism with authoritarian rule and are hostile to workers' rights. They are opposed by an alliance of middle-class democrats and trades unionists. Beijing would like to keep Hong Kong quarantined from the rest of China, but is unlikely to succeed, as the Hong Kong economy is so closely interconnected with neighbouring Guangdong. The democratic infection may well initially spread to the south China region in the form of trades unionism. Conditions in Guangdong's factories, many of them foreign-owned or joint ventures, are often appalling. Patriotic and anti-foreign feeling could possibly combine with trades union activity to create difficult problems for the government. Yet at the time of writing, the Chinese government appeared to be overall in a strong position, and no opposition group looked able to mount any serious challenge in the near future.

5

The Social System

For some thirty years following the 1949 revolution, it was difficult for foreigners to obtain first-hand information about developments within Chinese society. Even before the communist revolution, attitudes towards China were often based on fragmentary reports. European philosophers of the Enlightenment admired aspects of China's social system, but most of their information came from a handful of Jesuit missionaries. From the seventeenth to the mid-nineteenth centuries the Empire was virtually closed, and public opinion, at least in the West, was coloured by colonialist prejudice, as it was later by anti-Communist rhetoric. A good deal of foreign material on China dates from the period between the late nineteenth century and the 1940s, when businessmen, officials and missionaries travelled relatively freely throughout China; again since the late 1970s there has been a great improvement. Foreign academics have been able to work in China, albeit with some restrictions, and countless overseas journalists, business persons, and tourists have visited the country.

Depiction of Chinese society as stagnant or degenerate, or as a spawning-ground for Maoist clones, has largely been supplanted by more sober accounts of its main institutions. One stereotype that persisted for many years was of China as immutable, conservative, ultra-stable and tradition-bound. The persistence of time-honoured cultural practices among overseas Chinese, even after several generations' absence from the homeland, tended to support this picture. However, it should be heavily qualified. First, the concept of 'tradition' itself is nebulous, and can be misleading: while some Chinese customs may be ancient, others may date only from late imperial times. To label a practice or attitude as 'traditional' may obscure as much as it explains. Second, since the mid-nineteenth century, China has been shaken by wars and revolutions, by industrialization, migration to cities and, most recently, by radical economic reforms. The mass entry of women into the workforce in the Maoist period, the one-child policy and other factors have transformed many customs and attitudes at family level. Furthermore, although China started late in forming the institutions characteristic of a modern nation-state, the Nationalist government of the 1930s introduced them in embryonic form. After 1949 the Communists moved rapidly to construct health and education systems which, although under threat from current market reforms, rank as major achievements of CCP rule. Many of these new social institutions were modelled on those of Europe, Japan, the USA and the USSR. Contemporary China – like any other country – is a hybrid of the native and the imported: still unique, but not un-alloyed.

Another stereotype was that of the 'evil empire'. By the early twentieth century some foreign scholars, notably Weber and Witt-fogel, had concluded that Chinese society was uniquely oppressive, and the term 'Oriental Despotism' was coined to refer to societies which approximated to the Chinese paradigm. According to this view, the power of the state in Chinese society was universal and overwhelming: whereas in the West, private interests and religious organizations formed a counterweight to state authority, in China, where there was no national church and civil society remained undeveloped, the individual was crushed beneath the untrammeled and unmediated power of the state. Wittfogel, building on some observations in Marx's earlier writings, attributed the extraordinary power of the Chinese state to its role in organizing massive drainage and irrigation schemes, essential for agriculture in a monsoon climate. During the Cold War, stark assessments of the communist regime were widespread. Wittfogel regarded dictatorships of the Stalinist type as little more than a modern cloak for an ancient form of despotism.

While there are valuable insights in the various theories of Oriental Despotism, they are usually over-simplifications, and fail to take into account many lower-level social organizations, often formed for the purposes of mutual support and community integrity, that enveloped the majority of the population for most of the time. (Indeed, there are grounds for debate about the extent to which social-science concepts, developed for the most part with regard to Western industrial societies, may be of explanatory value in the Chinese context.) In any case, social developments, especially since the 1980s' economic reforms, have made such analyses barely applicable to contemporary China. The decentralization and deregulation of the economy are creating a diversified, complex urban society. Migration and media penetration have transformed attitudes in rural areas. A new middle class is growing, made up of entrepreneurs, professionals and other beneficiaries of the economic reforms, that may soon begin to assert its rights against the state. In this chapter we examine key institutions within Chinese society and the effects on them of recent policies. The reader will discern the complex interplay between traditional and contemporary factors. In the space available we can offer only a bird's-eye view of prevalent patterns – for example, of family structures. In practice, there are countless variations based on region, social class, local power-structures and so on. Community studies based on fieldwork can be consulted for information about specific local conditions.

Family and Clan

Traditional Chinese society was family-centred, rather than individualist or communitarian. The family dominated most people's economic and social life: sons would usually follow the trade of their fathers, and women would work under the control of male members of the family. Everyday social life was conducted in family settings. If a man was successful, his whole family would gain prestige; his failure likewise would reflect upon his family. Groups of unrelated families might cooperate closely for periods, but this was usually in response to external threats, and not the norm.

The idealized, and sometimes actual, traditional family structure is known as the 'big family' (or extended or expanded family). Until well into the twentieth century, arranged marriages were the norm. Often a matchmaker would connect two families which had a son and daughter of marriageable age and the arrangements would be made by the parents. Marriage was to a large extent a financial transaction, the groom's family paying an agreed tariff for the bride. There is a deeply rooted custom, which still holds in much of rural China, that adult sons remain with, or at least very close to, their parents. When a man marries, the new bride joins his household and has obligations towards her husband's parents as well as to the husband himself. Conversely, daughters effectively leave the parental home when they marry and become a junior member of the groom's family. The 'big family' thus comprises a father and mother living together with their male children and their wives and offspring, with unmarried daughters and with surviving members of the older generation.

In practice, this ideal was attainable only for the rich, since a poor family's land holdings were insufficient to support such a large group. More frequently, because of land shortage or perhaps because of a family dispute, sons would break away and set up independent households, a process known as 'dividing the home'. At the time of division, or on a father's death, property was usually divided equally between all male children. This practice led to the fragmentation of land holdings into ever-smaller units; the European system of primogeniture, although hard on younger sons, by contrast tended to conserve large estates.

Continuity of patrilineal descent was a central feature of the system. It was imperative for parents to raise male children, who would bear the same family name as their father and whose sons, in turn, would also bear it. It is useful to remember that Chinese names have the order family name/given name (although some overseas Chinese adopt the given name/family name sequence for convenience). The family name is almost always a single character, pronounced as a single syllable, common examples being Li, Chen, Wang, and Huang. The given name can be a single character, but is more frequently two: thus Zedong was Chairman Mao's given name. Women usually retain their own family names even after marriage, but children take their father's family name.

As mentioned, married women became members of their husband's family. This custom underlies the traditional low status of daughters and the strong preference for sons, since sons continue to live with and support their parents while daughters support others. In many social classes, and at different periods in Chinese history, women were treated more like property than autonomous human beings. They were sometimes sold as servants, concubines, or prostitutes. While males were expected to ensure continuity of the family, and earn much of its income, women were usually excluded from education and from public life. A Chinese proverb likens educating a daughter to watering another man's garden. Women derived their status from their association with males in the family: a wife from her husband, a mother from her son. One of the most extreme illustrations of male dominance was the practice, widespread well into the twentieth century, of foot-binding. From early childhood, a girl's feet were tightly bound with bandages, resulting in tiny, deformed feet, crippling the adult woman. Foot-binding graphically demonstrated a male's power over his females and was also a public display of his wealth, since a man would have to have surplus resources to feed a woman who was unable to contribute physical labour.

The ideological underpinning of the whole system of familial and clan authority was Confucianism (the term should be distinguished from the teachings of Confucius himself: see Chapter 6) which stressed hierarchy and harmony rather than individual rights and equality. Orthodox Confucianism taught that each person should play his, or her, role, by following appropriate behaviour as defined in the 'five relationships' of father–son, husband–wife, brother–brother, king–minister, friend–friend; the younger generation should obey its elders, women should obey men; the weak should be obedient and respectful; the powerful should be compassionate, upright and virtuous. Many of the rituals of popular religion, such as the worship of ancestral tablets, embodied obedience to elders and devotion to the family.

Such pious wishes may appear merely as a smokescreen for patriarchy, and some aspects of the traditional family, especially the treatment of women, will sound unacceptable to modern readers. Yet family relations were, and to a large extent remain, the key element in a Chinese person's life. There is an intense and usually unbreakable bond between parents and children, and very often between siblings. This warm and loving, yet hierarchical and sometimes stifling, family system tends to operate on guidelines that are well understood by all participants, to such an extent that it is not necessary to formalize them. To this extent, traditional, and even modern, Chinese society is self-regulating, and in many respects could dispense with written codes of law.

As Chinese anthropologist Fei Hsiao-Tung wrote in his classic study, *Peasant Life in China* (Fei, 1939: 27–8):

The basic social group in the village is . . . the expanded family. The members of this group possess a common property, keep a common budget and co-operate together to pursue a common living . . . It is also in this group that children are born and brought up and material objects, knowledge, and social positions are inherited. Larger social groups in the village are formed by combining . . . [families] along kinship or territorial principles.

Beyond the individual household in China's countryside lay the clan or lineage. Each clan comprised typically from a few dozen up to a few hundred households sharing the same family name and usually occupying one village (where several clans lived in the same village, they tended to inhabit different sections). Rich and poor households alike belonged to the clan, but it was likely to be dominated by the more wealthy. A great deal of ritual, legal, economic and social authority was vested in the clan elders, who were major power-brokers in their localities. Family disputes were settled, often harshly, by the application of local laws or clan traditions, upheld by generations of older men. There were few central constraints on local practices and most imperial edicts tended to reinforce the family- and clan-based pattern of authority with laws on obligations, and punishments for serious offenders. There were few institutions or civil procedures to which an individual might turn in the case of disputes, few intermediaries between family and state authority. Clans could also be important economic units, since clan-owned trusts often held land and property. Clashes, including violent ones, were frequent between villages, over matters such as land or water-rights.

Clans had their own internal control, regulated by written and unwritten laws and customs, overseen by local leaders and enforced by village militia under their control. The system thus appears to have been self-sufficient, a network of kinship-organized petty territories which perhaps for long periods paid scant attention to the authority of the central government. Throughout most of traditional China, and until very recently, family and kinship structures formed the closest and most powerful network of authority over the individual. Non-family associations and interest groups – sometimes referred to as civil society – have been slow to develop in China. There were no nation-wide religious institutions comparable with Western churches, and few political groupings, whereas in Europe from the Renaissance onwards an increasing number of people began to participate, even if in a restricted way, in local and national affairs of state.

State power in China, until the 1911 revolution at least, and arguably until now, has been perceived by most as remote and threatening. The state bureaucracy, represented at local level by the yamen or magistrate's court, meted out severe justice, and was otherwise responsible for affairs like military and taxation. It seemed to represent an alien structure, (sometimes literally, since the Mongols and Manchus were not Han Chinese) superimposed on the organic growth of family and clan. Among other duties, state officials were supposed to uphold the sacred order of the empire and of state Confucianism. They also cooperated with local military authorities on occasion when banditry, a recurrent problem in many parts of China, reached unacceptable levels.

Other networks that operated beyond the confines of local power structures were the sometimes equally powerful secret societies and sectarian organizations. These groups were often made up of people excluded from clan power, or those with mobile professions like traders or boatmen. Some sects were heterodox religious organizations, often entirely peaceful and espousing a synthesis of Buddhism and folk beliefs. Others provided mutual aid and support to their members. Some even had political aspirations, in late imperial times focused, in general terms, on the overthrow of the Qing regime. Secret societies certainly influenced imperial and early twentieth-century society and politics at times: for example, criminal gangs provided much practical support for the GMD in 1920s' Shanghai.

Scholars disagree on the extent to which the CCP has succeeded in carrying out an irreversible transformation of traditional social relations, especially in rural China. From 1949 onwards, the government made determined efforts to break up powerful lineages. Land reforms often pitted poor households against rich ones from the same clan, and Party cadres replaced leading clan figures as local power-holders. The Party constructed multi-family organizations like the People's Communes, in which work was organized by brigades rather than households. The government gave rights to women, allowing them a free choice of marriage partner and outlawing concubinage. But the rural reforms of the 1980s, especially the break-up of the People's Communes and the return to household farming, marked a definite retreat from the social reforming zeal of the Maoist years. Male heads of households are reasserting their authority and traditional practices are creeping back. Some argue that Maoist efforts to suppress the structures of the old society simply drove them underground for a time. By the late 1980s, parts of rural China had reverted in practice to some form of clan control, although the state certainly has more impact on family life now than it ever did before the revolution, for example through local officials' involvement in land allocation, village enterprises and family planning.

Social Stratification

Traditional Chinese society was unashamedly hierarchical but, unlike some other parts of Asia, China never developed an hereditary caste system. Early Confucian thought differentiated in a rudimentary way between high- and low-status individuals. One classical model grouped the population into four classes, where scholars were assigned the highest status, followed by farmers, then artisans and finally merchants. Later thinkers devised a somewhat more nuanced analysis, and the idea of a hierarchy of categories, with moral as well as occupational imputations, can be seen even in the communist era when a person's 'class background' often determined his or her fate.

Late imperial society was headed by a ruling elite comprising several hundred thousand people of Manchu origin. Below the dynasty, powerful landowners and merchants dominated the localities although, especially after the Taiping rebellion, military leaders began to wield increasing power. Scholar officials were usually posted to county towns for relatively short periods and in practice were forced to make accommodations with powerful vested interests. Landlords, tax-collectors, officials and military personnel were sometimes venal predators on the population. Extortion of money from peasants, and corruption in general, were endemic phenomena of successive Chinese regimes, and reached a high point under the Guomindang, whose officials siphoned off billions of dollars. Although there is little documented evidence, it is widely believed that conditions in rural China deteriorated from the mid-nineteenth to the mid-twentieth centuries, partly as a consequence of population pressure and war, but also because of ever-increasing exploitation. Desperate poverty, instability and famine were the background to the growth of the CCP.

The Treaty Ports and concessions controlled by foreign powers in the second half of the nineteenth century formed a new kind of urban centre which had tremendously important social consequences. Many Chinese naturally felt a sense of humiliation over lost sovereignty and resentment against colonialism. But the foreign concessions, as well as being strongholds of imperialism and based on cruel exploitation of the newly formed urban working class, were revolutionary. It was here that Chinese first came across the cinema, offices, buses, Western languages, clothes, consumer goods, production techniques and so on. Furthermore, the concessions provided a haven for Chinese radical intellectuals, who lived and worked in them, since the administration was more tolerant than that of warlords or the Guomindang. The Shanghai concessions were home to the most radical of May 4th journals, and to the numerous work and study groups that centred around the young CCP. Nevertheless, Shanghai and other cities retained some features of traditional China: they were crowded, picturesque, full of adventure, danger and squalor. Modern capitalist firms and avant-garde intellectuals had a role, but much urban life was still dominated by secret societies and gangsters, with narcotics a major source of income and employment, and by traditional occupations such as handicrafts and transport.

Under Mao, social structure was apparently simple and transparent. Workers, peasants (more specifically poor peasants and landless labourers) and soldiers were considered to be of 'good' class background. Individuals from these groups were usually safe from political persecution by virtue of their family provenance, and in many ways were the beneficiaries of the revolution. Urban workers in particular, between the 1950s and the 1980s generally had steady jobs with secure incomes and access to a reasonable range of welfare services. Their standard of living was, admittedly, spartan, but was nevertheless an undeniable improvement on pre-1949 conditions. Rural incomes generally lagged behind those of urban workers but, apart from the disaster of the Great Leap Forward, were usually high enough to secure basic needs.

The Mao years also saw the emergence of a new elite of Party cadres who began to carve out a comfortable life-style. Although politically committed to social justice, the Party leadership was not laggard in allocating resources to itself. Such trends had already caused discontent, harshly suppressed, in Yan'an, at the height of the guerrilla war. Hidden at first from the eyes of the public, cadres began to have rights to superior clothes, housing and food; private vehicles and holiday resorts; and high-quality schooling for their children. During the Cultural Revolution Mao attempted to excite popular resentment against the privileges of Party officials, but there is little evidence of spontaneous outburst of anger against the bureaucracy at this time. However, the relatively modest perks of the 1950s and 1960s appear negligible when compared with the massive embezzlement and corruption which accompanied the economic reforms of the 1980s.

By the late 1990s, market forces had rapidly generated new social strata. If China was perhaps the simplest society in the world in the 1950s, it had become the most complex by the 1990s. In both rural and urban areas, as well as suburban districts and industrialized parts of the countryside, the reforms produced new forms of economic and social organization. Peasants were now allowed to lease and sublet land, and successful families could acquire rights to large tracts (although the land itself remains state property and the market in land rights is subject to numerous restrictions). Village families also engage in all kinds of non-farm enterprises, ranging from trade to manufacturing and transport. Many local government agencies were commercialized and some set up joint ventures with foreign firms. Migration, and short-term regular commuting, became widespread as rural workers in poorer provinces set off to the booming coastal cities, while people from the coastal regions tried to find work overseas. At first, migrants to the cities worked in temporary jobs in construction, labouring, and petty trading. Long-term city-residents began to complain, in terms familiar in other parts of the world, that these new migrants were dirty, uneducated and unreliable if not actually criminal. There are now well over 100 million migrant workers who have become a permanent part of the urban scene and have taken jobs in all sectors of the economy. As labour retrenchment in work-units threatens job security for original urbanites, the structure of the urban working class has become more complex. Some have found relatively lucrative work in new and profitable firms, and there are financial incentives for the enterprising. Of those who remain in the state sector, some have taken second jobs, while a section of the workforce has been laid off and unemployment is growing.

Meanwhile, new urban elites were also emerging. At the very top, a clique known as the 'princelings' became infamous during the 1980s. These were the children or close relatives, numbering perhaps 3000 to 5000, of top CCP members, including Deng Xiaoping. The princelings were closely involved in promoting deregulation of the economy and, in the process, diverted massive sums to their own accounts. They became obligatory intermediaries for foreigners wishing to do business with many ministries, and would allegedly charge fees of up to US$ 100 000 for smoothing the path to a deal. The activities of the princelings caused popular outrage, and they were a prime target of the 1989 democracy movement. Their brazen and reckless profiteering reflected their determination to get super-rich quick, since their leverage depended on their parents' positions. A number of this elite group has now moved on to set up joint ventures with Hong Kong tycoons and other overseas partners.

Other top-ranking money-makers of the reform period have been senior military personnel. The PLA has moved aggressively into business over the past decade. Officially, the purpose of the army's commercial activities is to relieve pressure on the state's defence budget, by making the military partly self-financing. But what began as a limited form of self-sufficiency has grown into a multi-billion dollar business that some believe is threatening the military effectiveness of China's armed forces. The army is thought to control over 20,000 companies involved in transport, construction, medical services, hotels, farming and other sectors. It is China's major pharmaceutical producer. Some estimates put the income generated by these businesses as roughly equal to official state spending on defence, that is, around 40 billion renminbi. The military maintains numerous representative offices in the SEZ and is poised to mount big business operations in Hong Kong to support the garrison there. While even its legitimate businesses are often run in a corrupt manner, the military is also widely supposed to be involved in running massage parlours, smuggling, trading in narcotics and various other rackets. Although there has been some effort to purge the worst offenders, the army is largely a law unto itself.

CCP cadres have made substantial amounts of money, either by profiting from the sale of state property or making use of their access to subsidized materials and transport. In its crudest form, this may simply involve selling off state assets to investors and pocketing the proceeds: many Taiwanese investors are said to have acquired land and other assets in Fujian province in this manner. In the face of popular protests at such activities, the local authorities are quite prepared to resort to violence against demonstrators. Other, more or less corrupt, money-making activities include using state-owned offices and other facilities for their own or relatives' businesses. Officials may also be willing to sell favours and licences of various sorts, arrange an early release from prison, or even 'rent' Party membership. When criticized, the officials often claim they are promoting the reform programme.

Below the princelings, military officers, and leading cadres is a much broader social group with relatively high incomes derived from legitimate business and professional activities. The first wave of private entrepreneurs in the mid-1980s were from the poorer classes and mainly set up low-earning, one-man businesses. But in the 1990s increasing numbers of intellectuals and professional people began to 'jump into the sea' of private enterprise, often using official connections to smooth their path in business. Fairly sizeable groups in major cities can now earn incomes approaching those of the middle classes in neighbouring Asian countries. They include managers in joint ventures or large state enterprises, owners of private businesses, well educated accountants and other professionals. Indeed there are numerous cases, well publicized by the Chinese state, of private entrepreneurs who have become multi-millionaires. With their growing disposable income, the emerging professional and business classes have formed the nucleus of a new Chinese consumer culture. They send their children to nurseries, go out to restaurants and night clubs, buy fashionable clothes, eat in fast-food outlets, instal air-conditioners in their homes and, increasingly, own mobile phones and private cars. These new forms of social life are rapidly changing the face of urban China.

Social Control Mechanisms

One of the CCP's most remarkable achievements was the radical transformation of China's cities. In a series of reforms, the entire urban population became subject to an active, penetrative state apparatus, organized in people's homes and workplaces. The resulting urban life-style was almost unparalleled in the extent to which individual freedoms were curtailed and the social good, at least in theory, promoted. One may argue about the concept, the priorities, and the means of implementation, but there were undeniable successes. The standard of living increased very rapidly, and there were huge drops in infant mortality. Cities were relatively clean and public health massively improved, the food supply was rationed but adequate, education, health and welfare services were widely available, the crime rate low and unemployment (at times, and in theory) non-existent. This level of social control was accompanied by political mobilization on a national scale, and enforced through two key measures, 'household registration' and the 'work-unit'. The reforms of the 1980s and 1990s modified and weakened these systems, but they still exist, and they remain essential to an understanding of the Communist period.

The household registration system was developed through a series of regulations in the 1950s, the primary objectives of which were to control migration, especially from rural to urban areas; to manage the distribution of commodities like grain; and to keep close watch on all families. It built on an imperial system of mutual surveillance by neighbourhoods or family groups, with twentieth-century refinements adopted from Japan, from the Guomindang, and from Soviet Russia. Each household is obliged to maintain an accurate register of every member living at a particular address, and inform the authorities of any changes, visitors, etc. It is administered at grassroots' level by street committees and local cadres and carefully supervised by public security officials. It is difficult and time-consuming to change one's place of residence. In the past, migration from the countryside to cities was extremely difficult – as was, in general, any move to a larger population centre. Residency in cities like Beijing and Shanghai was extremely prestigious and desirable and was closely controlled.

In some ways the system was efficient and beneficial. It prevented the mass migration to major cities seen in some developing countries and led to reasonably equitable distribution of some consumer items and social services. On the other hand, it discriminated in favour of urban residents and kept rural residents tied to their villages and was also, of course, a substantial restriction of personal freedom. Implementation was most strict from about 1960 to 1985: until the early 1980s, an individual could not obtain ration coupons or employment without authorized registration documents. After 1985, regulations were relaxed and migrant labourers flooded into the cities. The subsequent abolition of ration coupons for basic foodstuffs dealt a further blow to the system. However, although it is now relatively easy to become a temporary resident or migrant worker in a city, it is still very difficult for an outsider to become an established urbanite with rights to city amenities.

The work-unit system is parallel to the household registration system, but based on an individual's place of employment. During most of the Communist period, work-units were responsible not only for production and other economic activities but also for the provision of many services for the workforce including, usually, access to social welfare, education, housing and documentation. At the same time, the work-unit, which might be an office, institute, school, hospital or factory, maintained a dossier on each individual, noting his or her views and reliability. It thereby ensured political orthodoxy within the unit, and could pass information to the security services. Finally the unit acted as a propaganda agency for government views, and held regular study sessions to study Marxist texts or to inculcate government policies. In 1989, for example, all work-units conducted propaganda meetings to promote the Party line during the democracy movement.

The work-unit system was, in some ways, relatively efficient in the distribution of services and goods and provided a secure and stable environment for the urban workforce. On the other hand, it led to a non-transparent and distorted pattern of authority in the workplace which hindered economic efficiency. Allocation of benefits by the work-unit in practice always came down to allocation by a Party cadre. Rather than rewarding efficiency or merit, the system tended to benefit those who could cultivate good relations with power-brokers. Political reliability was also a strong factor in determining the level of benefits, and loyal CCP members received more than other workers. The work-unit also exercised an intrusive level of personal control over its members including, in some cases, in domestic issues.

Until the 1990s, there were two common routes into a work-unit: one could be assigned directly after school or college; or one could inherit the job of a close relative, for example on the retirement of one's father. An employee would probably remain with the same work-unit until retirement, and thereafter would continue to depend on it for a pension and housing. Firms were often obliged to take on a certain quota of school-leavers, whether or not there was work available for them. Since it was, until recently, virtually impossible to dismiss workers, the work-units were usually extremely over-staffed.

These systems formed an integral part both of the centrally planned economy and of the CCP political control mechanism. They had important consequences for the whole population. In particular, they maintained a considerable distinction between ur-ban and rural standards of living. While urban residents were carefully monitored in all aspects of life, from home to work-unit, they did have secure employment and income and relatively good social welfare and education. The rural population, on the other hand, was prevented from physical relocation and, in many respects, exploited for the benefit of China's industrialization.

The work-unit system has been substantially weakened by the recent reforms. Radical changes in the economy in the past five years have already led firms to seek ways to cut costs by reducing their welfare responsibilities and laying off workers. If more radical reformers prevail, this will be the prelude to privatization of most state enterprises. Many urban Chinese are then likely to find that freedom from the intrusive and, in many ways, oppressive environment of the work-unit is balanced by increased economic insecurity. However, it may be that aspects of the system will be retained in some sectors of the economy. Similar, if less pervasive, systems proved compatible with private ownership of industry in parts of nineteenth-century Britain; and large sections of the South Korean workforce, even today, live in company houses and send their children to company schools. But an important characteristic of the Chinese system, its universal application to the urban workforce, has already disappeared.

Deviancy and Punishment

We have seen that under CCP rule society was tightly controlled, individual freedoms were severely restricted and emphasis placed on a reasonably equitable distribution of social benefits. The social priorities of the PRC were very different from those of liberal democracies in industrialized countries; but it might be argued that, taken as a whole, they were acceptable in the context of a developing nation. However, there is a dark side to modern China that has been concealed by the Chinese government. Since the early 1950s, the state has administered a system of labour camps which has rivalled those of Stalin's Russia in terms of brutality and terror, and perhaps surpassed them in numbers of victims. Although exact information is not available, it is probable that many million people have died in the camps since 1949, from starvation, exhaustion, execution, disease, and the effects of torture.

Conditions in the camps have been, and still are, appalling. There is almost universal over-crowding, malnutrition, brutality and routine torture of inmates. A system of enforced work placement after release means that many prisoners, at the official end of their sentence, remain trapped in the camp system with only a nominally changed status. The camps and prisons are spread throughout China, but some of the largest are in the remote border provinces of the northwest and northeast, where prisoners work on vast industrial and agricultural projects in terrifying conditions.

In the early 1950s, around 90 per cent of camp inmates were political detainees, usually supporters of the GMD, landlords, 'bad-class' elements, or others deemed to be 'counter-revolutionary'. In 1957 they were joined by many intellectuals who had been reckless enough to criticize the regime during the Hundred Flowers campaign. The Cultural Revolution sent another wave of political detainees into the camp system: the legal process by which they were sentenced was even more perfunctory than that prevailing in the 1950s. However, at the start of the reform period, many political prisoners were released; by 1985, police documents estimated that political detainees amounted to no more than 10 per cent of the prison population. A new generation of political prisoners was formed from those arrested after the suppression of the democracy movement in 1989 but, despite the existence of some high-profile political detainees in terms of overall proportions the situation is now the reverse of the early 1950s: political detainees form a small minority of prisoners, more than 90 per cent of whom have been sentenced for non-political offences.

Although most current inmates of China's prison system have been sentenced as 'common criminals', there remain enormous human rights problems associated with the criminal justice system. Amnesty International estimates that around 80 per cent of the world annual total of executions take place in the PRC. In the first six months of 1996 alone, more than 3000 executions were carried out as part of a high-profile 'Strike Hard' campaign against crime. Many of those executed were sentenced for crimes that would not be considered capital offences in other countries that apply the death penalty – for example, relatively minor thefts. Court proceedings provide little protection to the accused. Adversary tactics are not permitted, and defence lawyers generally cooperate fully with the prosecution: their role is mainly to persuade the defendant to plead guilty, and to request a lenient sentence on the grounds of good character.

Apologists may suggest that the failings of the Chinese justice system are the heritage of a cruel imperial system. Certainly, under the empire, torture was officially sanctioned as part of the judicial process, and court proceedings were heavily weighted against the accused: the shortcomings of the imperial system lay behind foreigners' demands for extra-territorial status during the nineteenth century. Equally, the GMD was extremely brutal in its treatment of political prisoners. But this legacy from earlier regimes cannot explain the sheer scale of the brutality under the Communists. The CCP always maintained that its political programme should be implemented without constraint and that norms of 'bourgeois' law should not prevail in the struggle against the class enemy; but endemic and systematic forms of abuse probably took root in the period of the Cultural Revolution, when the security services, police, and prison guards appear to have been almost completely above the law. The government has made no serious attempt since then to enforce humane treatment of suspects and prisoners, partly because an apparently tough stance on crime seems to be approved by the population at large.

A massive increase in criminality has accompanied the economic reforms: the admitted crime rate more than doubled between the mid-1970s and the early 1990s. Although relatively trivial juvenile crime accounts for around three-quarters of offences, serious crimes, such as murder, rape and armed robbery, are also increasing. China is no longer the strictly controlled environment it was under Mao Zedong. The market economy has provided both the temptation and the opportunity to commit crime. Organized criminal gangs have reappeared, some with covert links to cadres and official bodies. In some areas, Triads and other secret societies, as well as clan-based groups, have started to displace Party branches as the dominant local organizations. Grass-roots' Party branches, which were supposed to 'function as a fortress', are often moribund. The overall effect has been a general growth in lawlessness and, especially, racketeering in business.

In response to rising crime, the government has begun to reform the Public Security apparatus, the People's Police, and the People's Armed Police. In the relatively crime-free Maoist period, the security services used to function primarily as a political watchdog for the CCP. Legislation drawn up in 1957 laid down the primary duty of the police as the suppression of counter-revolutionaries (Wong, 1994: 5.5). The government now regards effective law enforcement as essential to create a stable environment for economic growth, and is attempting to re-focus police work on fighting crime, more specifically on protecting the property and management of private and state enterprises (ibid.: 5.7). The authorities claim to be encouraging higher standards of professionalism and have set up a number of specialized departments within the police force and promoted younger, better educated officers to leading positions. In the past, the police were poorly paid, but to some extent well respected and motivated by idealism. In a period when the population at large is being encouraged to get rich, ideological enthusiasm is no longer sufficient and the government has begun to increase pay and other material incentives for police officers. The claim is that, over time, the police will be transformed from an ideologically motivated service into a modern and accountable force. How successful these reforms may be is difficult to judge, as information on the police and security services is still extremely restricted.

One area in which the reform period has brought some significant and welcome change is in the treatment of certain minorities that were, and often still are, considered to be deviant. One example is the position of gay people in China. The Maoist regime was intensely puritanical and moralistic and hostile not only to homosexuality but to practically any manifestation of sexuality outside an extremely restricted framework. While the reform period may not have significantly changed intolerant attitudes among the population at large, it has at least created a social space, in some of the larger cities, in which life-style choices can be made. The 1990s saw the first flowerings of an alternative culture among young people in big cities, mainly associated with the nascent rock scene. Some improvements have also been seen in the treatment of mental illness, which in Maoist times was dealt with in an extremely repressive manner, with sufferers usually institutionalized and treated with heavy doses of drugs. Tolerance of religious belief and practices has also improved significantly in recent years (see Chapter 6).

The Changing Position of Women

As noted, in many respects married women in traditional society were treated as the property of their husband's family, while other women fell into even more severe forms of oppression, in some cases virtual slavery. By the mid-nineteenth century, even male nationalists started to argue in favour of improving women's status. To these men, Chinese women seemed to symbolize the weakness of China and the cause of national regeneration demanded their better health and welfare, in order to produce stronger children, if nothing else. Although many pioneers of the modern Chinese women's movement derived their ideas from contact with Western thought in the early twentieth century, there were a number of important indigenous contributions to the cause of women's emancipation. By far the best known is Qiu Jin, a charismatic figure who became one of the first Chinese women to study overseas when she left her husband and children to go to Japan. Qiu Jin attacked the traditional treatment of women, dressed as a man, and participated in a doomed uprising against the Qing. She was executed, but became famous throughout the nation as a model woman revolutionary.

By the early twentieth century, influenced by their experience of modern urban life, and foreign ideas, radical intellectuals – the great majority of them still male – developed forceful arguments in favour of women's' rights. Chen Duxiu and other leaders of the May 4th movement waged all-out ideological war against the hierarchical notions of Confucianism and made bitter attacks on arranged marriages, restrictions on women's education and rigid family structures. Many young intellectuals sympathized with these ideas, not least because traditional family values placed limits on their own personal freedom. The heroine of Ibsen's play *Nora*, who walks out of her family home in search of an independent life, became a great symbol for young Chinese feminists. Young women in Beijing and Shanghai in particular started to move into new areas of education and employment. A generation of women from the new bourgeoisie had started to graduate, mostly from mission schools and colleges, and found employment, often as teachers or nurses. In the working class, thousands of women found employment in the growing number of factories. By the early 1920s, young women also joined in revolutionary activity, for example in the radical networks that supported the young CCP.

The feminist movement remained confined for the most part to the cities. As we saw earlier, radical discourse was mostly suppressed after the mid-1920s; but the CCP retained a genuine, if ambiguous, commitment to women's rights. On the one hand, the ideas of women's liberation undoubtedly made their way into broader social layers through the CCP's political struggle. Even after the CCP fell under the control of a rigid and bureaucratic leadership, Marxist ideas of women's emancipation, expressed notably in Engels' work *The Origin of the Family, Private Property and the State*, continued, to a greater or lesser extent, to guide its policy. The Party was truly radical in promoting freedom of choice in marriage and the rights of women to education, property ownership and employment. Women joined in the anti-Japanese war, and many young female students from Shanghai and elsewhere undertook dangerous tasks in the revolutionary struggles.

After 1949 CCP rule led to immediate changes in women's lives, which improved in many respects in dramatic fashion. Mass propaganda campaigns to raise awareness of women's issues, and the promotion of such simple slogans as 'Women hold up half the sky', endorsed by Mao himself, played an important part in changing popular attitudes. First, the 1950s saw the massive induction of women into the workforce, including into regularly paid jobs in urban areas; girls had far better access to education than ever before in China's history. Women also played an active role in many urban campaigns, participated in street, health, and education committees, and worked as CCP grass-roots' cadres. Second, the 1950 Marriage Law, which outlawed polygamy, concubinage and enforced marriages, was a milestone in establishing protection for women within the household. The Land Law of the same year for the first time established women's right to own and inherit property. Perhaps most important of all, the land reforms of the early 1950s and subsequent moves towards collectivization of agriculture had a profound effect on gender relations in rural areas, which had previously been the most conservative and patriarchal. CCP policies meant that the collective took over roles that had formerly been controlled by male heads of households: ownership and management of land, deployment and remuneration of labour, decisions on health and education. In extreme cases, even collective canteens were established to free women from the drudgery of daily kitchen work.

Nevertheless, feminists have criticized CCP policy on several grounds, and with some justice. Some argue that since the Party drew much of its support from rural areas, it chose to compromise with the patriarchal ideas and practices of the peasantry rather than confront them and risk alienating potential supporters (Rai, 1995). More generally, Wolf (1985) puts forward the argument that the CCP, despite its rhetoric, failed women in at least two important respects. Although the Party promoted women's rights and promoted the creation of the All-China Women's Federation, there was never any doubt that the women's movement acted under the direction of the Party leadership which has remained overwhelmingly male. Thus women have not truly been in control of the reform agenda even regarding women's issues. The inevitable consequence was that women's issues were continually drowned amidst other pressing social priorities. The title of Wolf's book, *Revolution*

Postponed, indicates that women were always supposed to wait until other national goals were achieved – which never in fact happened – before being granted full equality.

The market reforms and modernization of economic life since 1978 have led to mixed results for Chinese women, and gender studies in China are becoming increasingly complex to take account of the diversity of issues in different strata (see, for example, Evans, 1997; Jacka, 1997; Judd, 1996). Women have certainly benefited from the increased social freedom that has accompanied the growing sophistication of urban life. Hundreds of thousands of women have now attained university-level education and many have studied overseas, while secondary education is the rule rather than exception. Women are increasingly literate, articulate and independent. There has been some welcome relaxation of what were fairly rigid gender roles: although the one-child policy is clearly a restriction of individual freedom, smaller families mean that women have more scope to pursue careers. There have been some negative consequences of the economic reforms, however. Enterprise managers have been forced to seek ways of cutting costs. Often, they target crèches, maternity-leave provision, and other legacies of the Maoist period, which they now see as 'extra' costs of employing female workers. There is evidence that this sort of covert discrimination is leading to reduced employment opportunities for women, even those with high qualifications (Rai, 1995).

In the countryside, the return to household farming has reinforced the authority of the head of the family, usually a man. Together with the revival of, largely male, clan organizations, this may signal a return to a more subordinate position for rural women. More generally, an overall 'retreat from ideology' and the association of progressive, feminist ideas with Party propaganda has encouraged all sorts of traditional ideas and practices to re-emerge. How these will affect social attitudes in the longer term, remains to be seen.

There are many areas where further research into important gender issues is needed. One is the role of the state in maintaining gender differences, and the interaction between administrative decisions – for example, on land allocation – and those taken within households. Another is the apparent failure of the state and its police apparatus to prevent the re-emergence of very serious crimes against women including kidnapping and enforced prostitution, which have been frequently reported in the media in the 1990s. On a more theoretical level, Evans argues that official discourse on gender in China even after 1949, dominated by male and reproductive priorities, does not present a real challenge to the Confucian ideal of social stability based on family harmony, underwritten by female subservience. Gender hierarchy and the stereotyping of 'correct' female behaviour may thus still be deeply ingrained in both official and unofficial contexts.

Education

Chinese society has always placed a high value on education. Imperial China allocated its posts on the basis of performance in examinations, so the route even to high office was theoretically open to all, through open competition. (The Chinese examination system, although imperfect, was admired by Western social philosophers and reformers as an exemplar of meritocracy.) In practice, the system favoured those rich enough to afford years of education and was, to varying degrees in different periods, open to corruption. Emphasis on rote learning of the Confucian classics encouraged formulaic thinking, as well as a kind of intellectual snobbery that disapproved of practical activity, commerce and the natural sciences. The ideal intellectual, or Confucian scholar, was one who concerned himself about art, education or social issues without thought for financial gain: servants of the imperial regime were meant to achieve office through merit and to govern according to high ideals. Such gentleman-scholars would feel morally superior to wealthy, but unlettered, merchants.

Traditional veneration of education was revived in the nineteenth century, when it became a key component of strategies for national renewal developed by patriotic intellectuals. Even many supporters of the imperial system recognized the need for scientific and technical training to support industrialization and build up military power. In the late Qing and early Republican periods, thousands of Chinese youth set off enthusiastically on 'work and study' programmes, some to Japan, others to the USA and France; the young Deng Xiaoping himself studied in Paris. During the 1920s, the focus shifted to Moscow where thousands of Communist Party and Guomindang youth attended Sun Yatsen University. Educational reform was one of most important elements of the May 4th period, encapsulated in Chen Duxiu's call for 'Science and Democracy'.

This period saw the elimination of the Confucian classics from university teaching, the introduction of a modernized written language, and the import of Western academic procedures.

In the Republican period, the authorities attempted to develop widespread primary education, down to the village level, and most towns acquired secondary schools. The system was chaotic and teachers' wages were often paid late, or by local subscription; but by the 1930s, the state had basically taken over the running of mission schools from church control and had put in place the rudiments of a national education system. A small, but highly influential, higher-education sector was established with the help of foreign aid, much of it from Protestant churches. During the Japanese occupation, the GMD government made heroic efforts, in appalling conditions, to relocate schools out of reach of the invading forces.

After 1949, the Communists made universal education a key priority. In the 1950s there was a massive drive to set up primary and junior secondary schools and teacher-training colleges. These efforts were accompanied by widespread adult education programmes that taught basic literacy, simple healthcare procedures and agricultural techniques. Soon, however, educational goals began to be compromised by the intrusion of political doctrine into the curriculum. At 'socialist high tides', academic values were downgraded and political education boosted, it being thought better to be 'red' than 'expert'. This conflict was most disruptive in higher education, where the lack of freedom of expression, constant political supervision and promotion and dismissal according to political reliability, all made for an atmosphere inimical to research. The situation was at its worst during the Cultural Revolution, now regarded by the authorities as a ten-year gap in educational process. Schools taught little except slogans; staff were demoralized and often too afraid of their pupils to turn up to work; the universities virtually closed down in the face of savage attacks on their staff; and all research except for a few military-related projects was abandoned.

One of the goals of the education system was to raise a generation of 'revolutionary successors' to continue the work of the CCP. An emphasis on political reliability meshed with the material interests of the bureaucracy to produce a highly elitist system. The children of cadres attended special schools, formed the intake of the top universities and moved on to senior official positions. Resentment against the privileged position of cadres' children was a factor in mobilizing other students during the Cultural Revolution.

In 1978 Deng Xiaoping revived the linkage between education and economic development. He insisted that the Chinese educational system abandon the emphasis on political education, class struggle and egalitarianism. These ideas were formalized in the 1985 Education Reform Decision and the 1986 Compulsory Education Act, which explicitly linked education policy with a strategy for modernization of the economy and the country. Their aim was to ensure at least nine years' compulsory schooling for all. There was increased emphasis on vocational and technical training and universities were given more autonomy to encourage research. 1993 policy statements not only reaffirmed that the primary role of education was to support China's modernization, but also made specific references to supporting, and participating in, the developing market economy.

The reforms have registered some successes, and China's progress in mass education outstrips many other developing countries. But still only around 70 per cent of children complete primary education, and there is a high illiteracy rate in remote and poor regions. In the past few years, as planned, there has been a dramatic shift to technical education in the secondary sector. The objective is to produce a huge pool of skilled labour. There have also been efforts to tailor education provision to local needs. For example, a campaign to 'improve the spiritual and material culture of rural areas' aims to integrate local education with local needs: it teaches agricultural techniques, for example, instead of looking towards unattainable places in distant city universities.

Despite these improvements, however, the education system is facing a funding crisis. Central government covers a smaller proportion of costs, and the burden of financing education is increasingly falling on parents, local governments and enterprises, welfare organizations and donations. There has been a gradual process of commercialization as schools are obliged to operate in the marketplace. Fees are almost universal and high enough to cause many parents to withdraw children from school, especially in rural areas. Although successful schools and colleges can strike lucrative sponsorship deals with local businesses, most teachers are poorly paid and often have to take second jobs to make ends meet. Many of the most able have left the profession, causing a decline in overall quality. The conflict between academic work and the need to make money also affects older students, who must meet their own living costs as well as pay fees.

There are many domestic critics of the new trends in China's education system. Sponsorship deals may bring in revenue, but some teachers regret the loss of independence and integrity that such arrangements may entail. More generally, in a context in which commercial success is valued above all else and in which uneducated peasants can become millionaires, education has lost much of its former social prestige. Low pay and cynicism is producing a high dropout rate of both teachers and students, especially in regions benefiting from the economic boom, where casual employment may be quite lucrative. For those who stay within the system, education is increasingly no longer undertaken for the sake of personal development or even for national goals, but as a means to social advancement. Students are often obsessively focused on exams, and choose subjects which are likely to mean highly paid jobs or foreign travel, such as management studies or accounting, while more traditional subjects are losing popularity. Some critics claim that Chinese education is facing a moral as well as financial crisis.

The crisis in education reflects widespread anxieties about social morality in general. The economic reform unleashed a rush for material wealth summed up by the slogan 'to get rich is glorious'. By the late 1980s, more or less everybody in China was admitting to consumer fever, and was desperate to get rich. There was a general increase in corruption and a rapid decline in the efficiency and honesty of public services. Chinese society became highly competitive and sometimes brutal, symbolized by the appearance of a new breed of gangsters and racketeers akin to the Russian mafia. Many commentators, inside and outside China, believe that all this amounts to a serious moral and spiritual crisis. On this view the Chinese in the PRC have lost all respect for government, law, morality and are in an unregulated struggle for profit. Disillusionment with socialism has been generalized into a deep cynicism about ideals of social justice. Dishonesty is so widespread that it has become a compulsory survival strategy. The market has created unemployment and polarised society; meanwhile unrestrained industrial development is destroying the environment. In the future we can expect rising criminality and social unrest.

An alternative and more optimistic view is that the essential feature of the reform period was the rise in living standards for the great mass of the Chinese people who 'never had it so good', making China rich enough to avoid famines and extreme poverty for the foreseeable future. Social morality may soon improve: the market economy demands the rule of law, which will spread into other areas of life and, most importantly, will temper the arbitrary power of the state. China has begun an unstoppable integration with the rest of the world, and the influence of overseas Chinese and Westerners is on balance highly beneficial. It could even be argued that the CCP has coped skilfully with the last two decades of upheaval: it may well find solutions to current problems, which on the whole are transient side-effects of a positive process of growth.

6

Chinese Culture

China is not only a nation-state: it is also home to one of the world's oldest and largest continuous cultures. For much of its history, the subcontinent was relatively little disturbed by outside influences and so developed a distinctive cultural life. This chapter examines characteristics of social dynamics and typical daily-life attitudes, discusses the arts and intellectual life and concludes with an analysis of religion.

Social Life

When outsiders make contact with Chinese people they are often aware of cultural differences, some of which can lead to quite unintentional misunderstandings; the same may apply to Chinese perceptions of non-Chinese. However, many of these misunderstandings are easily rectified. It is true that Chinese social life is subtle and the foreigner may never penetrate its depths; but a good start can be made by understanding some fundamental concepts. This section outlines characteristic family values and continues with discussion of 'face' and attitudes towards health, food and sex.

The reader should approach this section with great caution. First, Chinese society is rapidly becoming more urban, commercial and industrial, and a growing number of Chinese are exposed to foreign influences. Childcare practices and family structures are subject to radical change because of, for example, the one-child policy (and attempts to evade it). Are traditional cultural patterns relevant at all today? Second, there is a legitimate question whether such a thing as 'national psychology' exists, or whether it is possible to describe a culture without degenerating into national stereotyping. Third, there is no body of documentation to substantiate much of what is written below; the little literature that does exist tends to be either rudimentary academic work based on localized studies, or personal impressions by journalists or writers. Finally, without engaging in systematic cross-cultural studies, it is impossible to determine which practices are specifically Chinese and which are characteristic of, say, east Asia or even Asia as a whole.

A simple solution would be to dispense with this section altogether, but we feel on balance that more would be lost than gained. It is dangerous to stray into stereotyping, but it is also absurd to deny the existence of behavioural norms in a given society. We will be quite satisfied if readers, when they do have the privilege of moving in a Chinese society, feel a little better prepared than they otherwise would. This section is based partly on relevant literature and partly on personal experience; it is intended seriously, but it is inevitably partial and impressionistic. The reader should remember that there are many differences in different parts of the Chinese world, and above all that any person, Chinese or non-Chinese, is an individual who may, and probably will, differ radically from any preconceptions we may hold about his or her culture. Also, much of the Chinese world is changing very fast. Patterns that may have been prevalent some decades ago, and that may still play an important role in some communities, may well have been superseded elsewhere, especially in cosmopolitan cities.

The Chinese infant's environment tends to be close, warm, loving and highly controlled: a pattern of intense relations with a relatively small number of people, and of considerable indulgence. The baby is kept close to the mother and other family members, participating in social occasions, strapped to the mother's back where necessary. Until about the age of five, the Chinese infant is treated to the best available food, clothing and personal comfort, but is not much stimulated mentally. Babies are kept in restrictive clothing and restrained from much movement. They are frequently warned that the environment is dirty or dangerous, and control is exercised primarily by physical restraint rather than by words. One study suggests that Chinese infants, compared to children brought up in Caucasian households, are less vocal, less active and more content. This phenomenon may even reflect a genetic difference. One study found similar characteristics even among new-born infants, before socialization had taken place: Caucasians were more irritable, more changeable, more easily upset, more active, and less consolable than Chinese babies (Bond, 1991).

As the child grows, he or she becomes aware of many indicators of status, such as age, gender, family position and title. Prerogatives of the hierarchy are defined, and challenges promptly suppressed. The child quickly learns to acquiesce in preserving the status quo. Aggression, especially against senior members of the family, is not tolerated and children are usually disciplined if complaints are made against them. The child is brought up to feel emotionally secure, protected and happy in the bosom of the family. For many adult Chinese, much of their happiest social life is also spent in banquets, outings, or reunions with family members.

Compared to contemporary Western norms, most Chinese families have stricter views on sexuality and are more consistent in discouraging sexual behaviour among youngsters. Likewise, choice of spouse must always take place with the approval, if not the actual selection, by parents; the parents take precedence over the marriage partner, in display, if not in reality. The extent of physical and sexual abuse of children is unknown. Given harsh, cramped living conditions and strong patriarchal control in much of the Chinese countryside, it may be very extensive. Child abuse is almost a taboo subject, and reports of it emerged only very recently even in cosmopolitan Hong Kong.

Chinese society is collectivist and concerned about preserving hierarchy. It is risky for individuals to express opposition to the social order, and open displays of aggression are unusual. If an individual wants to make a challenge, he or she would often do so in a more subtle way, adopting passive–aggressive strategies – for example 'forgetting' to do things, playing helpless, falling ill. In the effort to avoid open conflict, people will generally be compromising. If it is necessary to challenge others, they will often do so in a roundabout way – for example, by sending hints through an intermediary, or by engaging in gossip behind the scenes. Objectives may thus be achieved without open dissent. Their own status in the hierarchy must be maintained, which may entail identifying and neutralizing potential challenges by a display of power. They value hard work and thrift, and achievement redounds not only on oneself, but on one's entire extended family, as does shame in the event of failure.

The importance of the family and of 'connections' leads to a relatively sharp distinction between in-groups and out-groups. Chinese are often extraordinarily loyal, generous and caring towards their family and closest friends. As a corollary, they can sometimes appear indifferent towards people outside this circle. The contrast between the two modes of behaviour is probably more marked than would be normal in some other societies. Apart from the emotional bonds, the network also has economic implications. Most Chinese prefer to conduct any kind of business with people they trust rather than in a purely commercial, impersonal way. Apart from sentimental considerations, this is obviously good policy in an environment where the legal system is often inadequate. Consequently, many groups of associates form loose-knit chains of 'connections' (*guanxi*, see also Chapter 3) whose relationship spans a certain amount of trust and personal friendship, but also includes trading favours, negotiating deals, locating resources, lending money, or helping in the various transactions of working life. These connections are wide-ranging, and extend to friends of friends, or even further afield. If one is a member of such a network (and almost all Chinese are members of several) it is vital to respond to requests for help as far as possible and not to cheat other members of the network; otherwise, one risks losing one's place and will thereby prejudice both emotional and economic support.

This leads on to the idea of 'face', often cited by outsiders as a characteristic of Chinese social behaviour. Face generally refers to a person's standing before his or her peers – for example, work-colleagues, neighbours, or friends. One can thus see that it is vitally important to maintain a positive social image of oneself as reliable, capable and smart. If one manages affairs well, one will gain prestige and consequently become even better placed in one's networks. Since access to resources often depends on one's connections, this is highly advantageous. On the contrary, if one loses the esteem of others, or gains a reputation for being clumsy or inadequate, one loses valuable status and access. To some extent, then, the Chinese social game is a kind of struggle to maintain or enhance one's own position, and possibly to demolish that of a competitor. One can 'gain face' in this game by such things as being praised by a superior, by hosting a meal, by running a successful project, or appearing on TV; one loses face by being exposed as mean or a cheat, by being criticized in public, by failing to fulfil a promise, or by making a serious social gaffe. Face may sometimes be more important than money; if one loses money, one can make it again. But if one loses one's position in a valuable network, one may never regain it. It is a friendly gesture to allow an acquaintance to 'gain face'. Thus, if a foreigner is ever asked to host an expensive banquet in China, it is not simply that the Chinese colleagues enjoy a good meal (although of course that may well be a consideration); it is also an opportunity for the foreigner to display financial clout. Failure to do so may reveal one, for example in business circles, as petty and possibly as an unattractive partner.

Many Chinese, especially men of some business or political seniority, take the question of face very seriously at a personal level. Some may respond extremely badly if their face is 'threatened', becoming intransigent and even belligerent. It is almost always counter-productive to criticize Chinese people in public, above all in front of their employees or juniors. On the contrary, they may respond very positively to polite, symbolic remarks praising their past performance, the delicious taste of a meal they host, or the imposing location of an office. Praise and approval in front of peers or colleagues are especially highly valued and the person giving it is noted as a potential associate. Thus, if one does have a potentially damaging issue to raise with a Chinese partner or business contact, it is usually far better to do so in a private, one-to-one conversation and to maintain friendly and warm appearances before anyone in his or her circle.

Some academics take psychological analysis of the Chinese character to an extreme, and argue that it is even a determining factor in the conduct of Chinese politics. Perhaps best known is Lucian Pye, who argues that Maoist idealism and Dengist pragmatism are essentially expressions of the Chinese psychological structure. He suggests, for example, that fundamental polarities at the heart of Chinese personality manifest in violent political swings: between egalitarian brotherhood at one extreme, and deference towards superiors at the other; between idealism and pragmatism; between protest and acceptance; between self-sacrifice and self-advancement; between pride and humility. Another contradictory tendency is belief in fate as opposed to human effort:

This means that Chinese can behave in quite contradictory ways. Sometimes they will be totally passive, apparently leaving developments to the play of impersonal forces; at other moments they act as though their personal effort is all that counts. In fact, however, the passive posture may reflect not fatalism, but the intent to wait for the propitious moment to spring into action. (Pye, 1988: 66)

Pye and analysts of this school thus interpret even national or international political decisions as arising from deep traits of the Chinese psyche:

> The Chinese have a distinctive capacity to create a world of make-believe, and to manipulate illusions rather than substances . . . Skill at feigned compliance makes it possible for leaders and followers to go along with collective pretenses. (Ibid.: 106–7)

The disaster of the Great Leap Forward, caused largely by massive use of falsified statistics, may be an instance to consider in this context.

Such generalizations are thought-provoking, but too vague and sweeping to be of use in social science or political analysis. Along similar lines, but with fewer pretensions, are the works of Lin Yutang, a doyen of 20th-century literature whose 1936 classic *My Country and My People* introduced China to a generation of foreign readers. Lin's brilliant prose (he wrote in English after a missionary education) presents an idealized, romantic, humorous, positive and charming account of the Chinese character; he surely reveals something about the self-perception of the Chinese, if nothing else. According to Lin:

> if we review the Chinese race and try to picture their national characteristics, we shall probably find the following traits of character: sanity, simplicity, love of nature, patience, indifference [glossed as refusal to meddle, especially in politics], old roguery, fecundity, industry, frugality, love of family life, pacifism, contentment, humour, conservatism, and sensuality. (Lin, 1936: 41)

He sees Chinese mental faculties as characterized by intelligence, femininity, lack of science and intuition. With typical wit, Lin deduces Chinese intelligence from their cowardice!

> The Chinese suffer from an overdose of intelligence, as shown in their pacifism . . . which so often borders on cowardice. But all intelligent men are cowards, because intelligent men want to save their skins. There can be nothing more silly . . . than a man popping his head 'over the top' . . . in order to meet a lead bullet

and die for a newspaper-manufactured cause. If he can use his head in reading newspapers, he will not be at the front. (Ibid.: 74)

Learning about, and learning from, the vast wealth of Chinese culture is one of the great joys of association with the Chinese world. There is no space to pursue details here, but the reader should at least be aware that Chinese attitudes to matters like health, food and sex may be different, sometimes obviously, sometimes subtly, to those of other societies.

In the case of health, for example, most Chinese, including those in the ultra-modern cities of Hong Kong and Singapore, are familiar with Western medicine and also with traditional Chinese medicine. According to the latter, the body's natural harmony may be disturbed by various factors: stress, bad weather, excesses of certain kinds of food and so on. The cure should not simply remove symptoms but rather return the body to its natural harmony by skilful manipulation of energies: balancing yin and yang, stimulating some organs and sedating others by a combination of herbs, massage, acupuncture, and diet. While Western medicine is widely practised, Chinese medicine is often seen as more effective for treating chronic ailments; and indeed it appears to have a good therapeutic record. As a rule, Chinese are interested in health and especially in techniques which may help them attain a Chinese ideal: a happy, long, and healthy old age.

Food is, of course, another major preoccupation of the Chinese who generally believe that their cuisine is the finest in the world. Again, without some knowledge of the philosophy of food, the foreigner may be at a loss to understand the significance of certain aspects of eating in China. Food-offerings are among the earliest expressions of Chinese religiosity, and the practice of offering food to ancestors and gods continues to the present. The use of food in the social context appears to bear some residual religious feeling. It is the prime symbol of family harmony, the sign of prosperity, togetherness, success and joy. Most Chinese families try to eat together, preferably seated at a round table. The conversation before, during and after meals tends to revolve around the food: the best way to prepare ingredients, the combination of dishes, their health-giving properties and so on. Each member of the party is constantly urged to eat more and choice morsels are fished out for the plates of young children, respected elders, or honoured guests. Extending from the family, shared meals cement most social relationships: many business negotiations are accompanied by banquets, and groups of friends often meet in restaurants. Hosting a banquet is a prime opportunity for splashing out on rare dishes and expensive drinks.

Apart from the social considerations, much attention is of course paid to the food itself. China has several regional cuisines which are nationally and internationally known: Cantonese, specializing in light cooking and fresh produce; Sichuanese with hot chilis; Beijing duck and so on. Chefs have to balance hot and cold dishes, salt and sweet, grain and meat. As well as taste, the art of cooking extends to health: according to Chinese medicine, some foods are especially healthy, while others taken to excess will quickly lead to illness. The Chinese love of symbolism is also given full play in food culture: for example, extra long noodles are served at birthdays, indicating an extra long life; and a particular kind of seaweed is prized because its name sounds the same as the words for 'make a fortune'! Altogether, a meal with a Chinese family or group of business associates may convey plenty of messages about social status, friendship, or even health, provided one is astute enough to receive them.

Finally in this section, Chinese attitudes towards sexuality may also differ from those in other societies. Pye's work, cited above, emphasizes that Chinese have a high tolerance for tension: they may regard contradiction as an integral part of human experience and know that it has to be tolerated and lived with, rather than resolved. With regard to sexuality, much of Chinese official culture has been extremely repressive. Until recently, even limited displays of affection in public were considered deeply offensive, and some regimes were extraordinarily puritanical: pre-marital sex was, for example, virtually a serious crime for part of the Maoist era. The official Confucian ethos was anti-sexual, reinforcing stereotypes of male supremacy and condemning females for diverting men's attention from higher pursuits. One thus finds areas of cultural life which are strictly desexualized, with relations between men and women apparently reduced to the demands of the extended family, where women are childbearers or workers and a man's primary obligations are to his parents or clan. In these circumstances women's clothing is correspondingly unrevealing, body movements demure and social freedoms restricted. Woman is, in the words of Lin Yutang, 'helpful wife and wise mother': loyal, obedient, and instinctively chaste (Lin, 1936: 152). Conversely, a man's primary emotional bond was supposed to be with his parents, and his secondary ones probably with his male peers. Survival of this attitude may be confusing to people whose culture values loyalty to spouse above all.

However, certainly in most periods of Chinese history, this is only one side of a far more complex picture. For the most part, the repression was of women's sexuality, while men were given much greater licence. Recent studies have investigated in detail the vast and usually sordid sex industry that arose in cities like Shanghai during the nineteenth century, which provided employment of sorts for millions of women. One of the remarkable phenomena of the 1990s, so far not subject to systematic research, has been the rapid revival of the sex industry, now reputed to be the largest in the world, encompassing pornography, brothels, and call-girls, often connected with the narcotics trade and, allegedly, frequently operating to the profit of the armed forces. There have also been many reports in the late 1990s of kidnapping of women into prostitution and even the export of young children to work in brothels overseas.

One may doubt that the image of 'virtuous wife and mother' in reality ever fitted more than a small number of sexual relations. There is a long tradition of eroticism in China, some of which openly discusses women's sexuality, usually acknowledging its superiority to men's. Well known examples from classical China include the *Yellow Emperor's Classic of Internal Medicine* and the *Classic of the Plain Girl*, both of which give explicit advice about sexual arts; typically, in Chinese terms, much concerned with the balancing of male and female energies to promote health, happiness, and longevity. This current of eroticism, influenced by Taoism, developed a subculture of sexual techniques and aids including aphrodisiacs, erotic pictures, toys, cross-dressing and so on. In the 1990s, sexuality appears to have burst the confines of both Confucian and Communist restraint. One finds sexually explicit material in films and videos, and sexual issues are discussed in the media.

The Arts and the Media

Many Chinese are justifiably proud of their artistic heritage. The writing system dates to about the fourteenth century BCE, and the same period gave rise to the first decorated bronze vessels. From then, successive generations of historians, poets, painters and musicians contributed to the great corpus of the artistic tradition. To summarize some Chinese aesthetic concerns, art should be subtle, allusive and symbolic, rather than overtly powerful or grandiose; artists frequently refer to earlier works in a given genre, embedding their own creations within the tradition; and there is a close relationship between poetry and painting, often mediated by the expressive capacity of calligraphy. To quote Lin Yutang:

> The Chinese artistic and literary genius, which thinks in emotional concrete imagery and excels in the painting of atmosphere, is especially suitable to the writing of poetry. Their characteristic genius for contraction, suggestion, sublimation and concentration . . . makes the writing of poetry natural and easy to them. If, as Bertrand Russell says, 'in art they aim at being exquisite, and in life at being reasonable', then it is natural for them to excel at poetry. Chinese poetry is dainty. It is never long, and never very powerful. But it is eminently fitted for producing perfect gems of sentiment and for painting with a few strokes a magical scenery, alive with rhythmic beauty and informed with spiritual grace. (Lin, 1936: 230)

Chinese artists, particularly in traditional pen and ink landscapes, have a vast repertoire of techniques for vague suggestiveness. Landscape paintings do not adopt the perspective techniques of post-Renaissance Western art. Rather, each part of the picture is a separate scene in itself, and the viewer should allow his vision to roam around the painting, visiting one aspect after another in a spiritual journey. Paintings often have tracts of cloud, empty sky, or water apparently overwhelming the tiny human figures. To the informed viewer, they represent Buddhist and Taoist concerns with the mind in meditation, with the relative insignificance of human striving in the greater cosmos, and with the beauty of nature. Some works of art are supposed to act as a mirror: a classical Chinese poem or picture often leaves unsaid more than it states explicitly, leaving the observer's imagination to project details onto the basic sketch left by the artist.

Often educated Chinese were, and many still are, connoisseurs of a variety of pastimes: tea-drinking, antiques, coin collecting, songbirds, calligraphy, gardens, miniature plants, ornamental fish and so on. Many of these arts and hobbies spread to other countries in east Asia: the Japanese tea ceremony and miniature trees derive from China. As an example, some Chinese scholars liked to keep a small piece of rock on their desk, and were willing to pay quite high prices for those with the right shape and quality. It served a purpose similar to the landscape painting: the scholar would allow his vision to move from one part of the rock to another, while in his mind's eye he would be roaming around a mountain range. Indentations on the rock might represent caves or pathways; colouring might suggest sunsets or vegetation. Thus he could use the rock to stimulate a flight of imagination into remote parts of China, perhaps to visit sages and hermits . . . Many such hobbies were almost destroyed in the first forty years of Communist rule, but some have revived and many of them survive among educated Chinese in Taiwan and overseas. It is often a pleasure when getting to know a Chinese person to find that he or she has impressive talents, perhaps as calligrapher or martial artist, that provide enjoyment to themselves and others.

Despite the glories of the artistic tradition, it also had its weaknesses, important among them a tendency to stereotyped imitation of past masters. By the late imperial age, poetry, painting and other arts were codified into elements that were inculcated in an artist's training (for example, the 'correct' way to paint bamboo, or to compose a poem): most artists appear to have been more concerned to reproduce them formalistically than to create new ones. The consensus of opinion is that the artistic tradition as a whole had stagnated, and that artists of the later Qing dynasty fell below the standards of their predecessors.

It was therefore natural that when the empire was overthrown in the early 20th century, the artistic tradition was also radically challenged. The May 4th period produced an outburst of activity profoundly influenced by Western artistic concerns. Among the best-known writers, Lu Xun produced bitter masterpieces, savagely attacking the old society in compressed short stories bordering on prose poetry. New novels, theatre and poetry appeared, often revolutionary in content and style, raising issues of women's rights, freedom of expression and social injustice. The new art addressed a new audience: the first generation of educated young urbanites, especially in the great cities of Beijing and Shanghai, who read literary journals and went to the theatre or cinema. However, political censorship soon restricted the brief flowering of culture in the 1910s and 1920s, since many artists sympathized with the left. New artistic techniques and concerns had certainly entered China, but were for the most part confined to relatively sophisticated sectors of the urban population. The great works of the Chinese tradition, however, maintained their prestige through the century: except perhaps in the most extreme period of the Cutural Revolution, the works of the classical poets, calligraphers, novelists, and painters continued to be held in high esteem. In the 1990s, classical Chinese literature, art, and music were still taught in universities and academies.

CCP domination over the arts, which lasted until well into the 1990s, was a new and, on balance, negative trend in Chinese artistic life. In 1942, partly to reinforce ideological unity and partly to promote his own personality cult, Mao initiated a 'rectification campaign' stressing discipline and Marxist orthodoxy. The question of art and literature was given priority, especially in a series of talks by Mao and other senior CCP leaders in the 'Yan'an Forum on Literature and Art'. Mao insisted that all literature and art should be revolutionary, national, and serve the masses. 'Revolutionary' implied that all artistic work should promote the interests of the Chinese revolution, for example by blackening the enemy and strengthening the resolve to fight, and by praising the contributions of ordinary workers, soldiers, and peasants who should be depicted in a glorious light. Writers could expose social conditions in areas under Guomindang or Japanese, and stir up resentment against oppression; but they should not mention any mistakes or problems in Communist-held territory: there was no place for any satire or criticism directed against the Party. 'National' meant that Mao disapproved of foreign, especially European, influences in art. Wherever possible, artists should adapt traditional Chinese artforms such as woodcut art, peasant stories and theatre, local folksongs and dances. 'Serving the masses' meant that artists should not experiment with refined or complicated modes of expression, nor pay much attention to aesthetic concerns. Rather, art should be couched in direct, simple formulas that could be easily appreciated by uneducated people, and should address the daily concerns of the masses, not of a sophisticated elite.

At the same time, Mao staged a vicious crackdown on a number of young intellectuals who had voiced mild concerns about some aspects of Communist policy. Most of them were pressurized into self-criticism and retraction; one, Wang Shiwei, was executed. Censorship or steering of art may arguably be justified in a national emergency, but the events in Yan'an presaged many decades of state repression. Mao's cultural dictatorship extended far beyond the war years and Chinese policy on arts was as destructive as that of Stalinist Russia. When the CCP took power, the guidelines on literature and art were translated into monolithic control over cultural life. The new government set up a Ministry of Culture, which oversaw organizations like the China Federation of Literature and Art. All writers and artists became state employees and were obliged to produce work that fulfilled Mao's instructions: to portray workers and peasants in the most positive light; to stir up hatred and resentment against class enemies and imperialists; and to praise and glorify the CCP and, in particular, Mao Zedong. It is perhaps exaggerated to write off the entire period from 1949 to the late 1980s as a wasteland, but certainly most commentators would regard it as a barren period in Chinese cultural history. A few writers and artists managed to negotiate the demands of the censors and maintain some semblance of artistic production, but the number of works from the period that may stand the test of time is small.

The nadir was reached in the Cultural Revolution, when stultifying artistic policies, imposed by Mao's wife Jiang Qing and others in the Party leadership, abolished even minimal scope for expression. Residual links with the Chinese tradition and with European impulses were crushed, and for a period artists had to produce works of a purely 'revolutionary' character. This diktat led to absurdly stylized portrayals of proletarian heroes and the promotion of the Mao cult; it was coupled with brutal physical attacks on many of China's most distinguished writers, musicians, and cinematographers.

Together with the censorship of literature and art, the CCP imposed blanket control over all news media, which became mouthpieces for the Party line. Censorship over the press and broadcasting was almost complete until the late 1980s. The national media demonized political enemies, promoted the Mao cult, exaggerated production figures, and concealed famines and crop failures. The population was deliberately kept in a state of profound ignorance about international and national affairs, more realistic news of which was circulated only to high-ranking cadres by a system of internal reports.

On the one hand, these policies contributed to the collapse of rationality in Chinese public life, where even senior government figures apparently believed the most absurd misinformation, or at least pretended to, thus in turn facilitating ever more absurd policy decisions. On the other, they contributed also to the public cynicism and disillusion that eventually spilled over into riots in 1989. By then, the contradictions between media reports and the perceptions of a better-educated public were too glaring. Chinese citizens knew, for example, that there was no mass starvation in Western Europe, as they had been reliably assured; they also knew that the children of Party leaders were amassing vast fortunes through illegal deals, which was never reported.

The cultural repression, extending from the 1940s until the 1980s, ties in with other aspects of the communist period. The combination of Stalinist politics, isolationism, and Mao's personal brand of megalomania, dominated art, as it dominated most of Chinese life. As in other areas, the rejection of the old proved easier than the creation of anything new. It is true that even in the Confucian tradition, literature was supposed to convey morality and ortho-doxy; however, it did so without the mind-deadening rigidity of CCP products. The policies led to a collapse in artistic standards, since works were evaluated by political rather than artistic measures, and issues of personal integrity, artistic exploration, and creativity were for the most part ignored. It was dangerous to experiment, safer to conform. This corresponded closely to the overall tenor of CCP control over urban life: intellectuals were under pressure to partici-pate in political study, prove their devotion to the new regime, denounce enemies, promote proletarian virtues, support the Party and forgo individualism. As mentioned in Chapter 5, the control over thought reached an extreme point in China between 1949 and 1978; it was severe in all walks of life and terrifying in the gulag, its ultimate expression and the repository of its victims.

After 1978, freedom of expression improved steadily. Reformers around Deng realized that it would be impossible to maintain such a level of control over the arts and the media, and gradually relaxed cultural policies through the 1980s. Fiction began to discuss emo-tional and personal issues. A new generation of poets, the so-called 'misty poets', produced in the late 1980s work of a high artistic calibre. Their poetry used the Chinese classical tradition and mod-ern European literature as reference points yet was characteristically modern Chinese in spirit. Even newspapers began to explore the limits of censorship and to publish more controversial material, although some of them courted trouble by doing so. Avant-garde artists in visual arts and cinema also began to explore controversial themes, occasionally having their exhibitions broken up by the police, or their films banned.

Not surprisingly, given the four decades of repression, experiments were cautious and progress was slow. However, a series of events in the late 1980s and early 1990s has totally transformed the art and media scene in China. First, the 1989 democracy movement finally blew the lid off the control of news. One of the students' key demands was for greater freedom of speech and expression and for an end to censorship of the news. In an astonishing development, staff of several major newspapers and broadcasting stations joined the protests, implicitly by positive reporting on the student movement, explicitly by criticizing the government, and personally by taking to the streets. In several protests by journalists, they made it plain that they were constantly obliged to print stories that they knew to be false, to cover up embarrassing facts and to mislead the public. The government of course cracked down on these protests and made media control a high priority immediately following the movement, but the wall of silence and misinformation had been definitively breached.

Another important factor was the Gulf War. In the run-up to the Allies' ground action, Beijing military spokesmen had been confidently predicting that the Iraqi desert would become another Vietnam, with hi-tech US forces bogged down by politically motivated infantry. The rapid and overpowering success of the Allies was devastating to Chinese government defence thinking, and also extremely embarrassing. A decade earlier, news of the US victory would doubtless have been thoroughly suppressed, and the public might have learned about it only from random gossip. However, by 1990 a dramatic development had taken place, the implications of which had perhaps hardly dawned on the government. A number of institutions in China by then had access to satellite TV stations, including CNN news broadcasts, which were received by major tourist hotels, universities, research institutes, government departments and even some private individuals, especially in south China. Overseas travel, and telecommunications with Hong Kong and the rest of the world, had become routine. Now, almost anyone interested could gain an entirely different perspective (in effect, that of CNN and other international media) on current events: the Chinese population was no longer restricted to government information sources.

Perhaps even more important was the commercialization of the media, starting from about 1992. In part this was driven by China's internal economic reforms. Along with many other previously state-subsidized units, media enterprises were obliged to enter the market and make a profit, or risk bankruptcy. They were in a precarious and at times desperate situation: sometimes, for example, the management was still obliged to provide an 'Iron Rice-Bowl' for employees, even where the unit was grossly over-staffed. However, these demands coincided with a period where Chinese companies were discovering the uses of advertising, which was one of the major growth areas of the economy in the mid-1990s, registering huge increases every year. Newspapers, magazines, radio and TV stations quickly seized the opportunity to commercialize and gain advertising revenue, which became the major source of income for many of them. A spin-off was the need to increase circulation by producing material more attractive to the far more sophisticated audiences of the 1990s. Since political debate was still strictly off-limits, this development stimulated a far wider range of writing.

Finally, international media burst onto the Chinese scene. The process had already started in two areas in the 1980s: areas around Hong Kong had been able to receive TV broadcasts and much of the Chinese population could, if it wished, receive foreign radio broadcasts like Gospel radios, Voice of America and the BBC. Following the introduction of stations like CNN, several media giants negotiated permission to broadcast material into China. Companies like Star and MTV are popular throughout the country: Chinese people are now free to watch domestic or international TV soaps and game-shows.

The arts and the media have undergone a radical transformation since the early 1990s. One question is how the government will retain some semblance of control over the news agenda, which is surely crucial for its survival. It seems that crude suppression is no longer feasible. Instead, the government may adopt techniques used in more sophisticated authoritarian states like Singapore, where the population is persuaded of state policies by a continuous drip-feed of positive news items and success stories, and frequently reminded of the defects of Western states riddled with narcotics, crime, and racism. In this scenario, slanted news would be combined with the retention of censorship against direct political attacks in the national media and commercial pressure on foreign media companies to toe the line. Investigative journalism would be suppressed as far as possible, and news-management would present a smooth flow of non-controversial items mixed with entertainment.

The future of the literary and artistic tradition looks promising. Although we have yet to see outstanding genius among the younger generation of artists since 1989, one might think that at least the preconditions for a new flowering of art and culture currently exist. There is an increasingly rich, lively, optimistic and educated urban society that would provide an audience; most art could find publishers or exhibition halls ready to risk hassle with conservative cadres; Chinese traditional art and the most modern Western and Asian works are readily available; many young people attend colleges of art and music or literature courses at universities. It appears extremely unlikely that the government will seriously clamp down on art and literature, and the environment may be more promising than at any time since the 1920s. Perhaps a major Chinese artistic renaissance is waiting to happen. So far, admittedly, the only forerunners of it are the successes of a number of film directors like Zhang Yimou who have begun to make an impact on the international scene.

Intellectual Life

What of China's intellectual life more generally? (The term 'intellectual' is loosely used in China to refer to anyone with a college degree or, in poor areas, even with a good secondary education. Many are state employees of various kinds, perhaps administrators in enterprises, political cadres, school-teachers, health workers. In a more restricted sense, the term applies to the graduates of China's elite universities, or those who have studied abroad.) Intellectuals in China have long had a precarious position in society, and a dangerous relationship with the state. Between 1949 and 1989, intellectuals were obliged to function as the state's loyal servants, whose role was to praise the Party leadership and to promote a vulgar Marxist–Maoist doctrine. Their life after the revolution was bleak: they were isolated from virtually all international contacts, they had limited access to books or ideas, their output was censored. Worse, intellectuals as a class were systematically targeted for harsh persecution. The Anti-Rightist Campaign, run by Deng Xiaoping with Mao's personal backing in 1957, sentenced more than half a million people to jail, hard labour, or internal exile. Most of them stayed there for twenty years; it was a terrifying lesson.

Intellectuals were again a target during the Cultural Revolution. One major difference from the Anti-Rightist Campaign was that the attacks reached to the heart of the CCP establishment. Certainly, those who carried stains of 'bourgeois' lifestyle were purged, but so were leaders, administrators and cadres. Universities were virtually closed; newspapers and books printed only Maoist propaganda. Perhaps around 3 million more intellectuals suffered persecution during the period, ranging from detentions and beatings to long-term imprisonment and execution. When Deng came to power, most intellectuals were cowed by thirty years of systematic persecution. Many had spent years in labour camps, and intellectual life had been ossified by censorship and isolation.

There has been an almost complete turnaround in the two decades since 1978. The new situation is perhaps even more radical than may appear at first sight because, although the Maoist state was an extreme example of authoritarianism, treatment of intellectuals in some ways mirrored that of its imperial predecessors. The 'intellectuals' of imperial China were the mandarins, senior civil servants whose role for the most part, despite some honourable exceptions, was to offer loyal advice rather than to generate independent ideas. Intellectual life was not commercialized as it had been in Europe since the Enlightenment; rather, it was a service purchased, sanctioned and supervised by the state which felt free at its whim to adopt or disregard proposals from its underlings, the hired brains of the intellectual class.

An independent intellectual community started to emerge in the 1920s but was aborted by authoritarian government; the 1980s marked an important resurgence of the 1920s' pluralism, and has taken it much further

> The relaxation of the Party's controls over ideology, intellectual activity and culture opened up public spaces into which spilled informal intellectual networks, salons, study groups and non-official journals and think-tanks . . . intellectuals were a potent and influential force during most of the Deng era . . . the major trend at the end of the century is towards a decrease rather than an increase in controls over intellectual and cultural life. (Goldman, 1996: 37–8 and 50)

The new generation of intellectuals displayed tremendous vitality from the early 1980s, seen for example in the vast range of foreign works published in Chinese translation. Successive waves of readers have now been introduced to feminism, post-modernism and most other trends in contemporary international discourse. The period witnessed the greatest import of foreign ideas certainly since the 1920s; perhaps even the greatest in Chinese history. Equally important has been the resurgence of free discussions – for example, on humanism and subjectivity in the early 1980s – that culminated in a wide-ranging debate on whether and how Chinese culture would survive into the twenty-first century. These debates cannot be isolated from the dramatic changes in life-style: no longer cowed by the state, many intellectuals lead independent lives working for newspapers or other media, no longer constrained by political masters.

The two reform decades thus saw 'an outburst of intellectual activity, the scope and intensity of which surpassed even the famous May 4th New Cultural Movement' (Lin, Rosemont, Ames, 1995: 728). Its protagonists commented on politics and economics, and also philosophy, literary criticism and aesthetics and the social sciences. The most illustrious critic of the 1980s was Li Zehou, who specialized in the history of Western philosophy and aesthetics. From 1984 Li started to pose questions that had barely been raised, and were virtually unthinkable, after 1949: explorations of humanity's essence, ethics, creativity, aesthetics and inner being. Li's influence soon began to make itself felt in literature, literary criticism and the social sciences, as well as philosophy. Along with these explorations of the inner world, Li wrote influential books on Confucius, whom he reinterpreted in a far more positive way than Communist orthodoxy permitted, and on Chinese culture more generally.

Further impetus came from the school of 'New Confucianists', mostly a group of Chinese–American scholars of whom the best known is Tu Wei-ming. Tu promotes an essentially philosophical, ethical and even religious reading of Confucius, and believes that only by a return to these roots will the Chinese be able to regain a solid cultural heritage. Although for most of the 1980s New Confucianism met with some indifference and even hostility from the bulk of Chinese intellectuals (and from the Chinese state), it gradually attracted more sympathy from mainland scholars. Among the themes raised were a revaluation of the Chinese tradition which had been so heavily criticized certainly by the CCP, but even before that by the iconoclastic May 4th movement. At a time when China is regaining its international prestige in political and economic spheres, it is natural that its cultural heritage should also be reinstated.

Together with the rescuing of the 'self' and the inner world after decades of oblivion, the mid-1980s also saw an important debate on the value and future of traditional Chinese culture, reflected and popularized in the cult television series *Heshang* ('River Elegy'), scripted by a group of people around Su Xiaokang and screened in 1988. *River Elegy*, though widely criticized even by opponents of the regime as a dilettantish and superficial mishmash, played a major role in preparing a climate of public support for the student protests. In September 1988 the National Vice-Chairman Wang Zhen comically denounced it for 'insulting the Yellow River and the Great Wall', and in July 1989 officials accused it of inspiring the turmoil. *River Elegy* argued that Chinese civilization is dead, and strongly implied that China's way to rebirth lies in all-out Westernization. 'Sea power is the key to democratic revolution', said Su Xiaokang; democracy is proper not to China's introverted continental culture but to the 'azure', seaward-looking civilization of the West.

The intellectual–cultural arena reflected the turmoil of a society which was deeply influenced by four strands of culture which interacted with, and sometimes contradicted, each other. First, as nobody doubts who has been to China even for a short time, the population has an abiding sense of traditional values, as discussed earlier. Second, these values came under radical attack at the time of the New Culture Movement: and many of them were found to be rotten. For certain, many Chinese wholeheartedly welcome such developments as the industrial economy, greater freedom for women, and modern technology. Third, both traditional and Western values were attacked, and sometimes destroyed, by the Maoist state, which itself contained elements of peasant rebellion, the Russian revolutionary tradition, Stalinism and imperial control. Fourth, and increasingly evident in the 1990s, cultural life was challenged, perhaps invigorated, by a brash new competitor. Along with the media influx from Hong Kong, China has been inundated with Canto-pop culture: popular songs and dance routines from Hong Kong, sometimes from Taiwan and other Asian countries. Videos and the karaoke phenomenon have stimulated an indigenous rock and pop industry in China itself. Chinese youth now has access to all the delights of a lively, commercialized, at times rowdy, romantic, sexy entertainment industry.

Religion

Religion in Traditional China

Chinese religion tended to be centred on the family and the local community. Even religions with well developed philosophies, like Taoism and Buddhism, were organized primarily in monasteries which had relatively little connection with each other. Religious believers seldom formed institutions, certainly nothing to compare with the powerful Christian churches of the West. Yet religion could form the ideology of revolt, as in the Taiping movement, the greatest insurrection in nineteenth-century China. The imperial state therefore kept a watchful eye on religious groups, and sometimes suppressed those – for example, underground sects – which overstepped boundaries.

From the earliest times, religious beliefs profoundly influenced society. Every district had its own particular traditions, but practices connected with gods, ghosts and ancestors were especially prominent. Gods included the spirits of deceased heroes, versions of Taoist or Buddhist deities and local animistic spirits. Particular gods were propitiated by members of certain professions, or by colourful community festivals and processions. As in many peasant societies, there was widespread fear of ghosts and evil spirits, and use of exorcism to cure illness. Ancestor worship was prevalent in south China, where it played a central role in family and clan systems: ancestors were thought to bring prosperity provided that their descendants protected their graves and performed ceremonies in the home. Popular religion has been evaluated very differently by outside observers. For some scientifically minded Chinese, it is merely superstition, evidence of backwardness, to be discouraged as far as possible. Others, including many Western anthropologists, take a more positive view and point to its social functions in promoting community identity, performing arts, and local solidarity.

Formal religions were more the concern of the educated elite, although elements filtered down into popular practices. Buddhism was introduced into China from India in the early centuries CE. It reached a peak in the Tang dynasty (7th–9th centuries) when it became almost a national religion. The most popular sects were the Pure Land and the Chan schools, the latter being well known through its Japanese derivative Zen. It is difficult to summarize Buddhist doctrines, but most of them stressed compassion, meditation, piety and devotion to the Buddha. Buddhism never fully recovered from a severe persecution in the ninth century, but it remains an integral part of the Chinese religious world. Hundreds of monasteries remained open until the 1950s, and many of them reopened in the 1980s. Buddhist philosophy exerted a profound influence over elite culture, and educated Chinese today still need a grasp of Buddhist ideas to understand their cultural heritage, for example the classical poets and novelists. Chinese culture as a whole has been deeply influenced by Buddhism, for example in a widespread acceptance of fate, belief in karma and respect for monasteries.

Taoism is a term applied to the philosophy attributed to two figures of uncertain historicity, Laozi and Zhuangzi, who asserted the existence of an unseen, inexpressible Absolute, known as the Tao, pervading the universe. Their works, dating from about the third century BCE, show how a person could become a sage by following the Tao, abandoning worldly desires and acting in accord with nature. Taoism later became a compendium of esoteric beliefs centred on the attainment of immortality. This quest was pursued by a variety of occult means including alchemy, rituals, yogic exercises and chanting. The poem attributed to Laozi, the *Tao Te Ching*, is one of the most celebrated works of Chinese spirituality containing famous lines such as 'Those who know do not speak; those who speak do not know'; 'The further one travels, the less one knows. Therefore the Sage arrives without going, sees all without looking, does nothing yet achieves everything'. If the quintessential Buddhist figure is the pious monk, the Taoist is a hermit. Taoism was regarded as an alternative to the conventional state philosophy of Confucianism. Scholars who became disillusioned with court life had the option of wandering away from the mundane world. Many such men, and a few women, wandered away to remote rural areas where they devoted themselves to meditation, the study of yin and yang, medicinal herbs, music, or poetry.

Confucianism could be considered a philosophy rather than a religion, but in either case is central to the Chinese world-view. The original teachings of Confucius (c. 550–480 BCE) focused on humanistic ethics and moral conduct. He dismissed speculation about the supernatural and insisted on the importance of human relationships between men and women, parents and children, rulers and subjects. In later centuries, Confucianism became the state orthodoxy and came to dominate official culture and education. Its political expression was the veneration of the emperor as supreme ruler by virtue of a heavenly mandate and the creation of elaborate ritual around him. (Its role in the social system is outlined in Chapter 5.)

Islam was taken to China by merchants and soldiers in the 8th century. By the 16th, many Muslims were integrated in Chinese society, although in the 19th, under the influence of militant Sufi sects, there were Muslim revolts against Chinese rule in the region known as Chinese Turkestan, present-day Xinjiang. As well as some 20 million Sinified Muslims, there are today important minorities in western and southwestern provinces, numbering some 15 million. Most of these people are of central Asian descent and ethnicity, and in the 1990s their growing discontent with Chinese rule finally resulted in armed protests and incidents.

Finally, Christianity has been known in China since the seventh century. The present Christian community can trace its origins to a sixteenth-century Jesuit mission. Christianity was proscribed in 1721 because of its condemnation of Confucianism and ancestor worship. After the Opium War in the middle of the nineteenth century, the European imperial powers forced the reluctant Chinese government to permit Christian mission work. This concession marked the start of a century of intense activity by, mainly, British and American Protestant missionaries and French Roman Catholic ones. Evaluations of the missionary enterprise vary. Chinese nationalists and Communists stress the pro-imperialist and reactionary political actions of many missionary groups; some historians have praised their contributions to education, medical work and rural development. By 1949 there were approximately 3 million Chinese Catholics and 1 million Protestants. Churches were suppressed by the Communists between 1949 and 1978, but in the reform period grew tremendously in strength, reaching perhaps 30 million believers by the 1990s.

A strange phenomenon of the Communist period was the elevation of Mao Zedong to godlike status, especially during the Cultural Revolution. His portrait inundated private and public spaces, adorning streets, homes, trains, docks, schools and factories. Some 4 billion Mao badges were produced and worn almost compulsorily. Prisoners and dissidents had to bow down before Mao's image and confess their sins. At the same time, the state developed a whole range of quasi-religious symbols, rituals, and scriptures (the Little Red Book). Some of Mao's personality cult can be traced back to the techniques of government promoted in the Soviet Union, but it is also a modern recapitulation of traditional Chinese patterns: emperor worship, the deification of heroes, and household cults.

The Communist State and Religion

The CCP vigorously promoted anti-religious propaganda in the 1920s and 1930s, although it seldom engaged in violence against believers. Its analysis of religion was based on a crude understanding of Marx and Engels, and on the anti-clericalism of the Bolsheviks. Chinese communists made few contributions to the Marxist analysis, and even after their rise to power added little of theoretical interest to Soviet orthodoxy. The true communist state is not only an egalitarian, but also an atheist utopia. Thus one task of the CCP is to liberate believers from their religious bondage and to offer them the freedom of atheism; Party members themselves must be die-hard and militant atheists. However, this utopian aim frequently conflicted with political realities – for example, the need to unite the majority of the population, under Party leadership, in the war against the Japanese, or in economic modernization in the 1980s. The ideological rationale for tolerating religion in the atheist state is the theory of the 'united front', which was formulated in a number of articles by CCP leaders: the CCP should at times work even with anti-Communist elements, for example religious believers, to confront a common enemy (Mao, 1966–77b: 232–48). The united-front approach to religion is also related to policies on national minorities. Many non-Han peoples of the PRC live in sensitive border regions, are antagonistic to Chinese rule and are fervent religious believers. To reduce the potential for conflict and to consolidate national integrity, the central government has at times accorded them concessions, including freedom to practise religion.

From the early 1950s state treatment of religion degenerated to outright persecution, partly with explicit state endorsement and partly through extra-legal suppression by security forces, cadres and Red Guards. Many religious believers were victims of political campaigns designed to purge elements of the old society. Many more were criticized, arrested and imprisoned or deported for long periods in the anti-rightist campaign of 1957–8. In the late 1950s Protestant and Catholic churches were virtually outlawed. Buddhist and Taoist monasteries were likewise continually pressurized, and almost all closed. Most manifestations of popular religion also stopped.

Anti-religious frenzy reached a height in the Cultural Revolution. Ironically, many religious believers, including professional personnel, were already in prison, internal exile, or labour camp and thus safe from personal attack. But the Red Guards in particular did irreparable damage to temples, churches, mosques, religious libraries and works of art. The Cultural Revolution vigorously promoted atheism and drove religion further underground. The CCP leadership after 1978 explicitly criticized these activities although, rather than acknowledging the Party's own role, it blamed them on its customary scapegoat, the Gang of Four.

Religious Life in the Reform Period

In early 1982, the Party announced a new policy on religion, repudiating the earlier suppression of religion and promising greater freedom. However, while the new guidelines tolerated religion, they also stated that believers would be closely supervised and that activities falling outside defined limits would be quashed. Two kinds of illegal activity were targeted: 'criminal and counter-revolutionary activities hiding behind the facade of religion', and 'infiltration by hostile foreign forces'. Despite sporadic abuses, state monitoring of religious groups is now vastly better than in previous decades. A well-researched recent study *China: State Control of Religion* (Human Rights Watch/Asia, 1997) notes significant improvement in the treatment of religious believers, except for Tibetan Buddhists.

By the late 1980s, the rapid growth of religion alarmed CCP leaders, who realized that religious activities, especially the so-called 'Christianity Fever', were getting out of hand. The Party's anxiety seems to be based on several factors, primarily the risk that religious institutions might form power-bases outside Party control. Second, religious beliefs tend to be anti-materialist and theist and they are therefore an ideological challenge to Marxism, the state orthodoxy. Third, religious organizations might strengthen demands for autonomy among non-Han Chinese, for example in Xinjiang or Tibet. Fourth, the Party leadership was worried by the overthrow of the Soviet government and its satellite states in Eastern Europe, and aware of the role played by churches in the opposition to communist rule there. Perhaps most significantly, the Party claims that many religious organizations are infiltrated by 'hostile foreign forces'. This view is linked to 'peaceful evolution', the notion that the West, in particular the USA, is using ideological penetration as a strategy to overthrow the Chinese government. Among the hostile foreign forces allegedly infiltrating religious groups in the PRC are evangelical Protestants (for example, the Southern Baptist Church has been accused of working for the CIA), Roman Catholics (promoting the Vatican's interests), and sectarian groups from Taiwan, such as the Yiguandao.

The 1980s and 1990s saw a remarkable growth in Protestant communities in China. Some 10 million Protestants were meeting in state-approved churches by the 1990s. There was also a dynamic 'house-church' movement. During the years of repression, the faith survived in small home meetings that appear to have spread their influence during the 1960s and 1970s. In the 1980s, house churches expanded far beyond their original scope. Some of them developed extensive national and international networks, with thousands of members and even publishing and educational facilities. Some overseas observers have claimed that the house-church movement has tens of millions of adherents. Such claims should be treated with caution, but it does seem likely that the number of Protestants in China may have reached well over 20 million, making it in some respects the most important religious community in China.

Other religions also revived or grew in the reform period. After 1979, a state-approved Catholic church resumed operations. It has been active in building and reopening many churches and seminaries and publishing a substantial amount of Catholic literature. By the 1990s, it presided over a dynamic Catholic community which reportedly numbered around 6 million. In addition there is a large and active non-official Catholic church, which has closer ties to the Vatican. Perhaps surprisingly, the indigenous religions were slower to revive, but they appear now to have developed substantial followings. There are Buddhist monasteries in all provinces of China, some of which attract millions of pilgrims every year, although their religious function is certainly mixed with, if not compromised by, the monasteries' role as tourist venues. Buddhists also operate many training centres and presses and organize groups of lay believers in major cities. Taoists were persecuted more heavily than Buddhists because of an alleged connection with secret societies and because Taoism was seen by the CCP as closely connected with old, feudal practices. But in the 1990s there were signs of a revival of

Taoism also, and of local religious practices such as ancestor worship, geomancy and processions: some of the latter even ended up in confrontations with local Communist cadres.

The revival of religion has been one of the great surprises of the period of reform. Religious belief and practice appeared to have been almost eliminated by the years of persecution, but are now widespread throughout the country. Besides the formal or institutionalized religions, there is a vast subculture of activities that may loosely be considered quasi-religious or, perhaps, superstitious. Countless Chinese practise meditation or 'internal' martial arts such as Taijiquan; many believe in geomancy and astrology, or use the concepts of yin and yang in matters of health or diet; many go to monasteries; classical ethical and philosophical ideas are still widely respected and religious literature of all kinds easily available. As outlined above, China's traditional religious life was multifarious, encompassing many kinds of beliefs and practices with all kinds of local and personal varieties. It seems that by the 1990s a modern version of the situation had emerged, with an equally multifarious, or even chaotic, kaleidoscope of religious practices under the watchful, and at times resentful, eyes of a hostile state.

7

China's International Relations

The extent to which China is re-emerging as the preponderant power in Asia, and the likely consequences of its new status, are controversial topics in contemporary international relations. Some analysts suggest that, by the mid-twenty-first century, China will have become not just the leading Asian power, but a superpower on the scale of the USA. The extraordinary Chinese economic boom of the 1980s and 1990s underlies these predictions. It is generally accepted that economic strength is a good guide to military–strategic capability. If the more optimistic assessments of its economic potential are realized, then the PRC, or more realistically, the so-called 'Greater China' conglomerate, would have a solid basis for military and diplomatic strength in the twenty-first century. Presumably such an outcome would imply some sort of political settlement between Beijing and Taiwan.

On the other hand, the perception of China as a regional hegemon, let alone a future superpower, is a recent one, and may reflect a short-term assessment of the balance of forces. It should be remembered that, since 1945, the USA has been, and still remains, by far the strongest military power in the Asia Pacific. The region was a major area of confrontation throughout the Cold War, and the USA maintained its military presence after the collapse of the USSR. Intellectual fashions change rapidly; until the late 1980s, most observers would have named Japan as the emerging regional force in east Asia. Despite economic difficulties in the 1990s, Japan remains far ahead of China in productivity and technology, and could rapidly expand its military capability if necessary. Looking more broadly at Asia as a whole, there is a long-term implicit competition for leadership between India and China, which has by no means been decided in China's favour. Furthermore, the internal foundations of Chinese power look more fragile when closely inspected; we have already described problems with China's aging rust-belt industries, the potential for social unrest and disaffection in Tibet and Xinjiang.

Despite these qualifications, the perception of a resurgent China has provoked a lively foreign policy debate in· the USA. Conservative politicians regard China as a threat to regional and global security, and call on the US government to adopt a strategy of 'containment' analogous to that applied to the Soviet Union during the Cold War. In the late 1990s, however, the declared policy of the US government was to 'engage' rather than 'contain' China. US officials several times reaffirmed that the USA did not intend to treat China as a Cold War enemy, but would carry on a strategic dialogue with China and expand areas of cooperation. A premise for both sides in the containment–engagement debate is that China is once again a force to be reckoned with.

Main Aims of China's Foreign Policy

The principal aim of China's foreign policy is the restoration and defence of territorial integrity, which for the PRC leadership necessarily implies the reintegration of Taiwan.

Since the May 4th demonstration of 1919, the recovery of lost territory and national pride has been a constant refrain of China's political movements. Almost the whole population has been taught about the century or more of humiliation and exploitation inflicted by imperialist powers. This view of history is rarely questioned and still plays a major role in shaping policy.

A Ministry of Foreign Affairs document published in Hong Kong provides insight into the views of the Chinese leadership (*Tung Hsiang*, 14 July 1996: 20–1). The document states that China will never tolerate:

> intervention or interference in state sovereignty and internal affairs by any foreign government or parliament, foreign group or international organization [and will not] compromise . . . on any issue which involves . . . state sovereignty and internal affairs . . . even at the expense of any political or economic relationship,

[and that] the Taiwan issue, the Tibetan issue and the Hong Kong issue fall entirely within the category of China's sovereignty and internal affairs.

In a personal addendum, the then chairman of the NPC, Qiao Shi, writes:

China will never tolerate interference and intervention by hegemonism and the West. The Chinese people will never forget the history of Western countries invading, plundering, bullying and oppressing China.

A note from Liu Huaqing, representing the military, reads:

We must solemnly tell hegemonism and Western powers that on the issues of Taiwan, Tibet and Hong Kong . . . any interference and intervention are futile.

The second major priority of China's foreign policy is to promote the national goal of economic development, which will also provide the advanced technology crucial for military–strategic reasons. China's economic strategy since 1978 has depended on attracting foreign investment and on maintaining access to export markets: this strategy demands a stable international environment and good relations with advanced economies. A central feature of foreign policy has been to improve China's international status – for example, by ending revolutionary propaganda and support for overseas communist groups; resolving many border issues; promoting diplomatic, cultural, and trade ties; and being flexible on a range of issues in the UN and elsewhere.

A third important strand of policy is to promote China's security interests in the Asia Pacific, a region where rapid economic growth has permitted massive increases in military spending in the past decade, and where there are several potential areas for conflict. There are obviously tensions between these three goals, although at least until the late 1990s Chinese foreign policy could overall be accounted relatively successful in combining them. In the longer term, it remains to be seen whether China will be able to complete its project of national reunification without, to a greater or lesser extent, upsetting the cordial relations with other powers on which its economic prosperity depends. While China defines the issues of

Taiwan and Tibet as internal affairs, other powers see them as legitimate causes for international concern.

The Taiwan Issue

Since Chiang Kaishek reconstituted the 'Republic of China' (ROC) on the island of Taiwan at the end of the civil war, the governments of the ROC and the PRC have both claimed to be the only legitimate government of the whole of China. The former claimed legitimacy as the regime that had united China and defeated the Japanese; the latter, as victors in the civil war and liberators of the oppressed. Until 1972, the ROC's claim was internationally recognized, and Taiwan was a key base in the US anti-Communist containment strategy. US commitment became evident when the PRC threatened invasion of the island in the mid-1950s: in spring 1955, the Americans explicitly threatened to use tactical nuclear weapons in the event of an assault on Taiwan, after which the PRC government defused the situation.

However, following the Nixon–Mao agreements of the early 1970s, the USA recognized the government in Beijing, which led to a rapid deterioration in Taiwan's international position as it was removed from the UN and lost diplomatic recognition by most foreign governments. The ROC's isolation was intensified because both Taibei and Beijing refused to have diplomatic relations with any state that recognized its rival. Most nations have followed US practice in handling this problem: they have formal ties with Beijing and conduct relations with Taiwan through a number of semi-official offices, institutes, councils, delegations, etc. which in effect conduct diplomatic business.

In the 1980s, relations between the two states improved. Neither government relented on its basic policy, but economic contacts increased dramatically, mainly through trade and investment from Taiwan into south China, filtered through Hong Kong. Taiwan's booming economy made it one of the most powerful states in East Asia. But despite improving relations with the PRC and an apparently peaceful international environment, Taibei maintained a high level of military preparedness, and the USA and other Western countries continued to sell it advanced military equipment. This policy proved to be a wise precaution because in the mid-1990s, Beijing became increasingly aggressive towards the ROC, in contrast to its conciliatory behaviour of the late 1980s. There were several reasons for this. The old generation of CCP veterans has effectively retired from politics, but the leadership remains deeply frustrated over their lack of success with Taiwan. They are especially alarmed at the growth of an independence movement on Taiwan which demands complete secession from China and aims to create a new nation-state. In March 1996, Beijing authorized highly provocative military exercises just outside Taiwanese waters, with warnings that any further moves towards independence would be met with an invasion. There are good reasons to take this threat seriously; as we saw above, Chinese leaders seem prepared to risk economic development to prevent Taiwanese independence.

There is a more optimistic scenario in the long term: that Taibei and Beijing could produce some kind of agreement along the 'one country, two systems' model, developed by Beijing with reference to Taiwan before being applied to Hong Kong. The Taibei government has responded with counter-suggestions, such as 'one country, two governments' or 'one country, two areas', and with the suggestion that the state of civil war should be formally ended. Many observers hope for a political reconciliation, that would allow both sides to retain face and postpone difficult decisions until a very distant future. However, the 1996 confrontations have certainly reduced the likelihood of such compromises in the short and even medium term. The bottom line for Taiwan is that it will not allow PRC armed forces onto the island. Beijing in contrast, is unwilling to allow a province to be militarily independent.

Taiwan has fought a determined rearguard action against diplomatic isolation. Its principal resource is its enormously successful economy, which to some extent compensates for its political weakness. It has upgraded its commercial, quasi-governmental offices in many countries to the level where they act as quasi-embassies. Another tactic has been to join international organizations, despite strong PRC objections (for example, the Asian Development Bank (ADB) and the Asia Pacific Economic Cooperation (APEC)). President Lee Teng-hui made a visit to the USA in June 1995. This was one of a series of high-profile, 'private' visits to states with which Beijing has diplomatic relations. The aim appears to be diplomatic recognition in all but name. In terms of formal diplomatic relations, however, Taibei continues to lose out. On 1 January 1998, Taiwan's last big diplomatic partner, South Africa, transferred its allegiance to Beijing. Only a few tiny states, including some Caribbean islands and the Vatican, still recognize the ROC government.

Review of Twentieth-Century Chinese Foreign Policy

Republican China

In the warlord period, when the central government was reduced to a legal fiction, China, by definition, did not follow an independent foreign policy. Rather, it was an arena within which other powers pursued their own rivalries. Japan's growing power was a major feature of the period; by the 1930s, the Japanese dominated northeast China, and were pushing south. Chiang Kaishek's government came under constant diplomatic and military pressure that culminated in the full-scale invasion of China by Japan in 1937. In response, Chiang sought support from the USA and, during the war years, relied heavily on the USA not only for military aid but also for revenue to underwrite the day-to-day operations of the regime. Despite evidence of massive corruption and misuse of funds, US support continued after the defeat of Japan, throughout the civil war, and after Chiang's retreat to Taiwan.

PRC Policy under Mao Zedong

Mao Zedong, notwithstanding misgivings about the Soviet leadership, decided to 'lean to one side' in the post-war confrontation between the USSR and the USA. In December 1950 China signed a thirty-year treaty of friendship with the USSR, despite considerable mistrust on both sides. The Chinese leadership's motives for signing the treaty included their commitment to communist ideology, and the fact that the Soviet Union was the only existing model for construction of a planned economy; they also expected to receive economic aid, technical assistance and concessions on disputed borders. Alliance with the Soviets was further intended to deter a US military adventure. Chinese leaders feared that a US attack was imminent: Western propaganda classed the PRC along with the USSR as part of the 'world communist threat'; and US and Chinese troops had already fought major battles in Korea.

By the mid-1950s China had begun to play an independent role in Asian regional affairs and in 1954, helped draw up the Geneva Treaty that ended French colonial rule in Vietnam. In 1955 it helped to organize a conference of Asian and African states in Bandung, Indonesia, which set up a grouping of non-aligned, third-world states. The initiative established China as an unofficial champion of developing countries.

In the mid and late 1950s relations between China and the Soviet Union cooled, and eventually degenerated into open hostility. The Sino–Soviet split developed gradually, starting with political and ideological disagreements. Mao was unhappy with the handling of the 1956 Hungarian crisis that culminated in a Soviet invasion. The Chinese were incensed that they had not been consulted before Khrushchev made his secret speech denouncing Stalin. Mao opposed Khrushchev's policy of peaceful coexistence with the West, and the 'reformist' policies being pursued by pro-Soviet communist parties. The Soviets, for their part, became increasingly horrified as the disaster created by the Great Leap Forward unfolded.

The USSR took the first step towards breaking the alliance by cancelling help in nuclear development and many economic projects. In response, China stepped up the ideological attack and encouraged Maoist factions to form within, and later split from, pro-Moscow communist parties around the world. In 1962, Moscow continued to supply military aircraft to India, as Chinese and Indian forces fought in the Himalayas, marking the transition from alliance to outright hostility. Increasing tension culminated in a large-scale battle on the Ussuri river in 1969. There is some evidence that the USSR considered carrying out major air-strikes on China that year. Some Russian sources also claim that defence minister Lin Biao's failed *coup d'état* was to have been accompanied by a Russian military thrust into China through Xinjiang.

By 1971, PRC courting of the developing and non-aligned states was beginning to reap diplomatic rewards. Pressure from developing countries helped reverse the anomaly that had allowed Taiwan to retain China's seat at the UN. As China had been one of the 'big five' powers at the end of the second World War, the PRC inherited a permanent seat on the Security Council. Such a dramatic shift could not have occurred without the agreement of Washington. By the early 1970s the balance of forces in Asia was shifting against the USA. US forces were facing probable defeat at the hands of the Vietcong and North Vietnamese forces. Victory for the Vietnamese would mean a massive increase in the influence of the Soviet Union in the region. This prospect was no more welcome to the Chinese than it was to the Americans; and it was in these circumstances that Washington and Beijing sought a rapprochement and laid the basis for President Nixon's dramatic visit to China in 1972. The deal worked out between Kissinger and Nixon on the US side, and Zhou Enlai and Mao, called for China to oppose the USSR in Asia; in return, the US government would use its influence to prevent a Soviet attack on China.

The Chinese leadership dressed their new policy in revolutionary Marxist clothes by calling for a 'global united front' against the USSR and what it termed 'social imperialism'. During the 1970s and early 1980s, the logic of this policy led the Chinese communists to adopt strange political allies. They expressed support for the CIA-sponsored *coup d'état* of Chile's General Pinochet against an elected socialist government; agreed to defend Thailand's right-wing military government against communist Vietnam; and supported the radical Islamist Mujahadeen against the Soviet-backed Afghan government.

Even before the 1970s, Communist rhetoric masked the fact that foreign policy was essentially based on national interest. Although the PRC had endorsed what it termed 'wars of national liberation' and supported some insurgency movements – for example, in the Philippines and Malaysia – it did so more often in words than by concrete assistance. It very seldom used its own armed forces overseas. On the few occasions when China and Chinese-backed parties became seriously embroiled in other countries' internal affairs, they usually formed alliances with nationalist leaders who, while not socialists, expressed anti-imperialist sentiments.

Such meddling was rarely successful and in Indonesia in 1965 led to disaster, when hundreds of thousands of communists and ethnic Chinese were massacred amid allegations of a Chinese-backed coup plot. During the Vietnam war, when a neighbouring communist country was facing the overwhelming firepower of the USA, China's involvement was limited to providing labour battalions, arms, and possibly military personnel. Mao, while publicly hailing the Vietnamese 'People's War' against the USA, privately argued against strong inner-party opposition, that China should restrict its aid to the Vietnamese (Karnow, 1990: 441).

One view of the Cold War period portrays a world divided into ideological camps, the 'free world' and the 'communist bloc', the latter divided between Moscow and Beijing loyalists. Another useful perspective is to view the USA, the Soviet Union and China as forming a strategic triangle, within which the three players shifted their allegiances, irrespective of ideology, to gain geo-strategic advantages. By far the weakest of the three players, the Chinese utilized the conflict between the other two powers quite skilfully. Certainly after the rapprochement with the USA, China profited from the deadlock between the two superpowers, which allowed it relative freedom from military threat to pursue its own modernization goals until the collapse of the USSR, by which time China had acquired a secure status in Asia due to its successful economic development.

In the end, Maoist China's ideological influence turned out to be limited and short-lived. Although it set up Maoist communist parties in many countries, with a few exceptions, most notably in India, the parties failed to put down roots. Maoism enjoyed a brief vogue amongst students in Europe and the USA in the late 1960s, but fledgling parties soon disintegrated. Ultra-radical, but futile gestures by Red Guards, such as attacks on foreign embassy personnel, helped to discredit the movement. Finally, in the early 1970s, China's apparent alignment with the USA, the chief 'imperialist' power, utterly confused and demoralized its overseas friends on the Left. From that time on, Maoism outside China remained little more than a sect. It had become evident to all, that support for 'world revolution' was a poor second to China's national interest as a factor in determining foreign policy.

Normalization under Deng Xiaoping

In Mao's last years, the entente with the USA in place, and the Cultural Revolution little more than a slogan, China ended its residual, limited support for communist insurgents in southeast Asia. Officially, the PRC announced a policy of establishing formal, state-to-state relations with capitalist countries, but reserved the right of the CCP to support insurgency. In practice, pro-China insurgents were abandoned, and China normalized relations with Malaysia, Thailand and the Philippines in 1974–5. A consensus emerged in the CCP leadership that economic recovery was the most urgent priority, and by the late 1970s Deng Xiaoping was working to improve relations with the USA and pro-US governments. The initial aim was to obtain advanced technology to carry out the 'Four Modernizations', but as the role of market mechanisms in its economy deepened China increasingly sought stability, investment and access to overseas markets. In November 1978, Deng visited Thailand and other southeast Asian countries to clarify that China sought cordial international relations and would not support communist insurgency.

While normalizing relations with former 'capitalist' enemies, China continued to pursue an aggressively anti-Soviet policy. In 1979 the PRC embarked on a costly military adventure, when it attacked the Soviet Union's ally, Vietnam. The attack was intended to punish Vietnam for ousting China's Khmer Rouge allies from power in Cambodia, but the PLA was soundly defeated by the battle-hardened Vietnamese: over 25,000 Chinese troops were killed in a short, bloody war that exposed the weakness of China's armed forces, above all the obsolescence of their equipment. Characteristically, Deng Xiaoping gained factional advantage from the setback by blaming the radical doctrine of 'people's war' for the army's poor performance. The isolation of Vietnam remained a principal aim of China's southern strategy: until the late 1990s, Beijing subsidized arms exports to Thailand, and vigorously supported the pariah Khmer Rouge.

In 1980, Chinese entry into the World Bank and the International Monetary Fund (IMF) appeared as a symbolic acceptance of the capitalist system and a statement of the leadership's intention to integrate China into the world economy. All pretensions to a foreign policy based on revolutionary Marxism were abandoned: China now sought, and largely achieved, peaceful, normal relations with all its neighbours. Within the context of an overall, pro-Western orientation, China also made an effort to normalize relations with the USSR from 1982 onwards. Peaceful evolution of Communist China into a prosperous, possibly even democratic state, seemed a realistic scenario to some Western analysts.

In 1989, however, the communist world, from Beijing to Prague, was convulsed by mass protests. Eastern European governments fell and the Soviet government received its notice to quit. Deng Xiaoping's regime survived at the cost of a bloody massacre of protesters. The collapse of communist governments in eastern Europe was a catastrophe for the Chinese leadership, all the more so because its envoys had recently visited East Germany and Romania to urge a crackdown (Foot, 1995: 237). Before Tian'anmen Square, China had been seen as leading the reform of the communist world. Now it was one of only a handful of surviving communist powers and, briefly, an international pariah after the repression in Beijing.

In 1991 the moribund Soviet government collapsed, and the Gulf war against Iraq demonstrated the overwhelming dominance of US military power. The bi-polar world of the Cold War appeared to have been supplanted by a uni-polar 'New World Order'. With one of the major players removed from the board, China could no longer exploit its position in the 'strategic triangle' with America and Russia. In the face of economic sanctions applied after Tian'anmen, some factions in the leadership feared that the USA planned to impose an economic blockade on China. In practice, the Chinese played a weak hand rather cleverly, exchanging neutrality in the Gulf conflict, and their all-important UN Security Council vote, for an early lifting of sanctions. By the mid-1990s with the economy booming again, the government had stabilized its domestic position and had mended its relationships with foreign governments, who were generally more keen to promote business than to preach democracy.

The Asian Context in the 1990s

Until the late 1980s, the confrontation between the USA and the USSR meant that regional rivalries in Asia were refracted through the prism of the Cold War. By the late 1990s relationships among the Asian powers had become more fluid, as states determined policy according to a calculation of their strategic interests, rather than 'camp' allegiance. Asia may be seen as a potential cockpit of conflicting powers, analogous to pre-1914 Europe, in which shifting patterns of alliance may lead to misunderstandings and a regional war. The principal players in the Asian balance of power game are the USA, China, Japan, Russia and India, with a supporting cast of Taiwan, Korea, Vietnam, Indonesia, Thailand, Malaysia, the Philippines and Singapore. Military spending is increasing across the whole region, except in crisis-hit Russia and North Korea. According to the International Institute for Strategic Studies, Japan increased its military budget by 87.5 per cent between 1990 and 1995 (Kalder, 1996: 140). Indonesia increased its spending by 73.3 per cent over the same period, and took over the entire ex-East German navy (Figure 7.1). China is already a nuclear power, and is building up a blue-water navy and acquiring ICBMs. India dramatically demonstrated an apparent nuclear capability when it exploded a series of test devices in May 1998. Despite its economic crisis, Russia retains large quantities of tactical and strategic nuclear weapons in the region; the USA has similar capabilities based in Okinawa. The Korean peninsular is the most militarized region on earth, with nearly 2 million troops under arms.

Figure 7.1   Military expenditure, 1991–4

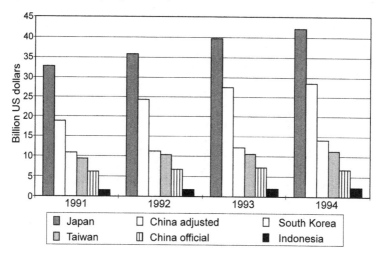

Japan   China adjusted   South Korea
Taiwan   China official   Indonesia

In contrast to most other regions, military expenditure in East Asia grew in the aftermath of the Cold War; for China, we give both the low, official figure and a PPP estimate: in either case, Japan's spending far outstrips China's.

Source: Calder, 1996: 14; original source of data Institute for Strategic Studies.

As well as large and growing armed forces, there are a number of flashpoints in the region which, if mishandled, could lead to confrontation. First in importance are the unresolved outstanding issues of the Chinese and Korean civil wars. An attempt by China to retake Taiwan by force would almost certainly lead to a major war. By the late 1990s the famine-ridden North Korean state was on the point of collapse but still capable of lashing out in its death-throes. Any outbreak of fighting might draw in China, Japan or the USA. There are also a number of unresolved territorial disputes. Most importantly, China claims the Paracel and Spratly islands in the South China sea, and has demonstrated its willingness to use force to counter rival claims by Vietnam and the Philippines, most notably when it occupied Mischief Reef in 1995. The Senkaku islands, northeast of Taiwan are also disputed between China and Japan, and there were fierce protests in Hong Kong and Taiwan in 1996 when a right-wing group raised the Japanese flag on the islands. Japan also claims the Kurile islands, near to its northeast coast, which have been administered by Russia since 1945 (Map 7.1).

Underlying some of the disputes over islands is the issue of oil. China is already a net oil importer and its consumption is set to grow massively. It is desperate to strike oil on what it regards as its own continental shelf, and determined to rebuff all counter-claims to the resources. Japan has no oil of its own and its oil imports pass along sea-lanes which run close to the disputed island groups. Free passage along these shipping routes is a matter of vital national interest to Japan. Conversely, control of these routes would allow China to exert pressure on Japan. China has close relations with Iran and other oil-rich Islamic states – a factor that could increase its leverage still further.

China's Key Relationships

The USA

No grasp of international relations in the contemporary Asia Pacific region is possible without understanding the enormous role played by the USA. US victory over Japan in the Second World War left it with overwhelming military superiority in the region. But American involvement goes back much further than the 1940s; the Spanish–American war of 1898 marked the arrival of the USA as a regional power. Amid patriotic fervour, the USA annexed the islands of Hawaii and took control of the Philippines. Since that time, US power, welcomed by some, opposed by others, has been an unavoidable reality in Asian politics.

There is a strong ideological element in US foreign policy and Americans were often perceived in Asia as less 'imperialist' than the European powers. In 1899 the USA proposed an 'open door' policy for China: instead of territorial concessions (sought by Britain, France, Russia, Germany and Japan), the USA insisted on equal treatment for each of the imperialist powers. In fact, this policy was designed to preserve US commercial interests, without entailing the difficulty of occupation. But the USA continued to promote itself as role model in Asia, especially during the presidency of Woodrow Wilson (1913–21), who believed that America had a mission to promote global peace and human rights. Ideals of human rights, self-determination, and racial equality are still upheld, in theory at

Map 7.1   China's neighbours, regional flashpoints, and disputed territories

least, by American foreign-policy officials: echoes of them could be glimpsed in President Bush's 'New World Order'.

In the late 1940s, President Truman initiated a new paradigm, which was upheld by successive administrations. The 'Truman Doctrine' stated that the USSR and its allies (then including China) were expansionist and totalitarian, and had to be 'contained' by economic, political, and military power. Communism would be confronted anywhere in the world, at almost any cost. An early initiative, support for the GMD in the Chinese Civil War, ended in bitter failure and recriminations; US military action in Korea ended in stalemate in 1953. These failures persuaded both political parties in the USA of the need for overwhelming military strength. Subsequent administrations authorized massive investment in submarines, aircraft carriers, nuclear and conventional weapons, and the maintenance of hundreds of thousands of American troops in Asia, mostly based in Japan and Korea. Additionally the USA distributed lavish economic aid to Japan, South Korea, Taiwan, and several countries in southeast Asia, including South Vietnam and the Philippines. Results were very mixed. The Philippines degenerated into the extremes of political decadence and corruption under Marcos and American efforts in Vietnam ended in humiliating defeat. On the other hand Japan, Taiwan and some other countries evolved into successful, prosperous, democratic states under US tutelage.

After the end of the Cold War, the US establishment appeared to be split as to its future role in the Asian security order. The US military presence in Asia is enormously costly. Some factions in Washington argue that it is a luxury the USA can no longer afford, and that responsibility for security issues should revert to the Asian powers themselves. However, there are also factions who insist on the need to enforce security and defend interests in the region, at almost any cost, often on the grounds of opposing a supposed threat from China.

Relations between the USA and China in the 1990s have been dominated by US concerns about trade and human rights. China's persistent trade surplus with the USA has been the cause of considerable political friction between the two powers. Washington accuses China of unfair trade practices, including dumping, counterfeiting goods and restricting access to its home markets. It has repeatedly blocked China's application to join the World Trade Organization (WTO) and grants Most Favoured Nation (MFN) status to China only on a year-by-year basis. Since 1989, groups of members of Congress have forced an annual vote on the issue, raising both economic and human rights issues. Although the objections have always been defeated, the votes are a regular occasion for airing anti-Chinese views in Washington.

There is a danger that political hostility to China will mesh with asymmetry in the trade relationship to worsen relations. There are sections of opinion in America that would like to destabilize the last major communist power. Others see China as a future threat to the USA's global position. A combination of economic, ideological and strategic premises underlie the arguments of the 'contain China' lobby. There is also a strong pro-China lobby in Washington. They argue that the US trade deficit is a temporary problem, and that the general direction of China's political evolution is positive. Above all, they point to the potential benefits to the American economy of China's enormous consumer market. Surveys suggest that a majority of senior business managers take a pro-China stance and support a positive approach to opening up China to American business.

In the late 1990s, the partisans of engagement rather than containment were in the ascendant in US government circles, and China for its part was determined to remain on good terms with its largest marketplace. Jiang Zemin made a successful state visit to the USA in 1997, reciprocated by President Clinton's visit to Beijing in June 1998. But the Chinese remain suspicious that Washington's engagement policy is part of a strategy to undermine the Communist state (see p. 201). However much they value friendly relations, they are determined to oppose what they see as US hegemonism. In 1990 the Chinese government, desperate to break out of its isolation, acquiesced in US-led action against Iraq. By contrast, in 1998, it played a leading role, with France and Russia, in forcing the USA and Britain to withdraw the threat of military action against Saddam Hussein.

Japan

Japan is one of China's major trading partners. It has enormous investments in China and is also host to many thousands of immigrant Chinese workers, many of them from Shanghai. Despite extensive economic ties, China's relationship with Japan is inevitably coloured by the traumatic experience of occupation in the 1930s and 1940s. The Chinese government exploits the war record to gain moral advantage in negotiations with Japan, but prevents public displays of anti-Japanese feeling. In the freer climates of Taiwan and

Hong Kong, occasional protests and boycotts demonstrate that hostility to Japan remains strong in a section of the public. China still uses Japan's wartime aggression to argue that special restrictions must be imposed on Japan's right to raise and deploy armed forces.

James Hsiung (1993) argues that the US–China–USSR triangle has been superseded by a US–China–Japan one. China benefited considerably by exploiting tensions between the USA and USSR: it hopes that in the coming decades it can again benefit from tensions likely to arise between the USA and Japan. In the early 1990s, China prioritized better relations with Japan, which was not as vocal as Western countries after the 1989 massacre. Since then, the Senkaku dispute (see above) has soured relations somewhat, but China badly needs Japanese investment and economic cooperation; alternate warming and cooling of relations are partly a bargaining strategy.

It is often assumed that the current military balance is heavily in China's favour. This is not necessarily so. According to the officially published figures Japan spends over six times more than China on defence annually (Kalder, 1996: 18). Even after adjustment, the International Institute for Strategic Studies estimates that China's real annual military spending is only just over half that of Japan. Energy is a possible cause of conflict between China and Japan. The Senkaku islands are believed to be rich in oil, and both sides have starting drilling in disputed areas. Taiwan and the Korean peninsula are other potential trouble spots. Both China and Japan see these countries as falling within their natural spheres of influence (both have been Japanese colonies during the twentieth century). Handling Korean reunification will be a crucial test of Sino–Japanese relations. China has had diplomatic relations with South Korea since 1992; it wants to see a peaceful reunification without humiliation of its long-term Northern ally. Its ability to wield influence on the Korean peninsula, where Japan desperately wants a peaceful outcome, adds to its bargaining powers. In the longer term, China and Japan are the two obvious contenders for hegemony in Asia, and there is clearly potential for rivalry and conflict if relations are not handled extremely carefully.

Russia

In the late 1990s Russia and China discovered a number of common interests. China wanted to modernize its armed forces and Russia was desperate to find markets for its arms, among the few of its industrial products that were saleable overseas. The Chinese found Western lectures on human rights irksome, while it suited the Russian government to occasionally adopt anti-Western positions to appease nationalist public opinion. Both governments were irritated by American rhetoric about a 'New World Order', with its implication that a 'uni-polar' world, with the USA as the dominant power, had replaced the bi-polar Cold War era.

These factors lay behind the announcement in April 1997 of a new 'strategic partnership' between China and Russia. Russian defence minister Rodionov and his Chinese counterpart, Chi Haotian, stated that the understanding was intended to last well into the twenty-first century. Its main points were that China would buy Russian weapons; Russia recognized Taiwan and Tibet as inseparable parts of China, and would oppose Western interference in China's internal affairs; China would support Russia in opposing the eastward expansion of NATO; and the borders between China and the former USSR would be progressively de-militarized. Rodionov stated that 'Russia and China want peace without the hegemony of some countries over others, without leaders or those who are led, and based on the principle of sovereign equality of all countries' (Interfax News Agency, 14 April 1997).

Some observers believe Russia took the initiative in proposing the agreement, after the West invited ex-Warsaw Pact countries to join NATO. The Kremlin saw NATO's eastward expansion as both a threat and a humiliation, and looked to the China for support. It is extremely unlikely that China would jeopardize economic links with the West by agreeing to anything approaching a military alliance with Russia, even if this was on offer; but appearing to consider the idea could serve China's purposes well. The announcement of a political understanding, leaving the door open to further developments, is a warning for Washington to adjust its policy.

Despite the new understanding, there are factors that tend to pull the two countries apart. Russia has long been concerned that its under-populated and remote eastern regions could be overwhelmed by attack, or simply large-scale immigration, from China. Given the long history of enmity, mutual mistrust between the two countries at grass-roots' level remains strong, despite the new friendship at the leadership level. The USSR trained a whole generation of military strategists and Sinologists on the basis of a China threat, and even highly educated Russians often express their fear of China in terms of crude, anti-Chinese racism. In Siberia and the Russian Far East, the population, impoverished by economic crisis, resents Chinese economic migrants and traders. These feelings are often exploited by local politicians and reduce the Russian government's room for manoeuvre especially on the question of settling territorial disputes with the Chinese.

Southeast and Northeast Asia

Although Chinese leaders do not spell it out openly, they probably believe China has a historical right to influence in southeast Asia. Since 1978, Chinese leaders have taken pains to build good relations with most nations in the region, and on the whole have been successful. Certainly, Chinese economic and political influence in southeast Asia is increasing rapidly, and China has attracted heavy investment from overseas Chinese businesses throughout the region. An ideal outcome for the Chinese would be to forge an under-standing, or alliance, with ASEAN, which would make a very powerful regional power bloc. In Indochina, a central objective has been the isolation of Vietnam, to prevent that country achieving significant power in the region. In pursuit of this aim, China has subsidized arms sales to Myanmar and Thailand and given massive aid to the Khmer Rouge in Cambodia. Apart from tension with Vietnam over other issues, the most likely point of friction in the region is conflict over the Spratly Islands and shipping lanes, discussed above.

China–Korean relations are complex, and important for the rest of the world because of China's influence on the renegade North Korean regime. China needs a peaceful Korean peninsula to continue with its own modernization and, to gain this, appears willing to pressure the North Korean regime when it threatens confrontation with the West, as has been seen a number of times in crises over North Korea's nuclear programme. Since the North Korean government admits few other outside pressures, this position gives China some bargaining power with the USA and with Japan. In 1992, China and South Korea took the historic step of establishing formal diplomatic relations which served Beijing by further isolating Taiwan: South Korea, like Taiwan, was a US client state in the Cold War, and the two shared extreme anti-communist sentiments. The PRC and South Korea share some economic objectives. Both are keen to promote Korean investment in China, especially in regions close to the border. In some ways, the division of Korea suits China, which has influence in both North and South. If unification comes about, China would like to see it take place at a pace and in a manner that is suitable to its own needs and avoids a humiliating collapse of yet another Marxist regime (Hsiung, 1993: 78–9).

India

Through the 1960s, and continuing into the 1970s, Sino–Indian relations were tense. In part, the tension arose from the 1962 war and unresolved border disputes. Another important factor was that India had a close relationship with the USSR, which had agreed large-scale deliveries of military materiel on a deferred payment basis. The Indian subcontinent was the scene of regional and international strategic rivalries, involving China, India, Pakistan, the USA and the USSR. It was not until 1976 that China and India resumed diplomatic relations, and there were few signs of rapprochement before 1980. Relations between the two greatest countries in Asia were, in effect, frozen, with little trade or diplomatic activity.

However the Deng regime took steps to improve relations and both sides made concessions at border talks, attended by Chinese premier Hua Guofeng, held in Delhi in 1980. More substantial progress was made in three rounds of discussions held in 1988 (when Indian prime minister Rajiv Gandhi visited Beijing), 1993, and 1996. The governments concluded a wide range of agreements in science and technology, civil aviation, control of narcotics and telecommunications among other sectors. There was substantial progress towards defusing military tensions. A high-level joint working group addressed the border issue, hotline communications and exchange visits were established between military commands and a series of confidence-building and arms-control measures for the border regions were agreed.

Further, China apparently stopped supporting separatist, anti-Indian, or insurgent movements in Kashmir, Nepal and elsewhere, while India indicated it would be less tolerant of pro-Tibetan activities. Trade between the two states increased dramatically. India permitted the first Sino–Indian joint venture, in steel production, in 1993, and overtook Pakistan as a trading partner in 1994. The Chinese rationale for improved relations is apparent: it conforms to a strategy for economic modernization by promoting a peaceful international environment. Although China's security preoccupations are more intense towards the east, policy-makers recognize the vital importance of stability on the Indian subcontinent. Moreover, major shifts in the international environment permitted the changes. India was obliged to make a strategic realignment after the collapse of the USSR which, among other consequences, meant that the Indian armed forces could not rely on subsidized weapons and even faced uncertainties in obtaining spare parts for their existing armoury. Another factor was the concern expressed by Western powers, headed by the USA, over nuclear proliferation on the subcontinent. The international community obviously favoured a reduction in tensions between Pakistan and India, and hoped that Beijing would perform a restraining role.

Despite the improvements, the two countries' interests have proved hard to reconcile. The formation, in 1998, of a government dominated by the Hindu nationalist Bharatiya Janata Party (BJP) appeared to herald a distinct cooling of relations. In May 1998, Indian defence minister George Fernandes strongly criticized Chinese policy in remarks widely interpreted as defining China as the principal threat to India's security. Within days, the Indian government braved international condemnation and probable economic sanctions when it carried out a number of underground nuclear test explosions. When Beijing's ally, Pakistan responded with its own tests, China appeared in danger of becoming embroiled in a regional crisis; India has long accused China of secretly supplying missiles and nuclear technology to Pakistan. The BJP appears determined to strongly reinforce Indian claims to hegemony in South Asia. Now developing fast, India is the only country in the region to come close to China in population, territory and economic potential. Apart from China's involvement with Pakistan, there are plenty of other issues that could act as catalyst for a return to conflict. There is a growing Chinese naval presence in the Indian Ocean (where China has acquired port facilities in Myanmar) which challenges traditional Indian preponderance. The Chinese still resent the asylum and support given by India to the Dalai Lama; and the important border dispute is still unresolved.

A Note on the 'Overseas Chinese'

PRC relations with the rest of the world, for example Europe, tend to focus on trade ties in the interests of modernization. It is a member of the UN Security Council and plays a role in other international organizations, but generally not a proactive one. In this respect, it is similar to several other Asian states. There may be cultural and political explanations for this relative passivity. Asian politicians tend to prefer agreements to be thrashed out in private, behind-the-scenes meetings between top leaders; the function of public meetings is to rubberstamp the decisions and disseminate them to the public. It is considered uncouth in some Asian societies to challenge leaders in public, and certainly unseemly for senior figures to be subjected to hostile questioning or challenge. ASEAN is held up as an organization that succeeds, by and large, in resolving contentious issues and promoting successful policies, but in an 'Asian' way, by consensus of leaders, avoiding undignified public squabbles. Another possibility is that Asian states may see the UN and most international organizations as basically skewed with a pro-West bias, because they were set up at a period when the world was Western-dominated. On this view, Asians would do better to focus on their local and regional economic growth rather than try to compete on the slanting playing-field.

For whatever reason, if the PRC has tended to underplay its hand in international organizations, it has certainly built on an extremely valuable 'asset' since 1978: the overseas Chinese community. There is no clear definition of what is an 'overseas Chinese', which is a vague term that can include citizens of Chinese 'territories' such as Singapore, Macao and even Taiwan; people with a recognisably Chinese ethnic background, of no matter what citizenship; and citizens of the PRC residing abroad. By some estimates there are around 30 to 35 million such people in southeast Asia alone, most of them descendants of earlier economic migrants. They control a large proportion of successful regional businesses, from small and medium-sized traders, through banks, to 'Chinese multinationals', some of the biggest companies in the world. This community contributed enormously to China's modernization drive in the 1980s. Many of them are believed to be emotionally and culturally close to China, but it is rather unclear whether or how this translates into practical help for the Chinese state. Many Chinese communities have been persecuted in southeast Asia, and are extremely keen to avoid being labelled as Chinese 'agents' of any kind; yet it is true that in some circumstances they find it easy to deal with a country whose language and culture they share. There is, incidentally, an interesting comparison with India, another major power with a comparable overseas community. Many successful overseas Indians tend to professions like medicine, teaching, and administration. The Chinese usually gravitate to the business world, partly because many southeast Asian governments have excluded ethnic Chinese from certain categories of employment and government service.

An important element of overseas Chinese economic activity has long been family and clan remittances. This capital inflow is impossible to quantify: we know only that countless millions of dollars have flowed back to China from workers overseas, particularly into areas of high out-migration on the southeastern coast. As well as cash, overseas family members doubtless provided information, education, and entrepreneurial skills that all contributed to economic and social dynamism. Likewise, there are no reliable data concerning investment by overseas Chinese businesses, although some guess that it forms around 70 per cent of total FDI since the mid-1980s. Starting in 1984 after the British-Chinese Joint Declaration on the future of Hong Kong, many Hong Kong financiers, industrialists and property magnates set up operations on the mainland. In the late 1980s, there was a wave of investment from Taiwan, especially in tourism and manufacturing; and in the 1990s major investments from huge conglomerates, 'Chinese multinationals', based in Indonesia, Thailand and Malaysia.

The great majority of investment was routed through Hong Kong and spread primarily in southeastern China, but some businesses, including some well known US Chinese firms, have preferred to go straight to Beijing. Anecdotally, business circles believe that overseas Chinese have generally been shrewd and successful in identifying profitable sectors, often in alliance with local politicians and not necessarily in accord with Beijing priorities. The hotel and tourism sector, which was very profitable in the 1980s, suffered a setback in 1989 owing to the Tian'anmen incident and the over-supply of hotels. Overseas Chinese FDI has since moved into labour-intensive, small-scale relocated industries, as well as major infrastructural projects. Many Western companies employ overseas Chinese as consultants or trainers in areas like law, management, or accountancy. Overseas Chinese move between Chinese and Western cultures, and may be best able to explain local operating conditions, negotiate in a style acceptable to both parties and so on.

A controversial theory subscribed to by conspiracy theorists is that the criminal activities of Chinese gangs are to some extent linked with the Chinese state (or states, since it would include Taiwan) though the intermediary of secret security forces. If true, it would be an unofficial and deniable element of Chinese foreign policy, whose objective would be to build up power bases in the black economy of major cities – for example, Moscow and Los Angeles – through gangs engaged in the narcotics trade and arms smuggling. Links between the GMD state and criminal gangs in the 1930s are well known, and there are frequent allegations in the Taiwanese media of criminal involvement in politics. Likewise, it seems to be well established that the security forces of the PRC and Taiwan have struggled for influence over the Hong Kong underworld. The extent of current underground activities may not be known for several decades, and may in any case turn out to be of limited significance.

In most countries, Chinese have the reputation of being extremely hard working, thrifty and law-abiding. Research on their real economic power is in its infancy, and the several overlapping roles of the overseas Chinese community are very hard to document or quantify. Nevertheless, they should not be neglected as an important component of China's global outreach.

8

China into the Twenty-First Century

At the end of the nineteenth century, China was widely seen as a comic-opera state, but by the end of the twentieth was emerging as a significant world power. Under Mao Zedong, the CCP unified the country and built up considerable industrial and military muscle. When Deng Xiaoping came to power in 1978, his radical economic reforms triggered two decades of rapid economic growth, and opened up China to the outside world after the isolationism of the Mao years. One of the most significant features of Deng's rule was his ability to mobilize the capital and expertise of overseas Chinese in a profitable crusade to modernize the homeland. By the mid-1990s there was a new mood of national confidence, at home and among the diaspora, and a growing belief that Greater China – a conglomerate of the PRC, Taiwan, and the overseas Chinese – would be setting the Asian, if not the world agenda in the twenty-first century.

As China integrated itself into the world economy, contacts between Chinese and foreigners multiplied. Hundreds of thousands of Chinese were sent abroad to study during the 1980s and 1990s, and many others were able to travel on business, or even as tourists. Foreign businesses sent their staff to live in China and tourists visited the PRC in increasing numbers. Chinese youth has been exposed to foreign popular culture, and all ages can now watch foreign satellite television, even if programmes are censored by agreement with the Chinese government. Unless there is an unexpected return to isolation, we can expect the further breakdown of linguistic and cultural barriers, as the Chinese population becomes increasingly mobile, and cosmopolitan. In many ways, circumstances have never been so favourable for increased understanding between China and the outside world.

International Opinion and the 'China Threat'

Despite this, the international community often sees developments in China in a negative light. It seems preoccupied with issues which are much less widely discussed within China itself: for example, China as a possible threat to regional security and the global environment; the possibility of a melt-down involving famine or disintegration; the problems of Taiwan and Tibet; and alleged trade abuses such as failure to protect intellectual copyright or the use of prison labour. Partly this is due to concern over human rights. Memories of the 1989 democracy movement, when innocent youth clad in trainers and T-shirts confronted a vicious and autocratic regime that called itself communist, have only partly been supplanted by China's new image as a capitalist New Jerusalem of a billion consumers.

Resurgent Chinese power also has implications for Asian and international security: it changes political spheres of influence in Asia, and most importantly has an impact on the interests and global strategy of the USA. Since the early 1990s a debate in US foreign-policy-making circles has spilled over into the media: is China a threat to peace, and should the USA attempt to contain China as it did the Soviet Union, or should it engage the Chinese government in a constructive dialogue? Engagement would mean integrating China into international organizations, making concessions where necessary and keeping frictions over trade to a minimum. Containment would mean building up an Asian security alliance that could be turned against China if necessary. Possible partners in such an alliance might be Japan, Taiwan, South Korea, and the ASEAN states, perhaps even Russia or Vietnam.

One of China's recurrent complaints is that the USA is attempting to change China by a process of 'peaceful evolution', meaning a low-intensity campaign to destabilize the Chinese government. According to the *People's Daily* the USA aims to 'promote US values and ideologies, sell the US economic and political system as the model for the world, and convert the entire world to capitalism' (*People's Daily* (overseas edition), 30 July 1991: 6). Certainly, if this is its intention, the USA has many classic Cold War techniques at its disposal: it could support separatist movements, create friction between the PRC and Taiwan, bring pressure to bear in international organizations, restrict exports of high technology, support the clandestine opposition, promote Christian evangelism and so on. China could still be promoted as a business environment but, from time to time, public attention at home would be drawn to China's negative points. Such ambiguity would allow a rapid mobilization of opinion against China if it became expedient.

On the face of it, foreign business wants to maximize profits by investing in, or selling to China, and it may seem outlandish to suspect foreign powers of hostile intentions. Does the USA really want to subvert the Chinese state, or is the Chinese attitude just paranoia? It is probably true that the USA and states near China fear that China might become irredentist or expansionist. The PRC claims Taiwan and the Spratly Islands as its own, and has threatened to use force to retake them. According to one US analyst, the CCP leadership has an outdated view of international relations as a 'quasi-imperial competition ... for hegemony' rather than a search for a stable security regime (Larry M. Wortzel, quoted in Roy, 1996: 761). On this view, China might at any time become embroiled with one of its many neighbours – India, Russia, Vietnam, or Japan, for example – in a territorial dispute, and therefore a policy of containment is prudent.

An alternative view, that supports a policy of 'engagement', is that as China modernizes, the process of foreign-policy formation is changing in ways that reduce the chances of confrontation. It is no longer safe to assume that foreign policy is the reserved area of a handful of elite politicians, such as Mao or Deng. By the late 1980s, the groups involved in policy-making had become far more diversified, as China had to deal with a wide range of specialized issues regarding military matters, technology transfer, capital borrowing, educational and cultural exchanges and so on. A degree of delegation of authority has become unavoidable. One symptom of this is the proliferation of think-tanks and advisers. For example, during the 1990 controversy over China's MFN status, Chinese leaders took advice from the Academy of Social Sciences, the China International Trade and Investment Corporation, and the city governments of Shanghai and Guangzhou. There are even signs of influence on foreign policy from 'interest groups', particularly firms that do business overseas. Given these developments, China could become an integral member, rather than potential enemy, of any developing Asian security regime (Hamrin, 1994).

Environmental Crisis

As reported in Chapter 2, China is suffering a severe environmental crisis, perhaps one of the most dangerous in the world. During the 1980s and 1990s, political leaders and the population of China were united in the goal of maximizing economic growth, and paid little attention to environmental controls. Inside China, the major causes for concern are water pollution and exhaustion of water supplies; poor air quality in urban areas; soil erosion; and deforestation. Fears have been expressed in the West (categorically denied by the Chinese government as a typical US slander) that within the foreseeable future China will be unable to feed itself, owing to a combination of water shortages, loss of arable land due to urbanization, desertification, changing consumer patterns and population growth. This could provoke a regionally destabilizing situation, with food shortages leading to famine, social unrest and a refugee crisis. In 1997 and 1998, the world saw apocalyptic pictures of forest fires raging out of control in Indonesia, darkening the skies in neighbouring Singapore and Malaysia; of hundreds of thousands of economic migrants being driven across southeast Asian borders to an uncertain future; might these events prefigure a catastrophe on an even larger scale in China?

From an international perspective, even more important issues are CFC emissions and fossil-fuel burning. China's massive industrialization is largely dependent on low-quality unwashed coal, much of which is used directly as fuel (instead of being converted to electricity); while power-stations themselves are usually antiquated and produce excessive sulphurous emissions. Meanwhile, China is also one of the world's greatest potential markets for CFC-producing equipment.

As may be expected, Chinese and Western leaders view the problem and its possible solutions very differently. To the West, China has a lamentable lack of political will to control its pollution, and appears to care little about the spillover into neighbouring countries and the global environment. However, in the Chinese view, this is just another example of Western hypocrisy: industrialized powers have no intention of relinquishing their high standard of living, but attempt to curb other states' development by bullying. The Chinese would, they claim, be entirely amenable to repairing their ecological damage if the West would cover at least part of the cost. As things stand, they see the Rio de Janeiro environmental summit and the Kyoto summit on climate change as clever ploys to sell – and not cheaply – Western environmental technology to 'the world's largest market for environment-related goods and services', as China can perhaps be described.

Prospects for the Economy

China's economic reforms have improved living standards enormously for most people. The government set itself the targets of quadrupling 1980 GNP and eradicating poverty by the year 2000: despite cyclical fluctuations in the growth rate, the former target will be met. The task of improving the lot of the rural poor will be more difficult, and there are many other outstanding problems, most importantly that of loss-making state industries. While important improvements have been made, by the late 1990s over 40 per cent were still running at a loss. This, in turn, imposes a huge burden on the banking sector, much of which, as a result of its non-performing loans to industry, is insolvent by international criteria. Resolutions carried at the 15th Party Congress in 1997 and elevation of Zhu Rongji to the post of state Premier in 1998 indicated that China was determined to press ahead with radical reforms even if this means mass layoffs. In this case, however, the leadership may solve economic problems at the cost of a social explosion.

It may be that the 1980s and 1990s will be seen in retrospect as exceptional decades, due to factors such as the favourable international trading environment, the growth potential in the rural economy, and low costs. Future Chinese governments may be unable to repeat the growth of output and rise in living standards. Among the most serious problems, some of which are now beginning to have a real impact, are low productivity and reliance on labour-intensive industrial processes; the rising costs of land, labour and energy; lack of innovation and high technology; dependency on world markets; weak infrastructure; costs of environmental degradation; and the social costs of a large population, a high and growing proportion of which is economically inactive.

China's economic development may also be subject to extra-economic constraints and, perhaps, disruption. Political factors can play a decisive role in economic development and we have already noted how popular anger at corruption and unemployment could derail the reforms. Prybla (1997: 16–17) makes the more subtle point that the most developed economies today are deeply involved with information technologies, and that free access to information, and its creative deployment in production, are essential components of the post-industrial age. Yet this aspect of the computer age is profoundly disturbing to Party leaders, who have adopted a series of administrative measures – doomed to partial or complete failure – to try to stem the flow of information into, and around, China.

Possibly the greatest challenge to completing the reform of the Chinese economy is the structure of the CCP regime. The boundaries between the command and the market economy are inextricably tied up with the legitimacy of the CCP and its ability to continue ruling China. Admittedly the CCP has shown itself to be more flexible, pragmatic and tenacious than some other communist parties, but there are some sectors of the economy which are virtually synonymous with CCP power itself. The industrial heartland of northern and northeast China largely consists of state enterprises that are over-staffed and inefficient; they are the centre of the state architecture of employment for tens of millions of workers and bureaucrats. At the 15th Party Congress it appeared that the leadership was prepared to take the political risk of industrial rationalization. But it is hard to see how the state could reduce its economic role to mere provider of a 'level playing-field'. If it did so, the ruling party would be at the mercy of a vast range of powerful economic interests. The CCP is entering uncharted waters and it appears far too late to change course; is the Party in danger of committing political suicide?

Prospects for Political Change

Following the collapse of communist regimes in Eastern Europe and the Soviet Union, it seemed clear to most political analysts that communism as a world movement had run its course, and that the remaining 'socialist' countries found themselves in a blind alley. On this view (that has many supporters inside as well as outside the country) the political problem facing China at the end of the twentieth century is how to manage its exit from communism. If the transition period is mismanaged, China may face chaos and, not for the first time, a prolonged period of disunity. In the early 1990s, the United States Central Intelligence Agency speculated that the Chinese state might break up before the end of the century, as had the Soviet Union, Yugoslavia, and Czechoslovakia.

Along what fault lines might China break up? The cultural and linguistic differences between Han Chinese from different regions are well known, and inter-provincial rivalries have been exacerbated by economic competition during the reform period. A certain amount of speculation in the early 1990s spoke of breakaway mini-states in South China predicated on their economic success and distance from Beijing, but there are few signs of this development in reality. A more likely scenario is occasional but essentially restricted conflicts of economic interests between different provinces, and between provinces and Beijing. It should be remembered that modern China is vastly more integrated both economically and culturally, by roads, railways, airlines, telecommunications, mass literacy, newspapers and television, than it was in warlord times, when many isolated peasant communities had only vague ideas of China as a political entity.

If the break-up of the core provinces of China seems a remote prospect, perhaps a more likely scenario is the separation from the core of the 'autonomous regions' of the major national minorities, above all the Tibetans and the Uighurs of Xinjiang. The Tibetan situation remains a running sore in Chinese politics, and nationalists in Xinjiang were boosted by the collapse of the Soviet Union and the creation of several broadly Islamic states, with which they have linguistic and cultural ties.

But proponents of a break-up theory may have made too much of the analogy with the Soviet Union. In the USSR Russians made up only around 60 per cent of the population. By contrast, Han Chinese account for over 90 per cent of the population of the PRC. Han colonization of the border regions accelerated rapidly after 1949. The state encouraged millions of Chinese to open up virgin territory agricultural land and built up extractive industries to harvest the rich mineral resources of outlying regions. Large troop garrisons, supported by associated supply and arms industries, were stationed in Tibet, Xinjiang and inner Mongolia. The result is that Han populations are now well established in the border regions and, despite a potential for disruption, it seems likely that nationalist movements could succeed in gaining independence only if there were a collapse of the Chinese state for other reasons.

There are a number of possible scenarios for fundamental political change. A mass privatization programme might be the flashpoint for a mass protest movement by workers threatened with layoffs. In a move that may reflect growing grass-roots militancy, in February 1998, veteran dissident Fu Shenqi announced that prodemocracy activists had set up an underground opposition party, the 'China Democracy and Justice Party' inside China itself. Although it claimed only 100 members, it had branches in more than five cities, making it the first national opposition party since the communist takeover in 1949. Significantly, most members were workers. The party vowed to push for independent labour unions and elections at all levels of government, and to fight CCP corruption. If a mass movement on the scale of 1989 developed, in the absence of an authoritative figure like Mao Zedong or Deng Xiaoping, a combination of inertia and factional strife might bring down the regime. The example of Indonesia, where the thirty-two-year-old dictatorship of General Suharto was ended by student-led mass protests in May 1998, will have been studied closely by Chinese dissidents. The parallels between the students' actions and the Tian'anmen protests of 1989 were not lost on the Beijing authorities, who instructed the Chinese media to play down the Indonesian events. Of course, if the civilian government is threatened, the military might intervene to 'restore order'. But what kind of 'socialism' would the military support, given its own widespread involvement in business?

Alternatively the regime may slowly liberalize itself, as did the Guomindang in Taiwan. In November 1997 the authorities released China's leading dissident, Wei Jingsheng, from prison, and the following April they released Wang Dan, a leader of the 1989 democracy movement. In 1998, a noticeably more critical attitude in the press, and the open discussion of political reform in think-tanks and universities, led some commentators to talk of a new 'Beijing Spring'. It would be wrong to exaggerate this; Wei Jingsheng and Wang Dan were immediately exiled to the USA. Those dissidents who remain in China, such as democracy wall activist Xu Wenli, are constantly harassed. Nevertheless, to characterize China as simply an authoritarian state is an over-simplification. For one thing, it overlooks local government and village politics that, in parts of China, are relatively democratic and efficient. In early 1998 the government announced plans for further democratization at local level. Any strategy for liberalization at a national level, however, would raise the problem of politically reassessing the Tian'anmen Square incident. Some gesture of apology and restitution would become necessary, and this will have to wait for the retirement of principal actors in the tragedy such as NPC chairman, Li Peng.

There may, of course, be no early change of regime. Since 1989, most Western prognoses for the future of Chinese politics have envisaged an end to the CCP regime within the coming decade. In the early 1990s following the collapse of the Soviet Union, and with the memory of Tian'anmen still fresh, some argued that the end would come more swiftly. Additionally, it was often assumed that loss of state power would effectively destroy the CCP. These days, the predictions of Western experts are less sanguine. We should remember that the Party is a massive organization with deep roots in society. In 1997 its membership was about 60 million, around one in twenty of all Chinese. The Party has recovered from the Tian'anmen crisis, and if it is able to deliver continuing economic growth, it may well retain power, possibly for several decades more. Furthermore, even if the CCP loses office for a period, it may well survive as an organization, and could even win back power. The experience of communist parties in Eastern Europe, for example in Poland, shows that such organizations can recover from seemingly crushing blows.

Socialism and Revolution: Fate of an Empire

For some 2000 years, the Chinese Empire was the greatest power in Asia, the world's longest-lasting empire, and the largest in terms of population. The Chinese made tremendous, if largely unacknowledged, contributions to the global development of science and technology, as evidenced in Needham's monumental *Science and Civilisation in China*. They have a documented cultural history of 3 000 years, which profoundly influenced the political and cultural life of most of east Asia. The transformation of the empire into a modern nation-state therefore marks a tremendous watershed in Asian and world history.

In some respects, one could view the governments of the Guomindang and of the Maoist CCP as the last throes of an imperial order. Institutions, recognizably similar to those of 'the modern world', were being formed, but until late in the century were not yet free of vestiges of autocratic rule, fetishistic attitudes to state leaders, rigid orthodoxy and isolation. By the 1990s, much had changed. Internally, the CCP, although still unwilling to allow political pluralism, governs a far better educated and articulate population; externally, the Chinese government accepts the norms of international relations, and acts as a nation-state in a world of peers, no longer as the 'Middle Kingdom'.

One characteristic of this transformation is that it was achieved under the leadership of the CCP, a 'communist' or 'socialist' party whose ideology is based on Marxist–Leninism, adapted to Chinese circumstances by Mao Zedong and Deng Xiaoping. Readers may wish to consider to what extent the concepts of 'revolution' (specifically 'communist revolution') and 'modernization' are useful interpretative tools for evaluating this historical process. Each term is loaded with rhetoric and with possibly unjustified assumptions. 'Communist revolution' implies a connection with working-class radicalism, with the October Revolution, with anti-colonial struggles in Asia, Africa, and Latin America, and with egalitarianism and social justice; it also implies hostility to 'imperialism' – that is, to the West. 'Modernization', on the other hand, suggests among other things the formation of a specifically capitalist industrialized economy integrated into world trade, some form of democracy, and the development of human resources through educational systems that conform to international norms.

If one reads texts on China written some twenty years ago, one finds that key analytical concepts were 'dictatorship of the proletariat', 'imperialism', 'Third World', 'class struggle' and so on. In most writing today, such terms would appear totally anachronistic, and most writers on China – not only in business journals, but even in academic journals – are much more likely to focus on the workings of the market economy. What has happened?

One scholar argues that the 'central event of the past decade is the repudiation in China of revolution in the name of modernization, or, stated differently, of socialist in the name of capitalist modernization' (Dirlik, 1996: 249). According to much contemporary writing on China, the 'revolutionary' element of modern Chinese history should be judged a failure in terms of economic development, of democracy and of ethics. Positive re-evaluations have been made of the Guomindang government, of imperialism, even of Confucianism. The paradigm of modernization, strongly reinforced by the economic boom of the Deng era and the collapse of the Soviet Union, 'is fundamentally in opposition to revolution and revolutionary transformation as concepts in history' (ibid.: 256).

Yet fashions change rapidly, and perhaps the Chinese revolution will again be conceptualized as such, and not as an aberration that wasted precious time between the roaring capitalism of the 1920s and that of the 1990s. It may yet be appropriate to debate whether the paradigm of 'revolution' is still relevant to understanding the modern world and specifically modern China. For those interested in political history and theory, China forms a tremendous case-study. Much of the century was dominated by 'communism': class struggle, revolutionary upheaval, state-driven industrialization, opposition to 'imperialism'. Yet since 1978, the reform programme has stressed 'modernization' with an entrepreneurial economy, foreign investment, exploitation of cheap labour, and world trade ties. A balanced discourse on contemporary China would have to be sensitive to both the 'communist' and 'capitalist' contributions – recognizing, for example, that the economic boom of the 1990s, with all its benefits and prospects, would have been impossible without the successful public health and education programmes of earlier decades; arguably, without the mass-mobilization of the population in the 'communist revolution'.

Recommended Reading

1 The History of Modern China

A readable introduction to this area is Moise (1994). Both Fairbank (1992) and Spence (1991) provide informative and detailed accounts of the development of China in the past two centuries. For background on nineteenth-century history, the Opium Wars and relations with foreign powers, see Waley (1958) and Gray (1990). Early twentieth-century history and the creation of the CCP are covered by Bianco (1971). Jenner (1992), Pye (1992) and Dreyer (1993) provide accounts of the Chinese political system and insights into the way in which modern China has been shaped by its past. There are also numerous personal accounts of twentieth-century events, the best known of which are perhaps Snow (1968) writing about Mao Zedong and communism in the 1930s, and Chang (1991) who relates her own experiences of the Cultural Revolution.

2 Land and People

For general information on land use, population, climate and geography, Howe (1978) provides details of pre-economic reform China. For more up-to-date information, Mackerras and Yorke (1991) includes a useful and concise gazeteer. Much more detail can be obtained from the Chinese Academy of Social Science series *Information China*, Cannon and Jenkins (1990) and Zhao (1994). Skinner (1974) examines the status of the city in China. Leeming (1985) provides a comprehensive explanation of rural issues whilst Ho (1994) presents a detailed case-study of one province during the period since reform. This period is covered also by Huang (1994) and Leeming and Powell (1990). Environmental issues are dealt with in Smil (1993) and Edmonds (1994). Croll (1994) provides insights into life in a period of change while Whyte (1992) looks specifically at changing family structure. Banister (1987) examines population matters since 1949 while Croll and Davin (1985) focus upon the one-child policy. China's national minorities are discussed in Heberer (1989).

3 The Chinese Economy

There is a full account of the period 1949 to the mid-1980s in Riskin (1987). The period after reform is dealt with by Feuchtwang et al. (1998) in two volumes which look at the rural and urban sectors respectively.The period after 1978 is covered in Lardy (1993, 1994), Wong (1993), Nolan (1993) and Naughton (1995). For specific focus on the agricultural sector see Lardy (1983), Parish (1985) and Leeming (1985). The industrial sector from 1949 to the mid-1980s is dealt with by Lee (1988).

Nolan and Dong (1990), Howell (1993) and Hannan (1995) look at the effects of reform on various sectors of the economy, while Vogel (1989) focuses specifically upon Guangdong during this period. The effects of decentralization are examined in Goodman (1994) and for information and analysis of the effects of economic reform upon individual provinces, Goodman (1997) is the first in a planned series covering the whole of China. An examination of the long-term prospects of the reforms together with analysis of current trends is contained in the report of the Economist Intelligence Unit (1990). A thought-provoking discussion of the more theoretical and normative aspects of economic reform can be found in Shih (1995). For up-to-date information on investment and new developments in China's economy, there are many journals providing reports and statisics. *Far East Economic Review* and *China Business Review* are particularly useful. The *China 2020* series (World Bank, 1997 a–g) includes clearly presented and readable reports on economic, environmental and other developmental issues which face China in the next century. It is also a good source of statistics about China.

4 Political Life

General texts include Wang (1988) and Christiansen and Rai (1996). Saich (1981) looks at politics in China for most of the twentieth century up until the late 1970s. For post-1949 institutions, structures and processes, Tung (1964) is comprehensive, whilst Brahm (1995) provides a detailed and useful overview of present-day power structures together with profiles of individual political leaders. The Chinese Academy of Social Science series *Information China* (1989) is a very useful reference for modern political structure and for related statistics. Pre-Cultural Revolution issues are dealt with in Chang (1978) and included by Harding (1981). The changing nature of relationships between centre and province during this period can be found in Goodman (1986), while an account of politics during the Cultural Revolution itself can be found in Robinson (1971). The transition from Mao to Deng is covered by Derbyshire (1987) and politics in the period of transition by Gardner (1982), Moody (1983) and White (1993). A biographical account of both China's leaders can be found in Salisbury (1993). Goldman (1994) and Sun (1995) examine the nature of political thought in China during the post-Mao period as do Kristof and WuDunn (1994). Hook (1996) looks at the relationship between the individual and the state. Discussions of democracy are contained in Nathan (1986) and Benton and Hunter (1995). There are numerous accounts of of the Tian'anmen events, many of them written by those who were personally involved, such as Tong (1991). Oksenberg et al. (1990) includes documents relating to this period, whilst Hicks (1990) is examination of the events and their aftermath. Unger (1991) looks at the pro-democracy movement in the provinces.

5 The Social System

Wittfogel (1957) is the classic exposition of the theory of Oriental Despotism. Two volumes dealing respectively with rural and urban life in modern China are Parish and Whyte (1978) and Whyte and Parish (1984). Focusing upon the inhabitants of one particular village, Chan et al. (1992) provides a view of changes over a quarter century. Several works that deal with the changing roles of women are Wolf (1985), Jacka (1997), Judd (1996) and Evans (1987). Baker (1979) examines family and kinship. Dernberger et al. (1991) looks at the way in which the Chinese people have had to adapt to deal with change. Education in contemporary China is the subject of Hayhoe (1984) and of Cleverly (1985), the latter also includes information about traditional education. The role of establishment intellectuals is the subject of Hamrin and Cheek (1986), who also look at the issue of alienated youth. The problem of youthful deviance is discussed in Ngai (1994). For information on China's social security system, see Sun (1996) and for legal reform see Lubman (1996).

6 Chinese Culture

For background on Confucianism, Dawson (1981) is both concise and accessible. Thompson (1979) is an introduction to Chinese religion and Sommer (1995) is an anthology of sources on the same subject. Fairbank (1992) and Needham (1978) provide extensive information on the development of China and Chinese culture through the centuries. Lin (1936) looks at both people and country while Spence (1992) is a series of essays on both history and culture. Two volumes dealing respectively with rural and urban life in communist China are Parish and Whyte (1978) and Whyte and Parish (1984). Focusing upon the inhabitants of one particular village, Chan et al. (1992) provides a view of changes over a twenty-year period up until the mid-1980s. Issues of identity are explored in Bond (1991), Tu (1994) and Hsu (1955). Popular culture in China, including the way in which this is affected by increasing exposure to non-Chinese influences, is the subject of Wu and Murphy (1994).

Hunter and Chan (1993) deal with Christianity under the communist government.

7   China's International Relations

Roy (1998), Garver (1993) and Robinson and Shambaugh (1994) are general works on China's foreign relations. China's place within the Asia Pacific region and its global context is explored in Hsiung (1993), Simone and Feraru (1995), Ball (1996) and Yahuda (1996). For a historical perspective and for information on recent past conflicts see Segal (1985). The end of China's isolationist foreign policy and the emergence of new relationships in the post-Mao era is the subject of both Yahuda (1993) and Kim (1984). Yang et al. (1994) is an examination of the potential effects of increasing regionalism within China upon security issues. The subject of Segal (1994) is the transfer of arms to and from China and the effect that this has in the post-Cold War world. The issue of Greater China and its potential future role is the subject of Shambaugh (1995). Useful journals in the field of China's international relations include *Pacific Review*; the weekly *Beijing Review* gives up-to-date official reaction and statements on current events.

8   China into the Twenty-First Century

The China Quarterly (London); *The Journal of Chinese Affairs* (Canberra); and *China Information* (Leiden, Holland) publish high-quality research on contemporary issues, book reviews, chronicles of recent events, etc. *Beijing Review* is a good source for official Chinese news. Finally, an ever-increasing number of Internet sites provide a wide variety of China-related information and debate.

China on the Internet

Because specific addresses on the Internet change so fast, it is probably more helpful to know about the general areas where one can find China-related information: it is easy to retrieve http locations from standard search procedures. (*But see 1998 addresses on the next page.*)

Academic Institutions

A number of major academic institutions provide on-line China re-sources; several of them as subsections of resources on Asia as a whole. Important ones are the Australian National University, the University of Leiden, the University of Heidelberg and the University Services Centre of the Chinese University of Hong Kong. The latter's services include statistical data about China and research assistance. From the main menus of these institutions one can find references to countless other information sources such as bibliographies, university libraries, government institutions and so on.

Business News and Journals

There are a number of services to the business community promoted on the Internet; of course, many of them are for paying subscribers only. The best-known business news magazine, the *Far Eastern Economic Review*, offers extensive on-line services.

Government Sources

Agencies affiliated to the Chinese government have recently begun to publish material on the Internet. They obviously promote official views, but nevertheless are a useful source of statistical information, statements by the political leadership, news stories from China and so on. Two of the better ones are the site maintained by Xinhua, the New China News Agency; and the site of the Chinese Embassy in Washington, DC. There are also many official sites in Japan, Singapore, Taiwan and the USA which may provide information about relations with China.

Democracy and Human Rights

The Internet is an excellent way to keep in touch with views of pro-democracy groups, many of which circulate information about their campaigns. Other groups which publish material about the Chinese government are the Tibet Information Network and various human rights organisations, especially Human Rights Watch/Asia. One web-site, based on the work of the well-known campaigner Harry Wu, focuses on the labour-camp system.

Voluntary and News Groups

Many groups offer on-line forums for discussion or act as resource centres for different kinds of China-related information. The biggest and best-established at present is the China News Digest, a voluntary organization specializing in China-related information. From the main menu one can select from a very wide range of options, including reviews of periods of history, sound and video-clips, discussion groups and a newsletter service. Apart from its own services, China News Digest is a good first port of call for information on the dozens of other China groups on the Net.

Internet Addresses and Home Pages (1998)

Far Eastern Economic Review
http://www.feer.com/

Xinhua New Agency
http://www.xinhua.org

Chinese Embassy in Washington
http://www.china-embassy.org

Tibet Information Network
http://www.tibetinfo.net

Human Rights Watch/Asia
http://www.hrw.org

China News Digest
http://www.cnd.org

Chinese University of Hong Kong
http://www.cuhk.edu.hk

Australian National University
http://www.anu.edu.au

University of Leiden (English home page)
http://www.leidenuniv.nl/index_e.html

University of Heidelberg (English home page)
http://www.uni-heidelberg.de/index_e.html

Bibliography

Baker, H. (1979) *Chinese Family and Kinship*, New York: Columbia University Press.

Ball, D. (ed.) (1996) *The Transformation of Security in the Asia/Pacific Region*, London: Frank Cass.

Banister, J. (1987) *China's Changing Population*, Stanford SCA: Stanford University Press.

Benewick, R. and P. Wingrove (eds) (1995) *China in the 1990s*, London: Macmillan.

Benton, G. and A. Hunter (1995) *Wild Lily, Prairie Fire*, Princeton: Princeton University Press.

Bianco, L. (1971) *Origins of the Chinese Revolution*, Stanford: Stanford University Press.

Bond, M. (1991) *Beyond the Chinese Face*, Hong Kong: Oxford University Press.

Brahm, L. J. (1995) *China Inc. A Concise Overview of China's Power Structure and Profiles of China's Leaders Today*, Butterworth—Heinemann Asia.

Breslin, S. (1995) 'Centre and Province in China', in Benewick and Wingrove, 63–72.

Brosseau, M. and Lo Chi Kin (eds) (1994) *China Review 1994*, Hong Kong: Chinese University Press.

Brosseau, M. et al. (eds) (1997) *China Review 1997*, Hong Kong: Chinese University Press.

Brown, L. R. and C. Flavin (1996) 'China's Challenge to the United States and the Earth', *Worldwatch Magazine* (September–October 1996), Massachusetts: Worldwatch Institute.

Cannon, T. (1990) 'Spatial Inequality and Regional Policy', in Cannon and Jenkins, 28–60.

Cannon, T. and A. Jenkins, (1990) *The Geography of Contemporary China: The Impact of Deng Xiaoping's Decade*, London: Routledge.

Chan A., R. Madsen and J. Unger (1992) *Chen Village under Mao and Deng*, New Haven: University of California Press.

Chang, J. (1991) *Wild Swans*, London: HarperCollins.

Chang, Pang-Mei Natasha (1997) *Bound Feet and Western Dress*, London: Bantam.

Chang, P. (1978) *Power and Policy in China*: University Park, Pennsylvania State University Press.

Chinese Academy of Social Sciences (1989) *Information China*, 3 vols, Oxford: Pergamon Press.

Christiansen, F. and S. Rai (1996) *Chinese Politics and Society: An Introduction*, London: Prentice-Hall.

Clarke, D. C. (1995) 'Justice and the Legal System in China', in Benewick and Wingrove, 83–93.

Cleverley, J. (1985) *The Schooling of China: Tradition and Modernity in Chinese Education*, London: George Allen & Unwin.

Constitution of the People's Republic of China, (1961) Beijing: Foreign Language Press.

Croll, E. (1983) *Chinese Women since Mao*, London: Zed Books.

Croll, E. (1994) *From Heaven to Earth: Images and Experiences of Development in China*, London: Routledge.

Croll, E. and D. Davin, (1985) *China's One-Child Family Policy*, London: Macmillan.

Dawson, R. (1981) *Confucius*, Oxford: Oxford University Press.

Derbyshire, I. (1987) *Politics in China: From Mao to Deng*, Edinburgh: Chambers.

Dernberger, R. F. et al. (eds) (1991) *The Chinese: Adapting the Past, Facing the Future*, Ann Arbor, MI: Center for Chinese Studies, The University of Michigan.

Dirlik, A. (1996) 'Reversals, Ironies, Hegemonies: Notes on Contemporary Historiography of Modern China', *Modern China*, 22(3), 243–84.

Dirlik, A. and M. Meisner (eds) (1989) Marxism and the Chinese Experience: Issues in Contemporary Chinese Socialism, Armonk, NY: M.E. Sharpe.

Dreyer, J. T. (1993) *China's Political System: Modernization and Tradition*, New York: Paragon House.

Economist Intelligence Unit (1990) *China Against the Tide*, London: Economist Intelligence Unit.

Economist Intelligence Unit (1992) *China to 2000*, London: Economist Intelligence Unit.

Edmonds, R. L. (1994) *Patterns of China's Lost Harmony*, London: Routledge.

Evans, H. (1997) *Women and Sexuality in China*, Oxford: Polity Press.

Fairbank, J. K. (various dates) *The Cambridge History of China*, Cambridge: Cambridge University Press.

Fairbank, J. K. (1992) *China: A New History*, Cambridge, MA: Harvard University Press.

Fairbank, J. K. and E. O. Reischauer (1989) *China: Tradition and Transformation*, Sydney: Allen & Unwin.

Fei Hsiao-Tung (1939) *Peasant Life in China*, London: Kegan Paul.

Feuchtwang, S., A. Hussain, and T. Pairault, (eds) (1988) *Transforming China's Economy in the Eighties*, 2 vols, London: Zed Books.

Foot, R. (1995) 'China's Foreign Policy in the Post-1989 Era', in Benewick and Wingrove, 234–44.

Gardner, J. (1982) *Chinese Politics and the Succession to Mao*, London: Macmillan.

Garver, J. (1993) *Foreign Relations of the People's Republic of China*, Englewood Cliffs, NJ: Prentice-Hall.

Goldman, M. (1994) *Sowing the Seeds of Democracy in China: Political*

Reform in the Deng Xiaoping Era, Cambridge, MA: Harvard University Press.

Goldman, M. (1996) 'Politically-Engaged Intellectuals in the Deng-Jiang Era: A Changing Relationship with the Party-State', *China Quarterly,* 145, 35–52.

Goodman, D. (1986) *Centre and Province in the People's Republic of China: Sichuan and Guizhou 1955–1965,* Cambridge: Cambridge University Press.

Goodman, D. (1994) 'The Politics of Regionalism', in Goodman and Segal, 1–20.

Goodman, D. (ed.) (1997) *China's Provinces in Reform: Class, Community, and Political Culture,* London: Routledge.

Goodman, D. and G. Segal (1994) *China Deconstructs: Politics, Trade and Regionalism,* London: Routledge.

Gray, J. (1990) *Rebellions and Revolutions: China from the 1800s to the 1980s,* Oxford: Oxford University Press.

Hall, C. *Daughters of the Dragon: Women's Lives in Contemporary China,* London: Scarlet Press.

Hamrin, C.L. (1994) *Elite Politics and the Development of China's Foreign Relations,* in Robinson and Shambaugh, 70–112.

Hamrin, C.L. and T. Cheek, (eds) (1986) *China's Establishment Intellectuals,* Armonk, NY: M.E.Sharpe.

Hannan, K. (ed) (1995) *China, Modernisation and the Goal of Prosperity: Government Administration and Economic Policy in the late 1980's,* Cambridge: Cambridge University Press.

Harding, H. (1981) *Organizing China: The Problem of Bureaucracy, 1949–1976,* Stanford, CA: Stanford University Press.

Hayhoe, R. (ed.) (1984) *Contemporary Chinese Education,* Armonk, NY: M.E.Sharpe.

Heberer, T. (1989) *China and its National Minorities: Autonomy or Assimilation,* Armonk: M. E. Sharpe.

He Zhou (1996) *Mass Media and Tian'anmen Square,* New York: Nova Science.

Hicks, G. (ed.) (1990) *The Broken Mirror: China after Tian'anmen,* Harlow: Longman.

Ho, S. (1994) *Rural China in Transition: Non-agricultural Development in Rural Jiangsu 1978–1990,* Oxford: Clarendon Press.

Hook, B. (ed.) (1991) *The Cambridge Encyclopedia of China,* 2nd edn, Cambridge: Cambridge University Press.

Hook, B. (ed.) (1996) *The Individual and the State in China,* Oxford: Clarendon Press.

Howard, M. (1990) 'Industry, Energy, and Transport: Problems and Policies' in Cannon and Jenkins, 168–202.

Howe, C. (1978) *China's Economy: A Basic Guide,* London: Granada.

Howell, J. (1993) *China Opens its Doors: The Politics of Economic Transition,* Hemel Hempstead: Harvester Wheatsheaf.

Hsiung, J. (1993) 'China in the Postnuclear World', in Hsiung, 73–92.

Hsiung, J. (ed.) (1993) *Asia Pacific in the New World Politics,* Boulder, CO: Lynne Rienner.

Hsu, F.L.K. (1955) *Americans and Chinese*, London: Cresset.

Huang, S. (1994) 'Rural China in Transition', in W. A. Joseph (ed.), *China Briefing 1994*, Boulder, CO: Westview Press.

Human Rights Watch/Asia. (1997) *China: State Control of Religion*, New York: Human Rights Watch.

Hunter, A. and K. Chan, (1993) *Protestantism in Contemporary China*, Cambridge: Cambridge University Press.

Huntington, S. P. (1998) *The Clash of Civilisations and the Remaking of World Order*, London: Touchstone.

Jacka, T. (1997) *Women's Work in Rural China: Change and Continuity in an Era of Reform*, Cambridge: Cambridge University Press.

Jenner, W.J.F. (1992) *The Tyranny of History: The Roots of China's Crisis*, Harmondsworth: Penguin.

Jiang Liu, Lu Xueyi and Shan Tianlun (eds) (1996) *Zhongguo shehui xingshi fenxi yu yuce 1995–96* (Analysis and Forecast of Trends in Chinese Society, 1995–96), Beijing: Zhongguo shehui kexue chubanshe.

Judd, E. (1996) *Gender and Power in Rural North China*, Stanford, CA: Stanford University Press.

Kalder, K. E. (1996) *Asia's Deadly Triangle*, London: Nicholas Brealey.

Karnow, S. (1990) *Mao and China*, Harmondsworth: Penguin.

Kim, S.S. (1984) *China and the World: Chinese Foreign Policy in the Post-Mao Era*, Boulder, CO: Westview.

Korski, T. (1997) 'Guangdong Plans China's First Tax Incentive for Controlling Pollution', *International Environment Reporter*, 20(2), 68–9.

Kraus, R.L. (1989) 'The Lament of Astrophysicist Fang Lizhi: China's Intellectuals in a Global Context', in Dirlik and Meisner, 294–315.

Kristof, N. D. and S. WuDunn (1994) *China Wakes: The Struggle for the Soul of a Rising Power*, New York: Random House.

Krugman, P. (1994) 'The Myth of Asia's Miracle', *Foreign Affairs*, 736.

Lardy, N.R. (1983) *Agriculture in China's Modern Economic Development*, Cambridge: Cambridge University Press.

Lardy, N.R. (1993) 'Recasting of the Economic System: Structural Reform of Agriculture and Industry' in Michael Ying-Mao Kau and S. H. Marsh (eds), *China in the Era of Deng Xiaoping*, Armonk, NY: M.E. Sharpe.

Lardy, N. R. (1994) *China in the World Economy*, Washington, DC: Institute for International Economics.

Lee, P.N.S. (1988) *Industrial Management and Economic Reform in China 1949–1984*, New York: Oxford University Press.

Leeming, F. (1985) *Rural China Today*, London: Longman.

Leeming, F. (1993) *The Changing Geography of China*, Oxford: Blackwell.

Leeming, F. and S. Powell, (1990) 'Rural China: Old Problems and New Solutions', in Cannon and Jenkins 133–67.

Lenin, V. I. (1988) *What is to be Done?*, Harmondsworth: Penguin.

Li Weihan (1981) *Tongyi zhanxian wenti yu minzu wenti* (Questions on United Front Policy and Nationality Policy), Beijing: Renmin chubanshe.

Lin Tongqi, H. Rosemont, Jr. and R. T. Ames (1995) 'Chinese Philosophy: A Philosophical Essay on the State-of-the-Art', *Journal of Asian Studies*, 543, 727–58.

Lin Yutang (1936) *My Country and My People*, London: Heinemann.
Long, S. (1995) 'Leadership Politics since 1989', in Benewick and Wingrove, 51–63.
Lubman, S.B. (1996) *China's Legal Reforms*, Oxford: Oxford University Press.
MacInnis, D. E. (1972) *Religious Policy and Practice in Communist China: A Documentary History*, New York: Macmillan.
Mackerras, C. (ed.) (1996) *Eastern Asia, An Introductory History*, 2nd edn, New South Wales: Addison Wesley Longman.
Mackerras, C. and A. Yorke, (1991) *The Cambridge Handbook of Contemporary China*, Cambridge University Press.
Madsen, R. (1993) 'The Academic China Specialists', in D. Shambaugh (ed.), *American Studies of Contemporary China*, Armonk: M E Sharpe, 163–75.
Mao Zedong (1966–77a) *Selected Works of Mao Tse-tung*, Beijing: People's Publishing House.
Mao Zedong (1966–77b) 'The Duty of the CCP during the Anti-Japanese Resistance', *Selected Works*, vol. 1.
McInnes, C. and M.G. Rolls, (eds) (1994) *Post-Cold War Security Issues in the Asia-Pacific Region*, Ilford: Frank Cass.
Meisner, M. (1989) 'The Deradicalization of Chinese Socialism', in Dirlik and Meisner, 341–61.
Moise, E. E. (1994) *Modern China: A History*, New York: Longman.
Moody, P.R. Jr. (1983) *Chinese Politics after Mao, Development and Liberalization 1976–1983*, New York: Praeger.
Nathan, A.J. (1986) *Chinese Democracy*, New Haven: University of California Press.
Naughton, B. (1995) *Growing out of the Plan*, Cambridge: Cambridge University Press.
Needham, J. (1978) *The Shorter Science and Civilisation in China* (an abridgement by Colin A. Ronan of Joseph Needham's original text), Cambridge: Cambridge University Press.
Ngai, N. (1994) 'Youth Deviance in China', in M. Brosseau and K.C. Lo, *China Review 1994*, Hong Kong: Chinese University Press.
Nolan, P. (1993) *State and Market in the Chinese Economy*, London: Macmillan.
Nolan, P. and F. Dong, (eds) (1990) *The Chinese Economy and its Future: Achievements and Problems of Post-Mao Reform*, Cambridge: Polity Press.
Ogden, S. (1989) *China's Unresolved Issues: Politics, Development and Culture*, Englewood Cliffs, NJ: Prentice-Hall.
Oksenberg, M., L.R. Sullivan, and M. Lambert, (eds) (1990) *Beijing Spring: Confrontation and Conflict: The Basic Documents*, Armonk, NY: M.E. Sharpe.
O'Reilly, E. D. (1997) 'International Environmental Concerns Applied to Chinese and ASEAN Development' Department of East Asian Studies, University of Leeds, unpublished manuscript.
Parish, W.L. (ed.) (1985) *Chinese Rural Development. The Great Transformation*, Armonk, NY: M.E. Sharpe.

Parish, W.L. and M. K. Whyte, (1978) *Village and Family in Contemporary China*, University of Chicago Press.

People's Republic of China Yearbook (annual), Beijing: PRC Year Book Ltd.

Phillips, Richard T. (1996) *China since 1911*, London: Macmillan.

Prybla, N. R. (1997) 'China as an Asian Economic Power', *Issues and Studies* 331.

Pye, L. (1988) *The Mandarin and the Cadre: China's Political Cultures*, Ann Arbor, MI: Center for Chinese Studies, The University of Michigan.

Pye, L.W. (1992) *The Spirit of Chinese Politics*, Cambridge, MA: Harvard University Press.

Rai, S. M. (1995) *Gender in China*, in Benewick and Wingrove, 181–92.

Riskin, C. (1987) *China's Political Economy: The Quest for Development since 1949*, Oxford: Oxford University Press.

Robinson, T.W. (1971) *The Cultural Revolution in China*, New Haven: University of California Press.

Robinson, T. W. and D. Shambaugh (eds) (1994) *Chinese Foreign Policy: Theory and Practice*, Oxford: Clarendon Press.

Roy, D. (1998) *China's Foreign Relations*, London: Macmillan.

Roy, D. (1996) *The China Threat Issue*, New Haven: University of California Press.

Saich, T. (1981) *China: Politics and Government*, London: Macmillan.

Salisbury, H. (1993) *The New Emperors, Mao and Deng: A Dual Biography*, London: HarperCollins.

Schell, O. (1995) *Mandate of Heaven*, London: Warner Books.

Schram, S. (1989) *The Thought of Mao Tse-Tung*, Cambridge: Cambridge University Press.

Segal, G. (1985) *Defending China*, New York: Oxford University Press.

Segal, G. (1994) 'China: Arms Transfer Policies and Practices', in McInnes and Rolls.

Shambaugh, D. (ed.) (1995) *Greater China: The Next Superpower?*, Oxford: Oxford University Press.

Shih, C. (1995) *State and Society in China's Political Economy: The Cultural Dynamics of Socialist Reform*, Boulder, CO: Lynne Rienner.

Simone, V. and A.T. Feraru, (1995) *The Asia Pacific: Political and Economic Development in a Global Context*, White Plains, NY: Longmans.

Skinner, G. W. (ed.) (1977) *The City in Late Imperial China*, Stanford, CA: Stanford University Press.

Skinner, G.W. (1974) *The Chinese City between Two Worlds*, Stanford, CA: Stanford University Press.

Smil, V. (1993) *China's Environmental Crisis*, Armonk, NY: M.E.Sharpe.

Snow, E. (1968) *Red Star Over China*, London: Gollancz.

Sommer, D. (ed.) (1995) *Chinese Religion: An Anthology of Sources*, New York: Oxford University Press.

Spence, J. (1991) *The Search for Modern China*, New York: Norton.

Spence, J. (1992) *Chinese Roundabout. Essays in History and Culture*, New York: Norton.

State Council of China.(1996) 'Resolution on Promptly Resolving Poverty in the Countryside', translated and edited in *October Review* (Hong Kong), (28 January 1997).

State Statistical Bureau (Annual) *China Statistical Yearbook*, Beijing: China Statistical Publishing House.
Sun, Y. (1995) *The Chinese Reassessment of Socialism, 1976–1992*, Princeton, NJ: Princeton University Press.
Sun, X. (1996) *China's Social Security System*, Beijing: Foreign Languages Press.
Szego, J. (1990) *Problems of Perestroika*, unpublished dissertation, Sussex University.
Thompson, L.G. (1979) *Chinese Religion: An Introduction*, Belmont, CA: Wadsworth.
Thomson, E. (1996) 'Reforming China's Coal Industry', *China Quarterly*, 147, 727–50.
Tong, S. (1991) *Almost a Revolution*, New York: Harper Perennial.
Trotsky, L. (1989) *The Revolution Betrayed*, translated by Max Eastman, 7th printing, New York: Pathfinder Press.
Tuan, Yi-Fu. (1970) *The World's Landscapes, China*, London: Longman.
Tung Hsiang (1996) Hong Kong (July).
Tung, W. (1964) *The Political Institutions of Modern China*, The Hague: M. Nijhoff.
Unger, R. M. (1976) *Law in Modern Society: Towards a Critique of Social Theory*, New York: The Free Press.
Unger, J (ed.) (1991) *The Pro-Democracy Protests in China: Reports from the Provinces*, Armonk, NY: M.E.Sharpe.
Vogel, E.F. (1989) *One Step Ahead in China: Guangdong under Reform*, Cambridge, MA: Harvard University Press.
Walder, A. G. (1995) 'China's Transitional Economy: Interpreting its Significance', *China Quarterly*, 144, 963–79.
Waley, A. (1958) *The Opium War through Chinese Eyes*, London: Allen & Unwin.
Wang Guiguo (1993) *Business Law of China: Cases, Texts, and Commentaries*, London: Butterworth Asia.
Wang Hongyu (1995) 'Sino–Indian Relations Present and Future', *Asian Survey*, 356, 546–64.
Wang, J.C.F. (1988) *Contemporary Chinese Politics: An Introduction*, Englewood Cliffs, NJ, Prentice-Hall.
Webber, M. (1968) *The Religion of China: Confucianism and Taoism*, New York: The Free Press.
White, G. (1993) *Riding the Tiger: The Politics of Economic Reform in Post-Mao China*, Stanford, CA: Stanford University Press.
Whyte, M.K. and W.L. Parish, (1984) *Urban Life in Contemporary China*, Chicago: University of Chicago Press.
Wittfogel, K. A. (1957) *Oriental Despotism: A Comparative Study of Total Power*, Oxford: Oxford University Press.
Wolf, M. (1985) *Revolution Postponed: Women in Contemporary China*, Stanford, CA: Stanford University Press.
Wong, J. (1993) *Understanding China's Socialist Market Economy*, Singapore: Times Academic Press.
Wong, K. C. (1994) 'Public Security Reform in China', in Brosseau and Lo, 5.1–5.39.

World Bank (1993a) *China: Managing Rapid Growth and Transition*, Washington, DC: World Bank.

World Bank (1993b) *World Debt Tables: External Finance for Developing Countries*, Washington, DC: World Bank.

World Bank (1993c) *China: Foreign Trade Reform*, Washington, DC: World Bank.

World Bank (1996) *Country Report: China*, Washington, DC: World Bank.

World Bank (1997a) *China 2020: Development Challenges in the New Century*, Washington, DC: World Bank.

World Bank (1997b) *China 2020: Clear Water, Blue Skies: China's Environment in the New Century*, Washington, DC: World Bank.

World Bank (1997c) *China 2020: At China's Table: Food Security Options*, Washington, DC: World Bank.

World Bank (1997d) *China 2020: Financing Health Care: Issues and Options for China*, Washington, DC: World Bank.

World Bank (1997e) *China 2020: Sharing Rising Incomes: Disparities in China*, Washington, DC: World Bank.

World Bank (1997f) *China 2020: Old Age Security: Pension Reform in China*, Washington, DC: World Bank.

World Bank (1997g) *China 2020: China Engaged: Integration with the Global Economy*, Washington, DC: World Bank.

Wu D. and P. Murphy (1994) *A Handbook of Chinese Popular Culture*, Westport: Greenwood Publishing Group.

Yahuda, M.B. (1993) *Towards the End of Isolationism: China's Foreign Policy after Mao*, London: Macmillan.

Yahuda, M.B. (1996) *The International Politics of the Asia Pacific, 1945–1995*, London: Routledge.

Yang, R.H., J.C. Hu, P.K.H. Yu, and A.N.D. Yang, (eds) (1994) *Chinese Regionalism: The Security Dimension*, Boulder, CO: Westview Press.

Zhao, S. (1992) 'From Coercion to Negotiation: The Changing Central–Local Economic Relationship in Mainland China', *Issues and Studies*, 28(10), 1–22.

Zhao, S. (1994) *Geography of China: Environment, Resources, Population and Development*, New York and Chichester: Wiley.

Index